Twayne's English Authors Series

Sylvia E. Bowman, *Editor*

INDIANA UNIVERSITY

Geoffrey Chaucer

GEOFFREY CHAUCER

Geoffrey Chaucer

By EDWIN J. HOWARD

Miami University

TWAYNE PUBLISHERS

A DIVISION OF G. K. HALL & CO., BOSTON

ISBN 0-8057-1088-4

Contents

About the Author

Edwin J. Howard received his A.B., M.A., and Ph.D. degrees from Cornell University, where he was elected to Phi Kappa Phi honorary society. He has taught at the University of Rochester, Beloit College, and the University of Washington summer school and is at present a professor of English at Miami University, Oxford, Ohio.

His publications include an edition of Chaucer's *Canterbury Tales*, of which he was co-editor; a volume of Elizabethan plays, Sir Thomas Elyot's *Of the Knowledge which Maketh a Wise Man* and the *Defence of Good Women*, the anonymous *Pleasant Quips for Upstart Newfangled Gentlewomen*, and a number of articles in journals on Old English and Elizabethan literature. He has also produced a number of editions of limited size of Middle English poems. He founded and for a number of years managed the Anchor Press, which pscialized in the reprinting of medieval and Renaissance literature from hand-set type.

The present volume, *Geoffrey Chaucer*, is a product of Professor Howard's major scholarly interest; he has always been an ardent student of Chaucer and has taught him to both graduates and undergraduates from the beginning of his teaching career until the present time.

Preface

The author of a book about Chaucer finds himself the possessor of an abundance of some data and an extremely meager supply of other information. Of actual facts the writer has few indeed, and those that he has do not usually bear on the matters about which he most desires to know. All of the biographical facts about Chaucer deal solely with his official life as a civil servant; we have nothing about his personal life as a private citizen and practically nothing about his relations with his fellow writers.

While we have few facts about Chaucer himself, we do know a great deal about the age in which he lived. For this reason I have divided the book into three main sections. The first deals with the background—political, military, social, economic, and religious—against which Chaucer is seen. Although the stormy fourteenth century is yet by no means completely understood, we must make some attempt to comprehend it if we are to see Chaucer in relation to his times. This section of the book is far shorter than I wish it were.

The second part treats of Chaucer's life. In it I have restricted myself to what is actually known about the poet. It must be admitted, however, that to tread the hard and dusty road of fact and to forego wandering in the beguiling bypaths of fancy, imagination, and speculation requires great resolution. I have had to draw some conclusions from the bare facts of his life, but I am reasonably confident that they are not too farfetched.

The third and major part of the book is devoted to critical evaluation of Chaucer's works. The opinions that I have expressed concerning the various poems inevitably owe much to the multitude of commentators I have read over the years. Because I have so many forerunners, I am now unable to sort out which bit of my current opinion derives from this scholar and which from that, and I am therefore unable to footnote every obligation. But my debt is large.

I have tended to minimize, but by no means entirely to neglect, Chaucer's use of sources. Anyone at all familiar with his works knows that many of them derive from older works and that from the beginning to the end of his poetry there is a constant quoting and paraphrasing of lines and passages from other writers. It is well that we know these facts, but they do not go far toward explaining his genius. We must look primarily at what he did rather than what he drew from. If, however, one separates Chaucer's works into those definitely deriving from known sources and those about which we must say that no source is known, it will be found that the greater number fall into the second category. And in spite of our ceaseless source-hunting, we must admit that Chaucer was a remarkably original poet.

It is to be hoped that anyone who reads Chaucer's works and also this book will feel impelled to do further reading about the fourteenth century and about Chaucer himself. The works listed in the bibliography have, with few exceptions, been chosen not only because they are informative but also because they are interesting reading. If paperbacked editions were available at the time this book was being written, I have so indicated, but no such list, of course, can be completely current.

The items in the bibliography have been selected from thousands that have been published. Usually they are books rather than articles from scholarly journals, for I have tried to list works that give a broad rather than a highly specialized treatment of Chaucer's works.

It will be noted that I have not tried to convert the money of Chaucer's time into today's sums. The matter can never be settled, and the interested reader is referred to John M. Manly's *Chaucer's Canterbury Tales*, New York, 1928, pp. 63-67, and to G. G. Coulton's *The Meaning of Medieval Moneys*, Historical Association Leaflet No. 95, London, 1934.

All quotations and line numbers are taken from *The Works of Geoffrey Chaucer*, edited by F. N. Robinson, second edition, Boston, 1957.

EDWIN J. HOWARD

Miami University
Oxford, Ohio

Chronology

1340- Chaucer born in this period, probably in 1343.
1345
1346 The Battle of Crécy.
1348 The Black Death first appeared.
1351 The Statute of Laborers was enacted.
1357 Chaucer is recorded as a page in the household of Elizabeth de Burgh, Countess of Ulster and Connaught.
1359 Chaucer was captured while on military service in France and was ransomed.
1361 The Black Death recurred.
1366 The conjectural date for Chaucer's marriage to Philippa Roet.
1367 Chaucer received a pension of 20 marks from Edward III and was described as a valet.
1368 Chaucer went on a diplomatic mission to the Continent. He was mentioned as a King's esquire.
1369 Chaucer was on a military expedition in Picardy. Blanche, Duchess of Lancaster, died. The Black Death recurred.
1370 Chaucer went abroad on a governmental mission.
1372 Chaucer went to Italy with two Italians to negotiate a trading port for Genoese merchants in England. He also went to Florence.
1374 Philippa Chaucer is for the first time officially mentioned as Geoffrey's wife. John of Gaunt gave Chaucer a pension of £10; Edward III granted him a daily pitcher of wine. He moved to the house over Aldgate. He became Controller of the Customs and the Subsidy on Wool, Skins, and Hides; he was also appointed Controller of the Petty Customs.
1375 Chaucer obtained two Kentish wardships.
1376 Chaucer went to the Continent with Sir John de Burley.

1377   Chaucer went to Paris and Montreuil, possibly also to Flanders, with Sir Thomas Percy. He was allowed a deputy for the controllership of the wool customs. Edward III died and Richard II became king.

1378   Chaucer commuted his daily pitcher of wine for a money pension. He and John de Beverley were mainpernors for Sir William de Beauchamp. Chaucer went with Sir Edward de Berkeley to Milan to seek military aid against France.

1380   Chaucer was sued for a *raptus* against Cecilia Chaumpaigne.

1381   Chaucer and others were sureties for John Hende. The Peasants' Revolt occurred.

1382   Chaucer assumed the controllership of the Petty Customs and appointed a permanent deputy.

1383   Chaucer appointed a deputy for the controllership of the wool customs for four months.

1384   Chaucer appointed a deputy for the controllership of the wool customs for one month.

1385   Chaucer appointed a permanent deputy for the controllership of the wool customs. He received black cloth for the funeral of Princess Joan.

1386   Philippa Chaucer was admitted to the fraternity of Lincoln Cathedral. Chaucer was elected to Parliament from Kent. The Scropes-Grosvenor court of chivalry began. Eustache Deschamps sent poems to Chaucer for criticism. Chaucer probably gave up the house over Aldgate. He severed connections with both customs services.

1387   The traditional year for the beginning of the *Canterbury Tales*. Philippa Chaucer died. Chaucer was granted protection from debt for a year. He went to Calais with Sir William de Beauchamp.

1388   Chaucer assigned his pension to John Scalby. Writs were issued enjoining his attachment for debt.

1389   Chaucer was appointed Clerk of the King's Works for certain buildings.

1390   As Clerk of the Works Chaucer supervised construction of scaffolds for two tournaments at Smithfield and by special commission saw to repairs to St. George's Chapel, Windsor. He was appointed to a commission to care for walls, ditches, sewers, and bridges along a section of the Thames. He was held up two or three times in four days.

1391   He loaned 100 marks to the Works office. He withdrew from Works office and became deputy forester of the Royal Forest of North Petherton, Somerset.

1393   He received £10 from the King for good services.

1394   The King granted him a new pension of £20.

1396   Henry, Earl of Derby, presented him with a valuable fur-trimmed robe.

1397   The King gave Chaucer the gift of an annual butt of wine.

1398   Chaucer was sued by Isabella Bukholt for over £14. He was given letters of protection against debt so that he could attend to royal business.

1399   John of Gaunt died. Henry IV, on his coronation day, renewed Chaucer's pension of £20 and the butt of wine and added an annuity of 40 marks.

1400   Chaucer died.

Geoffrey Chaucer

CHAPTER 1

Chaucer's Background

I *The Monarchy*

WHEN Geoffrey Chaucer was born, Edward III, of the
House of Plantagenet, was on the throne. Edward III was
the son of the weak Edward II and of Isabella of France, who,
while she was regent, had with her lover Mortimer misruled the
realm as badly as her murdered husband had done before her.
Although guilty of breaches of good faith, frivolity, extravagance,
and self-indulgence, Edward III made a sincere effort to reform
the government. He succeeded in large measure and on the whole
was a fairly good ruler. A man of imposing physique but of moderate intelligence, he kindled a spirit of patriotism in his people
by his stirring military victories against the Scots and the French.
Edward III was first of all an ardent soldier whose chief desire
was for military glory, but he was also deeply concerned with the
forms of religion. His excess of animal spirits, however, prevented
attainment of true spirituality. As he grew old, he turned from
military adventures to amatory ones; in his last senile years he
was completely dominated by Alice Perrers. When he died in
1377, the only fruit of his extensive conquests that remained in
English hands was the city of Calais.

Of Edward III's seven sons, two died in infancy, one was of
little consequence, and four were important men in their time.
Edward of Woodstock, Prince of Wales, who became known as
the Black Prince, shared his father's love of war and led several
victorious armies on the Continent. Although he died of disease
and exhaustion before his father, his son eventually inherited
Edward III's throne as Richard II. One of Richard's great mistakes was to surround himself with a band of flattering sycophants
who led him into disastrous misrule that ended in his abdication
in 1399. The naked tyranny that characterized the last years of
his reign alienated the hearts of his people. He had originally

been the idol of his subjects, but he lost favor by imprisoning men without trial, by terrorizing the realm with his private army, and by exacting taxes that Parliament had not authorized. He drove men into exile, seized their property for his own use, and pursued his enemies with implacable hatred. Perhaps his reason was giving way to madness in the last year or two of his reign; certainly it was time for him to vacate the throne. He died in Pontefract Castle in 1400, a prisoner of his cousin, Henry IV, who had forced his abdication. There were rumors that Henry had him murdered, but of that we cannot be sure. At any rate, Richard died at a highly convenient time for Henry's purposes.

The second surviving son of Edward III was Lionel, Duke of Clarence, who married Elizabeth de Burgh, Countess of Ulster and Connaught, in whose household Chaucer served as a page in 1357. Lionel, like the other members of the royal family, was a soldier, and it is not unlikely that Chaucer served under him on the Continent.

The third surviving son, John of Gaunt, so-called because of the English pronunciation of his birthplace Ghent, first married Blanche, Duchess of Lancaster, by whom he had a son. The son was Henry, Earl of Derby, also known as Hereford and Bolingbroke, who was the deposer of Richard II. He ascended the throne as Henry IV and was the father of Henry V and the grandfather of Henry VI. After Blanche's death, John next married Constance of Castile, by whom he had a daughter. His third wife was Katherine Swynford, sister of Chaucer's wife Philippa. By Katherine John had three sons and a daughter; the sons became the founders of the powerful Beaufort family.

John of Gaunt's association with Chaucer has been overemphasized, although Chaucer's wife was a member of John's household. John, incidentally, was probably more disliked by the common people, especially the citizens of London, than anyone else of the times.

Edward III's fourth remaining son, Edmund of Langley, Duke of York, an ineffectual creature, was the least important of the sons; his chief claim to fame is that he was the ancestor of Edward IV, Edward V, and Richard III.

Thomas of Woodstock, Duke of Gloucester and Earl of Buckingham, was the seventh and last son of Edward III. He took an active part in politics and was a bitter opponent of Richard II. At

[16]

one time he seized the reins of government, and to his ascendancy scholars have ascribed a fall of Chaucer's fortunes. As we are not sure that Chaucer ever experienced a fall of fortune, it is idle to attribute it to Gloucester or anyone else. The circumstances of Gloucester's death are somewhat obscure, but it seems certain that Richard II had him murdered.

II *Warfare*

Because of the royal house's interest in warfare and its willingness to employ innovations instead of the traditional methods of fighting, England in Chaucer's century became the dominant military power of Europe; it achieved its supremacy in the fourth decade of the century and held it for a hundred years. The tactical superiority that made the remote and little-known island of England a power to be reckoned with first manifested itself in some minor frays in Scotland, and these same tactics were used by the English to win the major battles of Dupplin Moor (1332) and Halidon Hill (1333). In these battles the small body of English cavalry was dismounted and, with a hill at its back, grouped between two wings of archers. The Scots, marching uphill in compact columns, attacked the center, and were massacred by the longbowmen on the flanks. Ironically, it was the Scots who had originated this battle formation; but they, having introduced it, immediately abandoned it, only to have the English adopt it and become a great military power.

In 1346 Edward III used this formation at Crécy in France; about 2400 dismounted men-at-arms, with 3000 or 4000 archers on the flanks, withstood sixteen onslaughts from the French mounted cavalry. Finally the French dead and their horses built up an insurmountable wall, but still the squadrons pressed on from the rear towards the English. About 1500 of the flower of French chivalry, together with 10,000 lesser men, were killed, at a cost of practically no English lives. At Poitiers, in 1356, the performance at Crécy was repeated, except that the French attacked on foot. The French suffered the same terrible slaughter, added to which their king, John, was captured.

The English system won other battles, but the French soon learned their lesson and avoided pitched fights. Consequently, English military history on the Continent was not quite so glorious during the second half of the century as it was during the first half—not that the English lost battles; they simply did not win them. The French learned to exhaust the English expeditionary forces by a practice of retreating and simultaneously devastating the land. This system was hard on the French economy, and it was especially horrible for the peasants who lived in the paths of the armies, but it had the result of so completely wearing down the English that they were forced to retire across the Channel.

In Chaucer's time gunpowder came into use, but cannons were so faultily made that they were as dangerous at one end as at the other. Moreover, they were so heavy that they were chiefly used to batter down walls and were rarely seen in the field. Small arms were a development of a period later than the fourteenth century.

As England assumed dominance as a land power, so did it achieve control of the seas. In the fourteenth century there was no regular English navy, although there were some royal ships. Every ship that sailed the seas was a combined merchantman and warship. When a ship of one nation sighted a ship of another power—and it did not necessarily have to be of a hostile power—it either engaged it in battle if confident of victory or else fled. What we consider piracy was then the accepted practice of the seas. Thus Chaucer's Merchant was interested in a protected route between Middleburgh and Orwell; and the Shipman, clearly a pirate, warred on all the vessels that came his way. To the best of Chaucer's knowledge, his Shipman was from Dartmouth, a nest of seamen notorious for their ravages on shipping.

Naval combat took place between fleets largely composed of impressed merchant ships. The sailors attended only to the running of the ships; the fighting was done by detachments of soldiers stationed aboard. Because of the nature of the weapons of the day, fighting was usually hand-to-hand after the ships had grappled and then been lashed together. There is a mention of cannon mounted on a ship at the time of Edward III, but the use of naval artillery was in the main a thing of the future.

The event that made England a commanding naval power was the Battle of Sluys (1340), which was fought on the coast of Flanders where the Zuwyn flowed into an estuary of the River Scheldt. French privateers were a constant danger to Channel shipping and frequently raided the towns of the southern coast of England. The English finally moved to clear out the French

pirates and collected a large fleet. The French, determined that
their profitable raiding should go on, also collected a huge fleet,
which, with additional Genoese and Spanish ships, awaited the
English at Sluys. The French tied their ships bow to bow, in
three lines, each line being securely anchored. The English ships,
not tied together, were able to maneuver; they attacked the
French lines and annihilated two of them; the third, freeing its
lashings and weighing its anchors, took to flight. The English
tactics were similar to those used at Crécy and Poitiers. Archers
shot clouds of arrows into the packed soldiers on the French ships
rather than dueling hand-to-hand with armored men-at-arms.
A Flemish fleet allied to the English helped pursue the French
ships that had not been destroyed in the primary encounter. Altogether, about 35,000 Frenchmen were slain, at the cost of only
4,000 English dead.

III *The Land and the Peasantry*

In considering the land and the peasantry, we must look at two
closely interrelated systems: the feudal and the manorial. The
feudal system was based on the theory that the king owned all
the land. As a practical matter, however, the monarch did not
hold the entire realm in his own hands, but apportioned it out to
important lords; the apportionment was made on the basis of
favor and friendship rather than of the desire for enrichment.
The individuals who received land directly from the king were
usually granted far more land than they could or wished to cultivate; so they, in their turn, divided their holdings, or fiefs, among
other lords. The lords who held directly from the king were
known as tenants in capite, or in chief, and the ones who held the
land under them were sub-tenants. Each lord did homage to his
superior lord and owed him fealty. The lords in general did not
render rent in money or in kind to their superior lords for the use
of the land, but paid for it in various services, the most important
one of which was to support the lord in time of war with a con-
tingent of armed men. It is true that when a king needed money
for a ransom, the tenants might be called upon to provide it, but
their primary obligation was not directly economic in nature.

There were, however, more people than the various lords involved in the feudal system. There were peasant freemen, some
of whom owned their own land, but most of whom held land

from superior lords under certain conditions. There were also the villeins (so-called because they were attached to a vill, or manor), who were neither free nor slave. In great measure they had reached the stage of villein by having at some period surrendered lands that they owned to a lord in exchange for protection. Periods of great civil unrest saw many men sacrificing their freedom for the security of a lord's protection.

The manorial system was, although closely associated with land, based on political considerations. A lord held an estate—usually a very complex one—which was a political unity, a salient feature of which was the manor court, in which many of the internal legal matters of the manor were settled. The land itself was frequently divided into three areas: the lord's private estate; the free tenants' estates, for which a rental of money or kind and a fixed amount of labor was paid; and the villein land, for which rental of money or kind and a highly uncertain amount of labor were paid. The free tenants were often hardly distinguishable from the villeins, but the free tenant had the right to appeal to the royal courts against the lord. The villein had recourse only to the manorial court, which, being totally controlled by the lord, was hardly likely to render many decisions in the villein's favor.

The land on an estate was subdivided in another way, namely, into arable land, which was divided into plots of various sizes; meadow land (common land) upon which the lord and the various tenants had rights of grazing a stipulated number of animals; and woodland, in which the various classes of the occupants of the manor had certain rights of securing wood.

When Chaucer was born, probably in 1343, England was a heavily wooded land inhabited by 2,500,000 or 3,000,000 people. In small enclaves in the forest were the estates, some large and some small. Although much has been written about the farm system of those days, a traveler was probably much more aware of the forests than he was of the open fields of the farms. The large estates or manors rarely consisted of one undivided piece of land; the holdings of the great landlords, lay or clerical, were likely to be scattered far and wide through a number of counties.

Among the important landowners were the monasteries, as the clergy constituted an important element of the feudal system. As continuing corporations, monasteries never relinquished what they owned; and, by means of gifts and purchases, they constantly increased the size of their estates. But not all of the land of England was in large holdings, for the peasants had a tremendous hunger for property. Slowly, but with almost a constant acceleration, many peasants rose from near slavery to full freedom. The slow pace of improvement of their lot was a constant irritation and was one of the causes of the Peasants' Revolt (1381).

For several centuries before the time of Chaucer the great estates were cultivated largely by the villeins or serfs, as the free tenants constituted a minority of the labor force. Villeins, as has been said, were not actually slaves, but neither were they free. In the early fourteenth century at least seventy-five percent of the population were peasants, and at least two-thirds of the peasantry—half the population of England—was not completely free. Usually they were not allowed to marry off their estates; to do so would jeopardize the lord's legal hold upon the children who came from the unions. It was not uncommon for one lord to transfer villeins to some other landowner; even monasteries did this, and the villeins were powerless to resist such transfers.

In compensation for the labor that peasants rendered their lord they were assigned plots of land for their own cultivation. They were subjected to a number of taxes or fines: *heriot,* or the claiming by the lord of the best beast of a villein who had died; *leywite,* a fine on a villein whose daughter became pregnant before her marriage; *chevage,* a fine paid by a villein who permanently left his lord's estate; *mechet,* a license fee for the marriage of the villein's daughter and sometimes for the marriage of the villein himself. There was also a *tallage,* or payment, a villein made to grind his grain in the lord's mill and sometimes to bake his bread in the lord's oven. The villein could not shop around to find where he could get his grain ground and his bread baked most cheaply—he used the lord's mill and oven or none at all. Another way of extorting money from the peasants was for the lord's servants to brew a great batch of ale and force the tenants to buy it; these were known as scot-ales and were a source of considerable vexation to the peasants. These monopolies were jealously guarded as the source of considerable revenue. There were also other fines that could be levied almost at the lord's whim; when such fines were not paid, the villein's livestock was seized. For such exactions there was no remedy, as the only court to which the villein could appeal was the lord's.

Educated serfs were usually lost as tillers of the soil, and lords were naturally reluctant to allow them to better their condition in life by acquiring education; lords therefore exacted huge fines to permit serfs to attend school. Some serfs did, however, succeed in becoming educated; such men frequently became minor clergy. It was extremely difficult—but not completely impossible—for a serf to better his condition. For one thing, he could rarely produce over his actual needs a surplus of goods to sell; for another thing, he was technically unable to own anything, since everything he had legally belonged to his lord. In practice this principle was often relaxed.

The lord-villein relationship underwent great modification during Chaucer's era. Agricultural produce steadily declined in value; as it declined, the landlords became willing, then eager, to accept money instead of labor service. When the visitations of the Black Death greatly curtailed the supply of labor, many huge estates could not be cultivated. This situation produced two contradictory results: First, the landlords exerted every pressure to keep their serfs and, in many instances, to bring back into villeinage men who had become free; and, second, landowners began to rent to newcomers to the district portions of their land they were unable to cultivate. Much land went out of cultivation and passed into sheep pasture, for herding needed only a small group of shepherds while cultivation required a much larger force of agricultural workers. As sheep pastures increased in number and size, powerful landowners encroached upon the common lands where the villeins had been accustomed to graze their animals. Every encroachment on the common lands was, of course, a form of robbery against which the villein had little or no remedy.

Working for wages became a fairly common practice among the lower classes. Serfs decamped from their home estates and became paid workers in other districts. Probably only a relatively small proportion of the working force, the adventurous and ambitious element, resorted to flight. If a runaway serf could maintain his freedom for a year, he became permanently free. If the villein could maintain himself in the new money economy, he might be able to accumulate the cash necessary to set himself up as a landed proprietor.

As the lord's servants were sometimes allowed to commute labor into money payments, so the practice grew of allowing the lord to discharge his feudal military duties to the king with money payments. Under the feudal system, money had not been a highly important sinew of war, but the character of warfare was revolutionized in Chaucer's time. The battles of Crécy and Poitiers rendered comparatively unimportant the fully armed knight on horseback who had previously been the dominant military figure and brought into great prominence the lightly armed archer. With this change in the character of warfare, the use of mercenary troops grew rapidly during the fourteenth century and money became more important than it had been. The monarch was willing to accept money in lieu of armed men, for large sums were essential to pay for the mercenaries. The mercenary companies usually served as long as they were paid, but the feudal levies had been obliged to serve for only forty days. The word "mercenary" has a bad connotation today, but this does not mean that the mercenary soldier of the Middle Ages was held in disrepute. Chaucer's Knight in the *Canterbury Tales* was clearly a mercenary, and he was probably the most respectable member of the entire pilgrimage.

The transference of the labor service on the farms into money payments was a great factor in the decay of the feudal system. And with the decline of the feudal system there was a corresponding decline in the institution of chivalry, although there were other factors involved. Among these was a series of epidemics that had tremendous effects upon the English social and economic systems.

IV *Plague and Labor*

In 1348-49 occurred the first visitation of the Black Death, apparently a combination of pneumonic and bubonic plagues. This dread disease, which is looked back upon with such horror, was apparently accepted calmly enough at the time, as we have no indication of any such terror as that which gripped Elizabethan London in the time of the sweating sickness. Although it is difficult to make an accurate estimate of the ravages of the plague, it seems likely that it killed between a third and a half of the population of England during the fourteenth century. The plague hardly touched some places and utterly wiped out others. The initial visitation of the disease exacted its toll mainly from mature persons, but subsequent ones killed mainly infants and children. This sequence of visitations first cut down the population and then did not allow it to build up again.

The immediate result of so many deaths was a great shortage of labor and a consequent increase in wages, which rose sharply after 1349. In the confusion caused by the Black Death, villeins deserted their ancestral homes to look for work where they could bargain for better working conditions. In an effort to keep wages stable, King Edward III issued an ordinance in 1349, and Parliament enacted a Statute of Laborers in 1351, to fix the price of labor at the rate that had prevailed before the plague; sometimes the rate was even lower than it had been in pre-plague days. In addition, all able-bodied men had to accept work at the prescribed wages if it were offered to them. And it was as much of a crime to offer more than the standard wage as it was to demand more.

For a time the Statute apparently worked, but as the rich could outbid the poor, and as workers constantly sought opportunities to improve their lot, the effort at regulation became progressively less and less effective. The large estate owners could not resist the temptation to hire workers at any wages demanded, for the alternative to violating the law was to see large portions of their estates go out of cultivation. When land is uncultivated for an extended period it reverts to the wild and loses its value. There was thus a double loss entailed: that from the normal produce of the land and from the deterioration of the land itself. Therefore wages, in spite of all the government could do, rose.

For thirty years after the enacting of the Statute of Laborers the peasants, especially those still on large estates as villeins, seethed in discontent. Throughout the country they began to collect in small groups to discuss what could be done to improve their condition. They had a vision of better things to come, and they took counsel to make their dreams a reality.

The lot of the English peasant was a hard one. He, his family, and his farm animals lived miserably in a one-room hut, frequently not much above the level of bare subsistence. Although he had some freedom of action, he was hampered and hindered in a large number of ways; there was always the galling realization that he was not legally his own man. Sentimentalists have pictured the English peasant of the Middle Ages as a happy, contented fellow with a buxom wife and a brood of rosy-cheeked children—one of the makers of Merrie England. But generally he had little enough to be merry about, and there is no reason to believe that he and his family were not frequently the victims of disease and malnutrition. Much has been written about his rough humor, but this was almost always town rather than country humor. At any rate, if the countryman was humorous, he left practically no records to attest to the fact.

V *The Peasants' Revolt*

One of the major events of the fourteenth century was the Peasants' Revolt in 1381. There has been much written in interpretation of the Revolt, but in essence it was an effort to get rid of unjust taxation (characterized by the hated poll taxes initiated by the Chancellor, Archbishop Sudbury), to commute labor services into a payment of 4*d.* an acre, and to allow the serf to work for wages. The Revolt was not an effort to institute a communistic system, nor was it an effort to level society by exterminating the upper classes; in fact, unless members of the upper classes had been notoriously oppressive, they and their property were not harmed. Above all, it was not a revolt against the government, for King Richard II was the hero of the common people. John of Gaunt, Richard's uncle, was, on the other hand, the chief object of the mob's resentment; anyone connected with John who fell into the hands of the rioters was speedily executed. It is noteworthy that Chaucer came through the violent time unscathed—probably an indication that his connection with John was very slender. So far as we can judge from his works, Chaucer does not seem to have been unduly alarmed by the insurrection; but, as he deals so slightly with contemporaneous events, we cannot tell much from his silence.

One of the chief fomenters of the revolt was a poor priest named John Ball; he was aided in his efforts to stir up the peasants by other members of the secular clergy, by friars, by peasants, and even by some of the gentry. Meetings were held throughout the country; messages couched in veiled allegorical terms were sent back and forth across the land; inflammatory sermons were preached; and in every possible way the discontent of the peasants was brought to a boil.

The actual outbreak of hostilities occurred in Essex in May,

1381, over what was thought to be an unfair and illegal imposition of the poll tax, at best a most unpopular way of raising money. From Essex the revolt spread into Kent, and soon all England was overrun by poorly armed bands of men moving on London. Although there was a considerable beheading of unpopular landowners, lawyers, and jurors, and the burning of some buildings, the Revolt was remarkably temperate, considering that it was conducted by unorganized mobs. The lawyers were executed, not because they had been especially wicked, but because they represented the enforcement of oppressive laws. There was a wholesale burning of charters and rolls of the manors, but usually the buildings in which they were kept were spared; the rolls were burned with the idea of confusing the ownership of serfs. An odd feature of the Revolt was the small amount of pillaging and robbing; of course there was some, but considering the chaotic state that prevailed, there was relatively little. In the early days of the Revolt, the peasants could have devastated the whole of England had they wished to do so.

The peasants converged on London in two main lines and finally entered the city over London Bridge and through Aldgate. Once in the city they burned several buildings, including the prisons, and just outside the city they gutted and burned John of Gaunt's favorite residence, the palace of the Savoy. The furnishings and works of art were completely destroyed but little or nothing was stolen, for the peasants asserted they were not thieves.

Finally the King met the rebels at Mile End and acceded to all of their demands: the abolition of serfage, the commutation of labor service into a payment of 4d. an acre, and amnesty for all the rebels. The peasants then poured back into the city and began a reign of terror against those whom they considered their enemies; among others, they murdered Archbishop Sudbury and all of the Flemish weavers they could find. The killing of the weavers—to which Chaucer refers in the *Nun's Priest's Tale*—was an isolated example of pure vindictiveness. The Flemings had been invited to migrate from Flanders to England to strengthen the English cloth industry. Because they were industrious and frugal, they aroused the ire of the native weavers, who believed that they were losing work to these foreigners. In this belief they were, of course, justified, since the output of a Flemish weaver tended to displace that of a native worker.

There was, however, much more to the matter than this. The Flemings were used to doing fine work and were willing and eager to continue doing so. The native weavers, on the other hand, although capable of doing excellent work, seemed to have an inborn reluctance to do so for extended periods. No sooner did the cloth of a district in England achieve a good reputation and come into general demand than the weavers began to engage in all sorts of chicanery such as weaving one end of a bolt of cloth well and the other end poorly; the buyer would judge the entire bolt by the good end, which was on the outside, and would find, when he unwrapped it, that he had been cheated. Another of their ruses was to weave a bolt shorter than standard and then stretch it in a rack to the proper length; this practice naturally ruined the entire piece of cloth. Whether the actual murderers of the Flemings were the men who believed that they had been injured by them will never be known; perhaps their killing was simply a piece of mob violence.

The King again met the rebels, this time at Smithfield, and it was there that Wat Tyler, who had assumed command of the Revolt, was struck down. Finally the King persuaded the rebels to disperse. As soon as they were back in their villages and were ready to take up their normal lives again, the government broke most of its promises. Revenge was the order of the day, and the wanton slaughter of peasants prevailed throughout the land for months. Because of this betrayal, the Revolt was for the most part a failure. The serfs were allowed to pay their 4d. an acre instead of labor service and they were released from the fixed wage scale of the Statute of Laborers, but they were not freed. But if the Revolt did not actually produce freedom, it did much to hasten it.

VI *Roads*

It is frequently assumed that the medieval English road system was either nonexistent or was at least very bad. From the amount of travel in the Middle Ages, we must, however, conclude that the roads were at least fairly adequate. We are constantly coming on records of the transportation of goods by wagon, and such a mode of transportation would have been impossible if there had not been passable roads. In addition, there are many references to bridges—who was supposed to keep them in repair, who was to receive the tolls, and so forth. Bridges are of importance only if there is a road system. Undoubtedly in the rainy season many roads became impassable; but we should remember that this condition prevailed in the United States well into the twentieth century and the era of the automobile, when hard-surfaced roads were needed outside as well as within cities. Probably the roads of the Middle Ages were not much worse than the roads of early twentieth-century America.

VII *London and the Artisans*

The London of Chaucer's age was not much more than a mile square. Although considerable population lived outside the walls, the population of the city itself is estimated to have been only about forty thousand. Yet London was larger than the next four cities combined and, small as we might consider it, was a genuine metropolis. It was the seat of England's government and religion, the country's great trading center, its great port, and the source of most of its manufactures.

One feature of life in fourteenth-century London was its riotous nature. In those days, when a dagger was part of the attire of every male over fourteen years old, the many street brawls tended to be sanguinary. The carnage was frequently augmented by people who had nothing to do with the initial quarrels. We have records of numerous citizens, motivated only by a love of sport who, at windows with bows and arrows, used the struggling gangs for target practice.

By no means were all the fights communal. Contests between pairs of combatants were common, although such private affairs had a tendency to become public; apparently no red-blooded Londoner could stand tamely by and merely watch a fight. A strange sidelight on these innumerable battles was that never, so far as we know, was a doctor summoned to minister to the wounded. We have records of scores of men injured in brawls who languished unattended for periods as long as a month before expiring.

A killer in a street fight, or a private one, usually decamped as speedily as possible and became an outlaw. In Chaucer's time the land swarmed with bands of robbers and lone pillagers. The tremendous forests and the lack of a national police force made apprehending evildoers almost impossible. The robber band has been romanticized in the tales of Robin Hood and his merry men in Sherwood Forest. Actually, the men were anything but merry, and, instead of remedying injustices, were intent only upon committing them. If they did not rob the poor, it was because the poor had nothing worth taking. But robbery was by no means restricted to the open country. The total absence of street lights made robbery by night a common feature of city life.

But the life of medieval London was far more than street brawls, duels, and night robberies. The city bustled with the movements of merchants, artisans, and those who made London the commercial center of England. The merchant guilds, mainly busy with wholesaling commodities such as wool and foodstuffs, frequently engaged in importing and exporting. The members dealt in large quantities of goods and were often wealthy. These merchant guilds were big business in contrast to the little business of the multitude of trades guilds.

Manufacturing goods and handling their retail sale were the province of many trades guilds. Not every manufacturer, however, was a retailer, as there was an intricate division of labor, and any article that came onto the market might combine the work of a number of guilds. A knife, for example, was the product of four guilds, not including those involved in the preparation of the raw materials. Cloth went through the hands of carders, spinners, weavers, shearmen, fullers, dyers, and was marketed by drapers and mercers. Before it could be of much use to anyone, it also had to pass through the hands of tailors, capmakers, or other artisans who worked it into useful forms.

The names of some of the guilds are still recognizable today: goldsmiths and silversmiths, grocers, spicers, pepperers, saddlers, fishmongers, butchers, skinners, painters, glovers. Others less familiar to us are fusters (makers of the wooden parts of saddles), vintners (wholesale dealers in wine), hafters (makers of knife handles), loriners or lorimers (makers of bits, spurs, and metal mountings for saddles and bridles), fletchers (arrow makers), tawyers (workers in fine leather), heaumers (helmet makers), cordwainers (shoemakers), mercers (dealers in cloth), and parmenters (dealers in broadcloth).

Although the guild is sometimes thought of as combining the features of a college fraternity and a labor union, it had many functions: its chief one was to preserve a monopoly of opportunity for its members. The right to practice a craft was a valuable property, jealously guarded in each city by the members of the guilds. This tended to restrict the movements of the working population, for a guild member of one city was decidedly unwelcome to the members of the same guild in another city. Generally it was either impossible for a worker to set up shop anew in a strange city, or so expensive as to be impracticable. A bladesmith of York would have all sorts of privileges so long as he stayed in his own area; if he came to London, he had absolutely no privileges as a bladesmith—and the London bladesmiths would do their best to see that he acquired none. We think of competition as a fine thing, but the medieval English guildsman wanted none of it.

Each trade tended to congregate in a restricted area. Thus in London there was Cordwainer Street in which Chaucer's ancestors had lived, Bowyer Row, the Mercery, the Poultry, Bread Street, Goldsmiths' Row, Honey Lane, Milk Street, Foster Lane, and many other thoroughfares indicative of the trades of those who lived in them.

Although England produced a great deal of the goods it consumed, it could not, of course, exist without entering into commercial relations with other countries. At the beginning of the fourteenth century England was mainly a nation of farmers, fishermen, and shepherds, with a small proportion of the population engaged in such activities as mining and saltmaking. The exports were grain, fish, wool, metals, coal, salt, and inconsequential amounts of other products. The great and basic export was wool. The uninitiated may believe that all wool is alike, but such is far from true. The wool produced in England in Chaucer's time ranged from that too coarse to be exported to that which was so fine that it was eagerly sought throughout Europe. In fact, England had a world monopoly of fine wool, and during the first half of the fourteenth century this wool was exported to build up the foreign cloth industry, mainly in the Low Countries. During this period some cloth was exported from England, but much more, especially cloth of the finer grades, was imported.

About the middle of the century the English weaving industry began to grow. There was a decline in the export of wool and an increase in the export of finished cloth; the cloth that continued to be imported was mainly fine material of interest only to the wealthy. This shift from the exporting of wool to the weaving and exportation of the woven cloth was revolutionary, the ramifications of which we cannot trace here. Weaving had been largely an urban industry until in the second half of the fourteenth century fulling mills driven by water power were developed. As the fulling mills could be established only in rural regions where water power was available, weavers moved into the country and the industry became predominantly rural.

The London artisan toiled from dawn till dusk, for a workday of sixteen hours was normal. His life was not, however, a monotonous grind. He frequently worked in the front of his shop where he could keep watch on what went on in the street, if, indeed, he did not actually work there. We have so many records of workers' establishments spilling out into the highways that we conclude such encroachments must have been the rule rather than the exception. And when a fight or the passing of one of the innumerable processions that were such a feature of the London scene took place, the master, his journeymen, and his apprentices were ready enough to suspend work until the excitement was over.

Although the hours of work were long, there were frequent holidays. There were wrestling and football matches to watch and take part in; both were bone-breaking, mangling activities that frequently caused the death of some participants. Even chess, backgammon, and other sedentary games often ended in fatal stabbings, for the hot-tempered Londoner's usual method of settling an argument was to lash out with his dagger. Executions, and they abounded, were attended in the lighthearted spirit usually reserved for going to the fair. Whippings, brandings, and maiming by cutting off ears, feet, and hands were also relished by the populace. Another recreation was observing or tormenting people placed in the stocks. Being put in the stocks was the punishment for a wide variety of misdemeanors and petty crimes. Drunkenness was far from rare, and, among Chaucer's Pilgrims, the Miller, the Summoner, and the Cook were guilty of it. Water drinkers were rare enough to merit comment; Sir Thopas drank water, but Chaucer is careful to make it clear that the doughty knight had a precedent in the Sir Percival of romance.

Pageants and plays drew large crowds of spectators. Wedding feasts were so riotous that it was not considered proper for monks to attend them. And funerals were just as jolly; wrestling bouts were held in the presence of the corpse, and the funeral feast was generally a drunken brawl. Dancing was popular, and if we can judge from the many condemnatory sermons it was frequently practiced in the churchyard. It was bad enough to have dancing after the service; what especially irked the clergy was to have to compete with it during service time.

Even the most irreverent of moderns would probably be shocked by a medieval church service. Gentlemen commonly brought to church as part of their costumes their falcons or other birds of prey, and many women carried their hawks also. Perhaps more disturbing than the hawks were the packs of hounds that frequently went to church with their masters. Nor did the medieval churchgoer give polite and quiet attention to the service. He roamed around the building; chatted with acquaintances; and, on occasion, transacted business. He never thought to keep his voice down to a reverential whisper.

Such celebrations as the Feast of Fools, the Feast of Asses, and the Boy Bishop were so boisterous as to shock the Church authorities of the Middle Ages, but they were powerless to eradicate them. Church ales were also condemned by the pious. Parishioners contributed ale or the material to make it to the church, which then held a community drinking party piously labeled a fund-raising enterprise. Drunkenness naturally resulted, accompanied by sexual immorality that scandalized the pure in heart.

The ales were not the only occasions for relaxing morals. Such old pagan holidays as May Day were simply thinly disguised fertility festivals that served as excuses for almost unlimited sexual indulgence. If we visualize what a dark, gloomy, cold, cheerless, uncomfortable time the English winter was, with its mists and snows and a pinched diet, we can understand the feelings of the people when release came with the passing of Lent and the arrival of the lovely English spring.

In winter the ill-constructed dwelling house of the poor was certainly a cold and frosty place. The occupants could little afford fuel for a roaring fire that might have made life bearable. Wintering meat animals was impractical because feed for livestock was scarce. Most of the beasts were slaughtered in the fall, and only salt meat or none at all was available during most of the winter.

VIII *Religious Organizations*

A popular opinion holds that the Middle Ages was a time of great spirituality. A reading of the *General Prologue* of the *Canterbury Tales* should correct this fallacy. The only member of Chaucer's pilgrimage who shows any spirituality is the poor Parson, and he is generally held to be so atypical as to be a satire on real parsons. And with the exception of the Parson, and perhaps his brother the Plowman, all pilgrims, especially the churchmen, have their eyes very much on things of this world.

In Chaucer's time the mysticism that had prevailed in the earlier Middle Ages had passed away, to be succeeded by the steady growth of materialism. The great religious movements, with their contempt for the joys and sorrows of earthly life, were a thing of the past. The road to the Renaissance, with its conviction of the worth of the individual in this world, was a long one, but England was on its way.

One of the great institutions of the Middle Ages was monasticism. In their early days the monasteries had been the homes of piety—a selfish piety, it is true, for the men who retired to the cloisters were motivated by a desire to save their own souls. Still, much good flowed from the monasteries; they were centers of learning and charity when there was not much of either in the world. But, as time passed, the monks became wealthy; their estates spread over the land. The old handwork, prayer, and meditation inevitably gave way to large-scale farming, accountancy, and commerce. Services were still held in the choir, charity was still dispensed at the gates, manuscripts were still copied in the scriptoria; but the spirit was that of an agricultural corporation rather than of a religious organization. The monasteries held their serfs as tenaciously as did the lay landlords—perhaps even more tenaciously, as the corporation tended to be more conservative than the individual. An abbot might refuse to manumit a serf on the grounds that he had no right to alienate monastic property; a lay landlord, having no one to answer to but himself, might well be more merciful and generous than the churchman.

The physical labor that had characterized the early monasteries was a thing of the past. Chaucer's Monk shows a great scorn for such an old-fashioned practice as working with his hands—he is a modern! Likewise, monastic poverty was obsolete. Not only did the monks have private possessions—Chaucer's Monk had fine horses and hounds for hunting, which at first glance might be thought an odd hobby for a monk—but they had regular allowances of pocket money. Instead of remaining in the cloisters, they were constantly abroad in the land; Chaucer's Monk, an outrider whose function it was to leave the monastery to oversee outlying farms, is on a pilgrimage. Likewise the monk of the *Shipman's Tale* does considerable traveling.

The sparse diet of the early monks had also given way to luxuriousness. Chaucer's Monk gives the impression of a man to whom the pleasures of the table are an important part of life; at any rate, his favorite dish, roast swan, indicates anything but poor living. Nor was he plainly clothed; his robe was trimmed with the finest gray fur in the land and was fastened under his chin with a gold love knot. In all of this Chaucer is reflecting the popular opinion of the monk as a man to whom the pleasures of life were paramount.

Although nunneries existed in fair number in Chaucer's time, there were no really notable ones and they seem to have been rather unimportant as part of the religious organization. Although Chaucer has more nuns on his pilgrimage than people of any other calling, he did not include them because they were a dominant segment of society. Because nuns could not travel alone, he had to have at least two if he was to have any. Nuns, for the most part, came from the upper classes of society: admission to a nunnery entailed so much expense that the calling was virtually closed to the daughters of the poor. The practice in reasonably well-to-do families was to dower as many daughters as possible and then shunt the remainder into nunneries. Therefore, the ones who took orders rarely had much calling for religion. Chaucer's Prioress, for example, is much more concerned about courtly behavior than she is with religious matters.

The orders of friars had been founded to do the works that the monks failed to do: that is, minister to the poor and the sick. The four major orders of friars were the Dominicans, also called the Friars Preachers, Black Friars, and Shod Friars; the Franciscans, called the Friars Minor, Minorites, Gray Friars, and Barefoot Friars; the Carmelites, also called White Friars; and the Austin Friars. There sprang up from time to time a number of short-lived smaller orders.

According to the original idea, the friar was to be a homeless ministrant to those who needed him, a man who lived so completely on the charity of the public that he was not allowed even to touch money. But within a generation the founders' ideals had been forgotten, and the friars became proud, arrogant hunters after money, and probably no other group was as thoroughly hated in the fourteenth century as they were. True, they did not touch money: they either wore gloves or, like the friar in the *Summoner's Tale,* had an attendant to receive the gifts. They built themselves splendid friaries: Black Friars of Elizabethan dramatic fame was one of their houses, and White Friars, the ruins of which can still be seen at Canterbury, was another. Like Chaucer's Friar in the *General Prologue* of the *Canterbury Tales,* they left the poor and sick to their own devices and cultivated the wealthy. If Chaucer actually beat a Franciscan in Fleet Street, he was only expressing the general feeling toward these friars.

But it must not be thought that all friars were simply guests, welcome or unwelcome, in the houses of the well-to-do. Some of them were among the most profound scholars of the age, especially at Oxford, and through their writing and lecturing they shaped theological thinking in England. In Chaucer's time, however, there were no friars of the mental stature of the recently dead Roger Bacon, Duns Scotus, and William of Ockham, who remain great figures in the history of thought. It was in the fourteenth century that intellectual leadership changed hands; it passed from the friars to the secular clergy.

The friars were popular preachers, holding forth both in churches and out-of-doors. Instead of dully expounding dogma, they exerted themselves to be amusing, and their efforts were appreciated—attending friars' sermons was one of the chief recreations of the populace. Their practice of telling stories, cracking jokes, and in general discoursing on a low intellectual level was constantly attacked by more orthodox preachers, and even as late as the reign of Henry VIII Erasmus was bitter against their methods. But they were not all bad, and we know that some of them were concerned enough about the wretched condition of the peasants to act as leaders of the Revolt of 1381.

The ordinary clergy were shot through with corruption, and visitations by authorities uncovered a staggering number of cases of immorality and theft of church property. There were undoubtedly good clergymen, and we have records of bishops who labored unceasingly—and almost always fruitlessly—for reform. A system that allowed a relatively small group of men to hold the population at large in ransom for tithes could not help promoting corruption. With the clergy, as with the laity, the desire for money was the root of all evil. And woe betide the small tither! He was harried as mercilessly for his shillings and pence as though he were the greatest sinner in the land.

Although the English people of this time were reasonably religious, they were anticlerical; and, as a nation, England was strongly antipapal. This may sound strange when we remember that the pope was the head of the Church, the only Church that existed, but there had always been a strong resistance in England to the paying of papal exactions.

IX *Religious Organizations and the Schism*

Religion was in a state of ferment in Chaucer's time. John Wycliffe, an Oxford scholar, emerged as a reformer. Although Wycliffe is now most famous for his translation of the Bible into English, probably he merely promoted and oversaw the work rather than doing it himself. This translation into English resulted from his conviction that the ordinary person should have at his disposal a Bible that he could personally read and understand. This was contrary to the Church's belief that the Bible was too dangerous to give to the uninstructed. The Bible, the Church held, should be read and explained to the people in accordance with accepted dogmas. If theologians who had spent their entire lives in Biblical study could err in their interpretations and so fall into heresy, what horrible fate awaited the unlearned layman? Wycliffe, however, had faith in the intelligence of the multitude. His so-called "Early Version," probably in the making by 1382, was direct and literal, and to some extent justified the official view, since it was largely unintelligible to the ordinary man. What part Wycliffe took in the actual preparation of the work is not known; it is believed that his disciples, John Purvey and especially Nicholas Hereford, were mainly responsible for it. The "Later Version," for which Purvey received the major part of the credit, was probably prepared between 1395 and 1397. Freer and with more explanatory matter, it was a greater success than the Early Version and remained current in England until the Tyndale and Coverdale versions rendered it obsolete.

Wycliffe was a puritan, bent on cleansing the Church of its impurities. One thing that he advocated was the expropriation of all Church property. Such a proposal, it hardly need be said, won him few friends in the Church organization. Wycliffe stood for a number of things, or, rather, against a number of things: for example, he opposed the doctrine of transubstantiation, as well as pardons and pardoners, pilgrimages, lawyers, friars, elaborate church services, the domination of state by Church, confession and penance, the pope's power to bind and loose, masses for the souls of the dead, the merits of the saints, the papacy, and the prelacy. In the face of such a list as this, one might well ask what he stood for. The answer is that he believed in a deeply personal religion based on the Scriptures. In advocating such a religion he was a forerunner of the Puritans who came into ascendancy in the sixteenth and seventeenth centuries.

Although for a time Wycliffe had support from important personages, notably John of Gaunt and the so-called Lollard knights, his followers were mainly poor uneducated wandering priests who exerted practically no influence on the Church hierarchy. Wycliffe was labeled a heretic, but such was the spirit of the age that he was tolerated. Instead of ending his life at the stake, he died peacefully in bed. It was not until the fifteenth century that Lollards, as the followers of Wycliffe were called, were burned for heresy. It has been speculated that Chaucer may have been a Lollard. It seems safe to say, however, that he was not an adherent of Wycliffe's, but it is entirely possible that he sympathized with certain aspects of Lollardry.

The Great Schism of Chaucer's time seriously weakened respect for the Church. It had its beginnings in 1305 when Pope Clement V, a Gascon, viewing with alarm the chaotic conditions in Italy, did not go to Rome upon his election to the papacy but instead established himself at Avignon in France. The succeeding popes also remained in Avignon, gradually building up a splendid residence, and more important, a thoroughly French cardinalate which became an instrument for political maneuvering against the Holy Roman Empire. Pope Urban V returned to Rome, then a vast ruin, in 1367 and stayed until 1370, when he returned to Avignon. Pope Gregory XI returned to Rome in 1377. When Gregory's successor, Urban VI, was elected pope by a conclave in Rome, the French cardinals realized that a truly Roman pope would mean the end of their indolent and luxurious life. In desperation in 1378 they elected their own pope, who took the name of Clement VII. He established himself in Avignon, and thus began the Great Schism, or the period of the two popes.

The English, inveterate enemies of the French, proclaimed their adherence to the Roman pope. The Schism lasted until 1417, and it quite understandably weakened the already tepid respect the English had for the papacy. Chaucer, who was probably as good a churchman as the average Englishman, makes very few references to the pope; in one he says you can teach a parrot to say "Wat" as easily as the pope can say it. There is probably a topical allusion here, for why either a French or a Roman pope would have occasion to say "Wat" is not clear.

CHAPTER 2

Chaucer's Life

I *Family*

GEOFFREY CHAUCER was the descendant of an apparently prosperous family which had originally lived in Ipswich. Known by the names of Malyn, le Taverner, and de Dynyngton, various family members had been occupied in the wool and wine trades and in the customs service, although the name Chaucer indicates that they were once shoemakers. Robert le Chaucer, Geoffrey's grandfather, who lived in London during the late thirteenth century, was the deputy for the king's butler for the port of London, which meant that he collected a certain percentage of the wine for the king's use from every wine ship entering the port. He was also collector of a special duty on wines from Aquitane. Robert was the second husband of Mary, who had previously been married to the well-to-do John Heyroun. Mary's third husband, Richard Chaucer, who may have been Robert's cousin, was a wealthy vintner.

John Chaucer, the son of Robert and Mary and the father of the poet, was the central figure of a fascinating adventure. His aunt, Agnes de Westhale of Ipswich, aided by Thomas and Geoffrey Stace and Geoffrey's servant Lawrence, kidnapped the twelve-year-old John, with the intention of marrying him to Joan, Agnes's daughter. The purpose of the project was to secure for the Westhale family a considerable amount of Ipswich real estate that John was to inherit upon coming of age. But John escaped unmarried; and, as a result Agnes and Geoffrey, who were married soon after the abortive abduction, languished in prison for several years until John signed their release. Seeking to avoid paying a huge fine of £250, Geoffrey very reasonably pointed out that John was still unmarried and that, anyway, the annual value of the land was only 20s., but his plea went in vain. Agnes and Geoffrey, having failed to get possession of John's property by skulduggery, finally purchased it.

John became a prosperous vintner and at an unknown date married a widow, Agnes de Northwell, heiress to her uncle, Hamo de Copton, a wealthy official of the mint. Although the family had formerly dwelt in Cordwainer Street, when the poet was born they were living in Thames Street in Vintry Ward, one of the wealthiest regions of the city of London.

Exactly when Geoffrey Chaucer was born is uncertain. All that we definitely know is that in 1386 in the Scropes-Grosvenor trial to determine who was entitled to bear a certain coat of arms, it was recorded that Chaucer was "forty years old and more" and that he had "borne arms for twenty-seven years." On the basis of these statements Chaucer is assumed to have been born between 1340 and 1345, the preferred years being 1343 and 1344. Many of the known facts of his life make 1343 seem reasonable, but in several places in his works Chaucer refers to himself as aged. Even if all of these references had been written in the last year of his life, he would have been only fifty-seven years old, surely not the antiquity that he attributed to himself.

II *Education*

Of Chaucer's education we know nothing. Certainly at an early age he learned French, as it was the language used in the schools of his youth. And whether he went to the school of St. Martin-le-Grand, of St. Mary-le-Bow, or of St. Paul's Cathedral, all fairly close to his residence in Thames Street, we know that he studied Latin, the basis of medieval education. Although he certainly acquired enough Latin to serve his needs, he seemed not to have had the facility in it that he had in French; for he tended to use French sources for his poems rather than the Latin originals. When Chaucer learned Italian is uncertain, but for a person of quick intelligence who knew French and Latin acquiring it probably presented no great problem.

The legend that formerly grew up around Chaucer held that he had attended both Oxford and Cambridge. In fact, many have considered the Clerk in the *Canterbury Tales* to be a self-portrait. This is fantastic, for the busy civil servant Geoffrey Chaucer was as different from the unemployed Oxford student of the poem as is light from darkness. There is not a bit of evidence to connect

Chaucer with either of the universities. If we are going to liken Chaucer to any of his Pilgrims, the most likely would be the young Squire, for he had a courtly background and a military career similar to Chaucer's.

There was another old tale to the effect that Chaucer had been a student in an inn of court. Speght, in the biography of Chaucer attached to his edition of 1598, said that a Master Buckley had read in the records of the Inner Temple that "Geoffrey Chaucer was fined two shillings for beating a Fransciscane fryer in Fleetstreete." This story fell into discredit as a myth and was so labeled until it was learned that Master Buckley had been, among other things, the custodian of the records of the Inner Temple and would have had an excellent opportunity to read such a document had it existed. Now there is a tendency to believe that the story might be true.[1] The inns of court were primarily law schools, but they were, in addition, similar to modern schools of business administration. If Chaucer attended an inn at all, it was probably for training in business rather than in law; he would be trying to number himself among the

> . . . *duszeyne in that hous*
> *Worthy to been stywardes of rente and lond*
> *Of any lord that is in Engelond.* (CT, I, 578-80)

Valets of the King, and Chaucer became a valet, were frequently admitted to the inns under special conditions. If Chaucer was admitted, we can account for the period of his life from 1361 to 1367 for which no records exist. Certainly Chaucer's parents could have afforded to send him to an inn of court, and, for a family with a long record of civil service, such a step would have been logical.

III *The Page*

We have brought Chaucer to his early maturity without having taken into account his boyhood. The first fact that we know about him is that in 1357 he was a page in the household of Elizabeth, Countess of Ulster and Connaught and wife of Prince Lionel, Duke of Clarence. It has been conjectured that Chaucer was in attendance upon the Countess on a number of notable court occasions both before and after 1357, but we do not know that he actually was. So far as we know, his appointment as a page marked the beginning of an association with the royal family that lasted until his death. Probably no other English poet had a longer or more intimate relationship with royalty than did Chaucer, yet we cannot find one shilling's advantage that he reaped from this association purely as a poet.

We know that Chaucer was in the Countess of Ulster's retinue because there is an entry in her household accounts for April, 1357, for the disbursing of money for a paltock (an abbreviated jacket), red-and-black breeches, and shoes for him. In May of the same year he received 2s. and later the same year 2s. 6d. "for necessaries at the feast of the Nativity." The Christmas season was spent at the royal hunting lodge at Hatfield, Yorkshire, and much has been made of the fact that John of Gaunt was a guest in the Countess's household during this same Christmas. We are told that "undoubtedly" John and Chaucer met and formed a friendship that lasted all their lives. This is pure romantic supposition; as a matter of fact, it is exceedingly unlikely that the royal prince would have been aware of the existence of the merchant-sired page boy.

IV Servant of the King

The next fact we have is that Chaucer was in military service with the English army in France in 1359. This invasion of France which the English began gloriously and lightheartedly soon, largely because of constant rains, turned into a dismal fiasco. During the campaign Chaucer was taken prisoner near Rheims, and the King contributed £16 toward his ransom. We do not know whether this was the total amount of the ransom, but it indicates that Chaucer was a person of importance, since valets of the Queen and of the Countess of Ulster brought only from £1 10s. to £2.

In the negotiations toward the Peace of Calais, Chaucer acted as a courier, carrying letters back and forth across the English Channel. For this he received 9s. from Prince Lionel. His activities in the matter of the peace are the last thing we know about him in the years 1361 to 1367. Some biographers have advanced the theory that he was with Prince Lionel in Ireland during this period, but his name does not appear on the very complete lists of that expedition. An alternative theory, as has been mentioned, is that he was studying law and business administration in an inn of court. It has been conjectured that he was married in 1366.

Our next certain knowledge of him is that he received on June 20, 1367, a pension of 20 marks for life from King Edward III. That Chaucer was referred to as *"dilectus vallectus noster,"* or valet, and was given a pension for life cannot be considered very indicative of his standing with the King, for it was the custom for the monarch to make such grants to his valets and esquires.

In 1368 Chaucer is referred to as an esquire. That same year, with a passport dated July 17, he went on a mission to the Continent. All we know about this expedition is that he took with him two horses and had 20s. for Channel passage and £10 for traveling expenses. Going on foreign missions was one of the regular duties of some of the esquires; hence we cannot attach much significance to this journey. Esquires were in general younger sons of important families, sometimes sons of secondary branches of important families, sons of well-to-do merchants, or men who had served in the households of the King's children. They were usually not very notable in their own right.[2]

In 1369 Chaucer was in the army under the command of John of Gaunt when it went on a raid into Picardy. This expedition was less eventful for Chaucer than his previous military campaign; he returned home uncaptured and, so far as we know, unhurt. It was in this year that Blanche, Duchess of Lancaster and the first wife of John of Gaunt, died—a significant event in Chaucer's career, for her death was the subject of his first lengthy poem.

In 1370 Chaucer went abroad on a governmental mission, the nature of which we do not know. On December 1, 1372, he set out for Genoa with Jacopo de Provano and Giovanni de Mari to negotiate a trading port for Genoese citizens in London. Since his two companions were Italians, it seems likely that Chaucer had to protect English interests. On the probability of this responsible role as a prime negotiator, many scholars have argued that he must have had legal training and are inclined to accept the story that he attended law courses at the Inner Temple. This is about the only piece of public business in which Chaucer participated that seems to have been more than merely routine—and, of course, we may be overrating his importance on this mission. The negotiations came to nothing, and Chaucer went on to Florence, where presumably he had more royal business to transact. This expedition into Italy is generally considered to have given Chaucer his introduotion to Italian literature. If it did, it was of tremendous significance in his intellectual development, for his knowledge of this literature helped to make him a great poet. On May 23, 1373, he returned to England.

V *Relations with John of Gaunt*

In 1374 Philippa Roet, daughter of Sir Paon de Roet (or Sir Payne Roet), a knight of Hainault resident in England, is first officially mentioned as Chaucer's wife. In that year John of Gaunt made a grant of £10 to Chaucer for his wife Philippa's services to Queen Philippa and to John's second wife, Constance of Castile. Philippa, who was in the service of the family of John of Gaunt, was the sister of Katherine Swynford, long the governess of John's children and for a number of years his mistress. John's eventual marriage to Katherine brought Chaucer into close relationship with the royal family.

John of Gaunt has often been referred to as Chaucer's patron, but he never acted in this capactiy and Chaucer never actually had a patron. Everything that he ever received came from his work as a civil servant. John was probably friendly to Chaucer, but the main relationship was between John and Philippa rather than between John and Chaucer. The fact that the *Book of the Duchess* was a memorial to John's wife Blanche has inclined scholars to assume a closer relationship between John and Chaucer than the records show. Why Chaucer wrote an elegy on Blanche is not known; it might simply have been that he liked her. We have no record showing that John commissioned such a poem, nor are there records of gifts to indicate such a poem had been ordered. John of Gaunt, so far as we know, had no interest in poetry.

VI *Public Service*

At Windsor on St. George's Day, April 23, 1374, Edward III granted Chaucer a pension of a daily pitcher of wine. This was an unusual gift, and some scholars have assumed, because this type of grant was later associated with the laureateship, that Chaucer received the pension for his poetical achievements and in effect was a poet laureate. Actually, the gift was for Chaucer's civil service and had nothing to do with his poetry. At this stage of his career he had not, so far as we know, written any poetry noteworthy enough to warrant a pension.

In May of 1374 Chaucer moved to the house over Aldgate. To say that he lived over a gate is mystifying to some modern readers, but in Chaucer's time city gates were elaborate structures. In Canterbury a city gate is still surmounted by a set of rooms used as a municipal museum. About a month later Chaucer became Controller of the Customs and of the Subsidy on Wool, Skins, and Hides at an annual salary of £10. The duties of a controller were to keep a set of records that duplicated those of the chief customs officers; the controller was thus a check on the honesty of the customs officer. He was to keep his records in his own handwriting, and one of the mysteries surrounding Chaucer is that there is no trace of the thousands of reports he must have submitted. Everything he did in a business way during his maturity would have called for written reports, and they are all missing. In this same year he was appointed Controller of the Petty Customs on wines, cloth, and other merchandise, but apparently did not assume the office for a number of years.

Chaucer would have received the controllership as one of the normal grants made as a matter of course to an esquire, and his receiving it does not indicate that he had any great influence at court. His subsequent appointment of deputies to do the actual work was also quite in line with accepted practice. The £10 he got as salary for the controllership of the wool customs was perhaps nominal, as he probably received more than this in fees. The customs officials, who were wealthy men able to equip fleets of ships from their private resources, received salaries of only £20 a year. Unless they were able to augment this sum, it is inconceivable that they would have bothered with the office.[8]

In 1375 Chaucer was granted the wardships of the lands and heir of Edward Staplegate and later in the year of John de Solys; both of these were Kentish estates. In the Middle Ages wardships of minor heirs were the sources of great profit to the guardians; it might be observed that administering large sums of money is frequently profitable. At any rate, Chaucer did well for himself. Again it must not be assumed that, because Chaucer was awarded these guardianships, he was necessarily of great political consequence. Such gifts were frequently made to esquires of very moderate importance.

In 1376 Chaucer accompanied Sir John de Burley to the Continent "on secret business." This description of Chaucer's occupation titillates our curiosity, which probably must for ever remain unsatisfied. "Secret business" was a fairly common term used in connection with foreign missions on which the king's esquires were sent.

In 1377 he went, possibly via Flanders with Sir Thomas Percy, to Paris and Montreuil, perhaps to treat of peace and to try to arrange a marriage for Prince Richard to a French princess. The same year he made another trip to France. Also in 1377 he was allowed to discharge his duties at the wool customs by deputy. There seems to have been no great feeling on the part of the government against deputies, and permission to employ them was even included in some appointments to office. The original stipulation that Chaucer was to keep the records of his office in his own handwriting was apparently not taken very seriously by anyone concerned in the transaction.

In 1378 Chaucer commuted his daily pitcher of wine for an additional pension of 20 marks a year. In this same year he and John de Beverley were mainpernors (surety) for Sir William de Beauchamp; this is a minor item in Chaucer's biography, but it serves to show that he was a solid and prosperous citizen. Also in 1378 Chaucer went with Sir Edward de Berkeley to try to secure military assistance against France from Bernabo Visconti, Lord of Milan. Before he left England, he gave powers of attorney to John Gower. There has been a good deal of speculation concerning Chaucer's relations with Gower, but this incident, combined with the friendly references that each made to the other in various poems, indicates that they were on familiar and amicable terms.

VII *The Lawsuit*

One of the highly controversial events of Chaucer's life occurred in 1380. He was sued for a *raptus* against the person of Cecilia Chaumpaigne, but was exonerated. The word *raptus* could mean either rape or kidnapping. Most biographers of Chaucer recoil in horror from the idea of rape, holding that the kidnaping interpretation is undoubtedly the correct one. We have no way of discovering just what it was that our poet was accused of; and, for all we know, it could have been a combination of rape and abduction. Since, however, two other men involved in the affair, Richard Goodchild and John Grove, signed deeds of release to Chaucer, and since Cecilia, upon payment of £10 from John Grove, released both Goodchild and Grove, we should probably interpret the word to mean abduction. Some biographers of Chaucer have, however, built up a pretty theory that little Lewis in *A Treatise on the Astrolabe* was the son of Chaucer and Cecilia as a result of this *raptus*. This theory, not supported by a single fact, except that Lewis was ten years old ten years after the *raptus*, is a good example of the legend building that associates itself with the life of a person for whom only scanty biographical data are available.

VIII *Further Business Activities*

In 1381 Chaucer, Ralph Strode, and two others became sureties for John Hende. In the next year Chaucer assumed the controllership of the Petty Customs on wines, cloth, and other goods to which he had apparently been appointed in 1374. This was a much less important position than his controllership of the wool customs, as wool, England's chief export, was the financial basis of the state at the time. He was allowed to discharge the duties of the Petty Customs by a permanent deputy. In 1383 he appointed a deputy for the wool customs for four months, in 1384 a deputy for a month, and in 1385 a permanent deputy.

Also in 1385 he was given black cloth for the funeral of the Princess Joan, widow of Prince Edward, the Black Prince.

On October 12, 1385, Chaucer was appointed a justice of the peace for Kent and was reappointed in June, 1386. This shows that Chaucer had moved from London to the County of Kent, perhaps to Greenwich, as only residents of a county were eligible for the office of justice. As a justice Chaucer would have been a minor judge, but that should not be construed to mean that he was expert in the law. There were usually a few full-fledged lawyers appointed as justices so that in fine points of the law their technical knowledge could be drawn upon by the layman justices. To be appointed a justice, Chaucer would almost certainly have had to own a considerable amount of land in Kent; otherwise, he would hardly have been given the appointment. We do not, however, have any record of his possessing land in that county.

[47]

Philippa Chaucer was admitted to the fraternity of Lincoln Cathedral on February 19, 1386. As the others who were admitted at the same time were all prominent people, this honor may be taken as an indication of Philippa's importance in her own right. But she hardly outshone Geoffrey, who that same year was elected as one of two members of Parliament from Kent. It was during this parliament that the Scropes-Grosvenor trial began. Had it not been for this trial we would have less of an idea when Chaucer was born than we do now.

In that same year Eustache Deschamps sent from France some of his poems through Sir Lewis Clifford to Chaucer. Deschamps asked for Chaucer's opinion of the works, a significant request because it indicates that Chaucer possessed sufficient poetical reputation to be known in France. Deschamps especially praised Chaucer as the translator of the *Roman de la Rose.*

On October 5, 1386, Chaucer had probably given up the house over Aldgate, and in December he terminated his long service with the customs services. There has been much speculation as to why he left the customs, a frequent guess being that he was discharged because his political friends and protectors at court had lost power.

The traditional starting date for the *Canterbury Tales* is 1387. Whether or not the death of his wife Philippa in this same year motivated him to begin the *Tales* is another matter of speculation. It has even been suggested that Chaucer made a pilgrimage to Canterbury in connection with her death. Here again we know nothing definite, although we can confidently assume that he had often traveled the Pilgrims' Way to Canterbury when passing between London and Dover to start his foreign missions.

In July of 1387 Chaucer was granted protection from debt for a year so that he could go to Calais in the retinue of Sir William de Beauchamp. This bit of information perhaps indicates that Chaucer was not in as flourishing a financial condition as he could have wished to be. His going to Calais for an extended time raises a question about his doing any hard and concentrated work on the *Canterbury Tales,* although we do not, of course, know anything about his methods of composing poetry.

Chaucer assigned his pension to John Scalby on May 1, 1388. This action is taken to indicate that Chaucer needed a lump sum of money; the series of writs enjoining his attachment for debt hint that his finances were not in the best condition. Assigning a pension was, however, by no means anything very rare. We have numerous records of esquires signing over pensions, grants, and positions of all kinds. The next year Chaucer was appointed Clerk of the King's Works for certain royal residences and other properties. This was a responsible position, entailing much travel, handling large sums of money, and overseeing hosts of workmen; presumably he received sufficient money from the position to ease his financial difficulties. Chaucer was never, it may be remarked, paid very highly for his governmental work in either salaries or pensions. A few of his fellow esquires were less liberally rewarded than he, others received about as much as he, but many received far more for comparable services.[4]

As Clerk, Chaucer supervised the construction in 1390 of scaffolds for two tournaments held in Smithfield and by special commission saw to the repairs of St. George's Chapel, Windsor. Also in 1390 he was appointed to a commission for the care of the walls, ditches, sewers, and bridges along the Thames between Woolwich and Greenwich. This job, if he did it conscientiously—and we have no reason to believe that he did not—would have taken a great deal of his time. In September he was held up and robbed two or three times in four days, and on one of the occasions he was beaten and wounded. A considerable sum of money belonging to the Works was taken in each holdup. Later he was officially forgiven the repayment of the money that was taken from him. On April 6, 1391, he lent to the Works office 100 marks, which was not repaid to him until May 22, 1392. That he was able to make such a large loan, or any loan at all, indicates that he was not in dire financial condition at this time. On June 17 he gave up the clerkship of the Works. There have been many conjectures about why he resigned: one is that his performance of the office was unsatisfactory; another is that he resigned because of the holdups the previous year. We do not have the answer.

IX *The Forestership*

In June, 1391, Chaucer was appointed deputy forester for the Royal Forest of North Petherton in Somerset. Perhaps receiving the forestership was what induced him to quit the Works office, for he was expected to maintain his residence in the forest during his term of office. The gift of this office belonged to Roger Mortimer, Earl of March and Ulster and grandson of the Countess of Ulster in whose household Chaucer had begun his career. But Chaucer received his appointment not from Roger, who was a minor, but from Sir Peter Courtenay, who was acting as administrator of the forestership and who had been Constable of Windsor Castle while Chaucer had been Clerk of the Works and had directed the repairs referred to before. This fact should amply refute the charge that Chaucer was let out of the Works position because of his incompetence, for Sir Peter would have been in an excellent position to judge his competence.

In this new position Chaucer was not involved in logging, silviculture, or any of the other work we now associate with foresters; he was closer to what we think of as a conservation officer or head gamekeeper than to a custodian of a woodland. This is not to say that Chaucer himself prowled the woods in search of poachers; rather, he supervised the work of the gamekeepers—men like the Knight's Yeoman in the *Canterbury Tales*. It is not at all improbable that Chaucer's Yeoman was the portrait of someone whose work he had overseen at North Petherton. In addition to his probable dwelling in the Park House in the Forest, Chaucer apparently also maintained a legal residence in Kent, as is attested by his serving in April, 1396, on a board of Greenwich freeholders representing Gregory Ballard in a legal action concerning land.

X *Pensions*

On January 9, 1393, there is a record of a gift of £10 for "good service rendered to the King during the year now present," a type of grant regularly made to esquires. On February 28, 1394, Chaucer received an annual grant of £20 for services rendered and to be rendered, and here again we have a typical grant to an esquire. Chaucer received so many advances from the Exchequer on this pension that scholars have been led to believe that he was in financial straits. But the explanation may be that he drew as much of his pension as he could when there was money in the Exchequer, since there were times when it was empty. Also since he was probably not in residence in London, he may have drawn money whenever he made visits to the city, even though the payments were not yet due. There are so many records of people who drew money when it was available and before it was due that it seems to have been a common custom and does not necessarily indicate financial embarrassment.

In December, 1397, the King granted Chaucer an annual butt of wine, another type of gift frequently made to esquires. On April 24, 1398, Isabella, widow of Walter Bukholt, who had been keeper of the king's manor of Clarendon and also Clerk of the Works there, sued Chaucer for over £14. It has been assumed that this suit arose out of something connected with Chaucer's clerkship of the Works. At any rate, Chaucer was given letters of protection against debt for a period of two years so that he could attend to "many difficult and pressing matters" and not be hindered by "certain jealous persons."

XI *Chaucer and Henry IV*

The coronation of King Henry IV occurred on October 13, 1399. One of Henry's first acts on the very day that he received the crown was to renew Chaucer's annual pension for £20 granted in 1394 and the butt of wine granted in 1397. Henry added to these grants an annuity of 40 marks "for services rendered and to be rendered." Apparently Chaucer had been closely associated with Henry of Derby for a considerable length of time before the latter's accession to the throne. At Christmas, 1395, and in February, 1396, Chaucer had conveyed £10 to Henry from the Clerk of the Wardrobe, and in early 1396 Henry had given him a splendid fur-trimmed scarlet robe costing £8 8s. 4d. That Henry saw fit to give Chaucer a piece of wearing apparel that cost the equivalent of thousands of modern dollars could only mean that Chaucer was respected and prosperous; were he not, such a gift would have been a mockery. It also indicates that Chaucer's relationship with Henry must have been more than that of a casual servant.

As Chaucer was presumably a trusted employee of King Richard II at that period, we may well wonder what his connection was with Henry. It may have been that Chaucer saw the ruinous career that Richard was pursuing and decided to attach himself to a worthier man. But Chaucer, so far as we can judge from very scanty evidence, does not seem to have been very active politically. He had friends in all of the warring factions of the time, and we cannot point to a single incident in which a blow was dealt him by any faction for his adherence to some other group.

It has been conjectured that he lost his controllership of the wool customs because of the enmity of the Gloucester faction toward John of Gaunt, but this is pure speculation. He must have been able to maintain a strict neutrality that offended no one; to do this would have been no mean feat, since in politics those who are not for us are against us.

On Christmas Eve of 1399 Chaucer signed a lease for a house in the grounds of St. Mary's Chapel at Westminster Abbey at an annual rental of 53s. 4d. Because the house was close to a religious building, there have been conjectures about Chaucer's feeling toward religion, but we know nothing definite. The lease was to run for the duration of his life.

XII *Death*

According to the inscription on his tomb in what is now called the Poets' Corner of Westminster Abbey, Chaucer died on October 25, 1400. We do not know if the plague that struck that year was the cause of his death. Certainly he did not die of old age, as he was, according to modern belief, but fifty-six or fifty-seven years of age and still a presumably active and valuable servant of the King.

XIII *Chaucer's Children*

How many children Chaucer had is not known. By some scholars the "Lyte Lowys my sone" of *A Treatise on the Astrolabe* was thought to be a godson, the son of Sir Lewis Clifford, Chaucer's good friend. But Professor Manly's discovery of a record linking Lewis with Chaucer's known son Thomas makes it almost certain that Lewis was Geoffrey's son.

Much is known about Thomas Chaucer, who is now generally accepted as the poet's son. Even so, there still remains about him an element of legend. This legend is based on the fact that John of Gaunt made numerous rather valuable gifts to Philippa Chaucer. From this meager evidence biographers have assumed that John fathered Thomas. But even John of Gaunt, morally loose as he was, cannot be imagined guilty of such an act, for Katherine Swynford, Philippa's sister, was John's mistress. According to the mores of the times, sexual intercourse with sisters was incest; and from incest even the most immoral of those days drew back in horror. Contemporary chroniclers were only too happy to record John of Gaunt's moral lapses; and, as they said nothing about an affair between John and Philippa, we can be reasonably confident that there never was one.

Thomas Chaucer was appointed chief butler to Richard II on March 20, 1399, and served until the end of the reign. On November 5, 1402, he was appointed to the same office under Henry IV. Upon the accession of Henry V in 1413, he received the butlership again, but was superseded in March, 1418. When Henry VI came to the throne in 1422, Thomas was reappointed to the office, which he held until his death on March 14, 1434. He represented Oxfordshire in Parliament at frequent intervals from 1400 to 1431, and he was four times speaker of the House of Commons between 1407 and 1414. Upon the accession of Henry IV, he too was appointed forester at North Petherton; and in January, 1424, he was made a member of the Council. He became a very wealthy man, but, like his father, never rose above the rank of esquire. His daughter Alice first married Sir John Philip or Phelip, then Thomas de Montacute, Earl of Salisbury, and finally William de la Pole, Earl and afterwards Duke of Suffolk. One last interesting fact about Thomas is that in 1411 he rented the house in Westminster in which Geoffrey had passed his last days.

Chaucer may have had either one or two daughters. One was an Elizabeth "Chaucy" who became a nun at Barking in 1381; John of Gaunt contributed £31 8s. 2d. toward her expenses. The other was an Agnes Chaucer who was one of the *domicellae* at Henry IV's coronation in 1399. We do not know whether either of these women was actually Chaucer's daughter.

CHAPTER 3

The Short Poems

CHAUCER'S works fall into two main categories: the transla- tions—the *Romaunt of the Rose,* Boethius' *Consolation of Philosophy,* and *A Treatise on the Astrolabe,* which is in the main a translation; and the poems, which are here subdivided into short poems, minor poems, *Troilus and Criseyde,* and the *Can- terbury Tales.* The short poems, our concern in this chapter, in- clude the *Book of the Duchess,* the *House of Fame, Anelida and Arcite,* the *Parliament of Fowls,* and the *Legend of Good Women.* Classifying these poems as "short" is an innovation, for this term is generally applied to those poems which in this book are grouped under the heading of "The Minor Poems." Some of the works classified as "short" are in fact fairly extensive; but, in con- trast to *Troilus and Criseyde* and to the *Canterbury Tales,* they are short. It is with this comparison in mind that they are classi- fied as they are.

I *The* Book of the Duchess

The *Book of the Duchess* (*c.* 1369) is probably Chaucer's first serious narrative poem. How many minor pieces he composed before he attempted it we are unable to say; in the Retractions at the end of the *Canterbury Tales* he indicates that he had written a large number of poems—"many a song and many a leccherous lay"—but these are now lost. It is not unreasonable to believe that these lost works were the first things that he composed and that the *Book of the Duchess* is therefore not an absolute begin- ner's work. It cannot be denied that the *Duchess* is apprentice work, the production of a poet still learning his trade, and as such it is sometimes viewed with a certain amount of condescen- sion. It is far from being a perfect work of art, but, had Chaucer produced no other poem than this one, he would be entitled to a high position in the ranks of Middle English poets. His greatest works, *Troilus and Criseyde* and the *Canterbury Tales*, so completely overshadow the lesser works that we sometimes fail to see their very considerable merits.

The *Book of the Duchess* contains some of the most charming passages in all of Chaucer's works. It begins with Chaucer, who, as the narrator, reflects upon the sleeplessness that has afflicted him during his eight years of unrequited love. One night he seeks to pass away the time by reading the old story of Ceyx and Alcyone, of which he gives a summary: Ceyx, a king, goes upon a journey, leaving at home his wife, Alcyone, sorrowing at being parted from him. Ceyx is drowned, and Alcyone becomes distraught at his continued absence. Finally, in a dream, she learns of his death and in three days she herself dies. Upon finishing the reading of the story Chaucer offers, among other things, a beautiful feather bed as a gift to Morpheus if only he can sleep. Almost immediately he falls asleep and has the following dream —the substance of the rest of the poem.

It seemed that in the dawning of a May morning Chaucer is awakened in a beautiful chamber by the song of the birds and the sounds of the preparations for a hunt. Upon the walls of the room in which he lies are depicted stories about the war at Troy, Jason and Medea, and matter from the *Roman de la Rose*. Chaucer, gladdened at the idea of going on a hunt, dresses and mounts his horse, which he rides from the room. He learns that the hunt is being held by the Emperor Octavian, and soon he is in a wonderful woodland abounding with wild animals.

Chaucer finds a stray little hunting dog, and when it flees from him he follows it. Suddenly he comes upon a man dressed in black, who, sitting with his back against an oak tree, unaware of Chaucer's presence, is singing a song about his lady love. For a long time the man does not notice Chaucer, who, motivated by the desire to relieve the man's obvious sorrow, finally engages him in conversation. At first the man uses the symbolism of a game of chess and says that he has lost his queen. When, however, Chaucer incredulously asks if all this woe is for the loss of a chess piece, the man tells of having loved a wonderful woman in whom all virtues united. When she finally accepted him as her servant in love, his long-continued woe turned to utter bliss. Chaucer, interested in such a paragon, asks where she is. When informed that she is dead, he receives the announcement with quiet sympathy. A concluding paragraph of the poem indicates in thinly veiled language that the man in black was John of Lancaster, whom we know as John of Gaunt; and the fair lady White, his love, was Blanche of Lancaster.

There is little of the majestic in Chaucer that is found in Homer, Dante, Shakespeare; there is, instead, an abundance of pure delight that puts him in a class by himself. He solves none of the problems that have vexed the minds of men from time immemorial; he does not set right the ills of the world, nor does he give us a code of morals by which to live. He looks calmly at the world, records what he sees, and gives us a collection of works that have been joyfully read for 600 years.

When Chaucer wrote the *Book of the Duchess*, he was strongly under the influence of the French school of dream poets, and his poem draws directly upon a number of French works for ideas, phrases, and words. But considering this, he showed considerable independence in modifying for his own purposes the material that inspired him. His dream poems are sometimes considered to be slavish imitations of his French originals. Yet a comparison of any one of Chaucer's poems with any French poem should convince even the most skeptical that he was an innovator, not an imitator. The dream was not for Chaucer merely the mechanism to provide the setting. Rather it had for him an enduring interest—from the *Book of the Duchess* through the *House of Fame*, the *Parliament of Fowls*, the *Legend of Good Women*, the *Knight's Tale*, and the *Nun's Priest's Tale*. In some of these works Chaucer, as narrator, merely falls asleep and dreams the substance of the poem; in others he wonders what causes different kinds of dreams, and why one dream has great significance and another none. He, in fact, shows a modern psychologist's interest in dreams.

Although Chaucer is held in great esteem, even those who love him best sometimes fail to realize the magnitude of his achievement. In English there were no models for him to follow—at least no models that he apparently wished to follow. It is true that when he began to write there was extant a considerable body of Middle English poetry, but the poems were mainly of but moderate quality. And not only were good models in English lacking, but all of his sources were in alien tongues. Chaucer, with foreign sources as his raw material and with only that mysterious thing called genius to guide him, refined his ore into the gold of his finished works. It was this genius that caused succeeding generations to consider him the "father of English poetry," a title he does not really deserve. He did not create English poetry, and still less did he create the English language. What he actually did was to realize the full potentialities of the London dialect of his time.

Scholars have pointed out that for the *Book of the Duchess* Chaucer made extensive use of Guillaume de Machaut's *Jugement dou Roy Behaingne* and perhaps drew upon eight other of Machaut's poems, including the *Dit dou Lyon*, which, in the Retractions to the *Canterbury Tales*, he intimates he at one time translated. He also relied heavily on the *Roman de la Rose*, Jean Froissart's *Paradys d'Amour*, the anonymous *Le Songe Vert*, and Ovid's *Metamorphoses*. Such an array of sources might give the impression that Chaucer assembled his poem with a pair of scissors and a pot of paste, but he did no such thing. What he produced is marked by his own genius, immature as it was.

Why Chaucer wrote a poem in praise of the dead Duchess Blanche of Lancaster will probably always remain a mystery. As was said earlier, there is no reason to believe that the work was commissioned by John of Gaunt. From the tender and loving tone of the poem we might conclude that Chaucer wrote his tribute to her from no more mercenary motive than a strong affection. Blanche, if she was like her description in the poem, was just such a person as to appeal to Chaucer's gentle heart. Scholars have shown that practically everything Chaucer said about Blanche can be found in his French originals, that the description is purely conventional.

The verse form of the *Book of the Duchess* is the tetrameter couplet, of which Chaucer's mastery is at this point less than complete. There are irregular lines that defy scansion, which H. Frank Heath believes are not the result of Chaucer's lack of skill, but echoes of the rhythmic system of verse that prevailed in England until Chaucer's time.[1] It is true that many of Chaucer's predecessors wrote verse lines with four strongly marked beats that do not scan, but upon the whole, Heath's assumption is rather doubtful. After one more poem, the *House of Fame*, Chaucer was to turn his attention to the iambic pentameter line in the seven-line rime royal stanza and in the rhymed couplet, both of which forms he eventually wrote with fine skill. If *An ABC* is, as we believe, earlier than the *Book of the Duchess,* he was already writing the pentameter line with considerable mastery.

At first glance, the *Book of the Duchess* seems somewhat badly organized and disjointed, but actually it has a neat structure and a subtle unity woven around the theme of love-longing. For the narrator's opening reflection on his long-continued sleeplessness, the cause of which was an unattainable lady, Chaucer drew directly on Froissart, who in turn had drawn on Machaut. Chaucer, however, imparted such a complete authenticity to his plaint that many critics believe it to be autobiographical.

The narrator's (or Chaucer's) unrequited love, then, is set against the pitiful tale of Ceyx and Alcyone, which, to pass the time away as he lies in bed, he reads and relates to us. Morpheus responds promptly to the narrator's offering of the furnishing of a bed, and the narrator falls asleep to dream of love-longing as it appears for the third time in the poem in the complaint of the man in black for his lost love. It can be seen that each episode is unified with the others; the theme of love-longing is common to the narrator, Alcyone, and the man in black. Perhaps the *Book of the Duchess* is too spun out and takes too long to reach the climax, but we must admit that its structure is more tightly woven than a quick first glance indicates.

The beginning of the narrator's dream is justly admired. The bedchamber in which he finds himself, mounting the horse in the room, riding forth into the outdoors to join the Emperor Octavian's hunt, and the tidy, symmetrical forest fairly bursting with various animals are all subtle distortions of reality that make this dream a masterpiece. Literature is filled with dreams, many of them artificially contrived devices. Few of them have the validity and the fresh charm of this one.

The hunting scenes are so authentic that critics have assumed Chaucer was drawing upon experience when he depicted them— as an esquire of the King, he would be quite familiar with field sports. Yet, even though he probably had a surfeit of talk about hunting in the court of Edward III, it should be noted that most of the details he gives can be found in his French sources. It might strike the reader that the little lost whelp is somewhat of a digression, but it is not. Following the fleeing whelp is a highly realistic detail; it was always the duty of anyone on a hunt to capture any young dogs that strayed from the main pack. There is a fine artistry about this little episode; Chaucer uses the straying whelp to effect a smooth transition from the preliminary matter of the poem into his main theme. The device of the dog may also be found in French literature, but nowhere will one find such a genuine little whelp.

The dealings of the narrator with the man in black have led many readers to assume that Chaucer was a remarkably naïve fellow. Passages in several other poems apparently confirm the impression: the narrator's conversation with the eagle in the *House of Fame,* his humility before the angry God of Love in the *Legend of Good Women,* and his bumbling incompetence in telling the *Tale of Sir Thopas.* What should be borne firmly in mind is that this naïveté is that of characters whom Chaucer has created, not of the man Chaucer himself. The one thing that a really naïve poet never does is depict himself as naïve; he invariably tends toward the other extreme and pictures himself as worldly wise. A poet must have a complete awareness of the ways of the world to make a butt of himself as Chaucer did; and if we had nothing of Chaucer's but the *Book of the Duchess,* we would know that he was anything but simple-minded.

One might think that the narrator was remarkably obtuse to believe that a grown man would be cast into the depths of despair over losing a game of chess. But this is to overlook what Chaucer was telling us. When the narrator approaches, the man in black is singing an elegy to his dead lady; the narrator recognizes, when the song is finished, that something extremely serious has occurred in the life of the man in black. The narrator says:

> *And telleth me of your sorwes smerte;*
> *Paraunter hyt may ese youre herte,*
> *That semeth ful sek under your syde.*   (BD, 555-57)

In other words, the narrator, seeing that the man in black is filled with woe, invites him to seek release from sorrow by telling what is on his mind. Thereupon the man begins with the symbolism of the game of chess. This soon gives way to his adven-

tures in love, which culminate in the lady's accepting him as her
servant-lover. It is worth noting that there is never so much as a
hint of marriage in this recital, although, of course, John of
Gaunt and Blanche of Lancaster were husband and wife. Chaucer
preferred to deal with courtly love, which is much more ro-
mantic than married love. Marriage is, as a matter of sober fact,
singularly prosaic in its literary presentations. The *Clerk's
Tale* deals with marriage, but until Grisilde was reunited with
her children it can hardly be termed a happy one from her point
of view, and when the turning point from sadness to gladness occurs, the Clerk dismisses the matter with two lines:

> *Ful many a yeer in heigh prosperitee*
> *Lyven thise two in concord and in reste.*   (CT, IV, 1128-29)

Even these lines do not indicate anything in the way of wild
ecstasy. Arveragus and Dorigen are happily married, but the
emphasis in the *Franklin's Tale* is on the skirmishing between
Aurelius and Dorigen rather than upon the love of Arveragus and
Dorigen.

The *Book of the Duchess* is a tale of love and not of death. It
is an elegy, it is true, but death is of secondary importance to
life. The chief concern of the poet is the loveliness of the living
Blanche. The emphasis is not on the coldness of the grave but on
the warmth of the living woman. Thus we are sad that Blanche
passed from the land of the living, but our sadness is tempered by
our memory of a charming and delightful woman.

II *The* House of Fame

The *House of Fame* (*c.* 1374) begins with a "Proem" in which
Chaucer speculates upon the meaning of dreams and then announces that he will relate a wonderful dream that he had on
December 10. Before launching into his narrative, however, he
invokes the god of sleep; he wishes well to all those who take
his dream aright and ill fortune to those who scorn it.

The dream begins with Chaucer in a glass temple filled with
rich images of such figures as Venus and Cupid, with tabernacles,
portraits, and so on. On the walls is portrayed Dido's love for
Aeneas and how he betrayed her. The latter part of the *Aeneid*
is very briefly summarized, and, after he has observed these

things, Chaucer goes outside to see if he can get more information about this wonderful structure. As he stands on the field of sand in front of the building, a golden eagle swoops down from the sky.

The eagle seizes Chaucer and bears him aloft, and Chaucer is for a time numbed by fright. The eagle, who proves to be extremely talkative, explains that no harm will come to him. Because he sits dumb as a stone before a book after his day's work is done and thus only writes in honor of love without experiencing it, Chaucer is being transported to a region where he can observe the behavior of love's folks. He is being taken to the House of Fame, to which everything that is said on earth comes. When Chaucer admits that he does not understand how this could be, the eagle delivers a lengthy explanation of the theory of sound; for this he smugly congratulates himself as having spoken plainly and simply to an ignorant man.

After seeing the sights of the cosmos, Chaucer is deposited on a hill of ice in front of the elaborate House of Fame. From within there issues a tremendous confusion of sounds. On the hill of ice many names are engraved, although some are now so melted away that they are hardly legible.

Inside the house are minstrels, poets, musicians, historians, heralds, sleight-of hand artists—all sorts of people who have spread news from the earliest days of mythology down to Chaucer's time. Finally Chaucer sees Fame, a woman who is covered with eyes and who continually fluctuates in size. She is attended by Aeolus, regent of the winds, who has two trumpets, Clere Laude, or praise, and Sklaundre, or ill fame. To Fame come company after company of people, some of whom deserve fame, some shame. Some desire reputation; others are indifferent to it. They make their requests for fame or silence concerning their names; and Fame, in a completely whimsical and illogical fashion, gives them whatever she wants to by having Aeolus blow on either Clere Laude or Sklaundre.

After Chaucer observes this scene, the eagle deposits him through a hole in the roof in the House of Rumor, a whirling wickerwork structure sixty miles in diameter. In this building there is to be found everything that is said on earth, no matter how quietly it may be whispered. As the various speeches are passed from person to person, they become modified beyond recognition. A man of great authority appears, and he is surrounded by the occupants of the building. Chaucer cranes forward to see what is going on, but at this point the poem is broken off.

In some ways the *House of Fame* is similar to the *Book of the Duchess;* in some ways it is superior and in others, inferior. It is similar in that it is a dream poem in octosyllabic couplets. Both poems begin with the extensive retelling of a classical tale, and both work up to a surprise ending. Although in the *Book of the Duchess* the reader is aware of what ending to expect the narrator does not seem to suspect, for he receives the information about the death of White as if he were surprised. Undoubtedly the ending of the *House of Fame* was to be a surprise; unfortunately the poem breaks off short of the conclusion and the narrator—and we, the readers—are left in the dark.

The verse of the *House of Fame* is essentially the same as that of the *Book of the Duchess,* but Chaucer handles it with greater skill. It has a naturalness and ease lacking in his first essay with this particular meter. The meter has the advantage of being far better suited to the subject of the *House of Fame* than to that of the *Book of the Duchess.* The comparatively rapid movement of the four-foot line, not particularly well adapted to an elegy, suits the rushing subject matter of most of the *House of Fame.*

A good case can be made for using the tale of Ceyx and Alcyone to begin the *Book of the Duchess,* since this classical prologue and Chaucer's continuation both deal with the death of loved ones. Just what application the classical story of Aeneas and Dido has to the story of the *House of Fame* is a matter of speculation. As the poem exists, in its unfinished state, we can see little connection between the two parts; it is possible that a connection might have become manifest had the poem been completed. The story of Aeneas and Dido is one of love, and Chaucer specifically told us that the *House of Fame* was to be about love; the trouble is that he never got to deal with his announced subject.

Interest in the *House of Fame* far exceeds that in the *Book of the Duchess.* Our fascination with some things Chaucer tells us in the *House of Fame* is unrivaled in all the rest of his works. This statement could hardly be made for the *Book of the Duchess.* The pure fantasy of the *House of Fame* is delightful, and the autobiographical details are both informative and charmingly told. The talkative eagle is, of course, one of the great characters of English literature; he is worthy of a place beside Pandarus and Criseyde in Chaucer's gallery of inventions. From this poem we also get some idea of Chaucer's interest in science: his curiosity about psychology when he speculates on the nature and causes of dreams in the "Proem," and his knowledge of physics when the eagle explains the nature of sound. And had the narrator not balked at listening to it, we would have had a treatise on astronomy, as the eagle was quite eager to deliver one. We do not know whether this engaging fowl would gladly learn, but there can be no doubt that he would gladly teach.

Throughout his writing career, as has been said, Chaucer was fascinated by dreams. He was familiar with much of the extant literature concerning them, but, more important, he evidently thought deeply about the subject. His speculations were to culminate in the immortal *Nun's Priest's Tale*. His interest in the physical sciences is not perhaps so obvious as that in the mental sciences, but it also was deep. His description of the nature of sound has often been called "modern," but there is much of the medieval in his idea that there is a place for everything and everything strives to reach its place.

The *Book of the Duchess* was written in 1369 or soon thereafter; the *House of Fame*, if we can trust the reference in Book II to reckonings:

> *For when thy labour doon al ys,*
> *And hast mad alle thy rekenynges,*   (652-53)

must have been written no earlier than 1374, in which year Chaucer received his appointment as Controller of Customs. An event of great impact on Chaucer's development as a poet had occurred between 1369 and 1374; in 1372 he had visited Italy, where he became acquainted with the works of Dante.

The similarities between the *House of Fame* and the *Divine Comedy* have many times been mentioned by scholars, although the two are extremely different entities. Both are divided into three sections; both deal in some way with Aeneas; both involve travel into strange regions; both poets are borne aloft by golden eagles; and both have guides. These inconsequential similarities pall in the face of the really vital relationship between the Italian and the Englishman—their powers of description. When Chaucer learned from Dante how to employ realistic description, he became the first English poet to use this technique successfully, an achievement that set Chaucer apart from his forerunners and contemporaries. When we pause to consider how much his works owe to the vivid pictures they contain, we can in large measure appreciate what Dante did for him. The *House of Fame* is loaded with description; a modern reader, to whom description is commonplace, is often unaware of its presence and certainly of its importance, but it is there.

Just how Chaucer intended to end the poem we will never know. Some writers have suggested that the ending was lost. A likelier supposition is that Chaucer actually had no definite ending in view when he began and never formulated one as he progressed. Of all his works, this one has the loosest structure and the least unity. It is true that the narrator as an observer of the shifting scene throughout the work gives unity to the point of view, but there is never any sign of a plot or story line. Chaucer is not even consistent in his use of the word "fame"; in his first observance of the goddess Fame she is the equivalent of reputation or renown; in her second manifestation she is gossip or rumor.

What the man of great authority at the end of the poem was going to say or do we do not know. We are, if we admit the truth, at a complete nonplus about his function. Some writers believe that he was going to say something about love, but there is little in the poem to support this theory. There is another theory that this is an occasional poem and that the man was going to make some statement concerning a well-known person, perhaps Philippa of Lancaster, John of Gaunt's daughter.

Though the poem admittedly is structurally faulty, it contains much to delight us. The beginning of the work, a résumé of the early books of the *Aeneid*, is not among the best passages of Chaucer's works, and we are hard put to justify its use as a prologue to a work about fame. Chaucer informs us at the beginning of Book II that he is going to be told about matters of love, since he writes about them without experience. If, then, the poem is to deal with love, perhaps the story of Aeneas's betrayal of Dido could be justified. But Chaucer is so speedily diverted from love to fame that it is difficult to see the appositeness of the

Aeneas story. It is really remarkable how quickly and completely Chaucer gets away from his avowed purpose of receiving news about love's folk. From line 605 to line 699—almost a full hundred lines—the eagle explains why Chaucer will be given tidings of love, and he also goes into exquisite detail about what the tidings will include. And that is practically the last we hear about love!

The retelling of the Aeneas-Dido story is, as was said, not in Chaucer's happiest vein. He is constantly hurrying himself along, and at the end he jams the last eight books of the *Aeneid* into about forty lines of verse. He writes this part of the poem with little inspiration; it is as if the subject bored him. This prelude does not prepare the reader for the amazing explosion into the magnificent second book. Rarely has there been a sharper contrast between two books in a single poem. John L. Lowes has given a logical explanation for the difference between the books: Book I is in the French vein, but Book II is filled with the influence of Dante.[2]

The second book of the *House of Fame* is pure delight, one of the high points of English literature. There is such a contrast between the taciturn, stodgy narrator and the brisk, talkative eagle that we can read and re-read the book with never-ending joy. It is here that we have a bit of autobiography—a rare thing from Chaucer's pen—for there is little doubt that we are being treated to a fairly accurate picture of Chaucer's daily life. Nowhere in English literature do we get such complete self-abasement by an author, and nowhere else do we get such an amusing self-portrait.

The House of Fame, with the enthroned goddess distributing or withholding good reputation and slander in a wholly whimsical and illogical fashion, is interesting, but it is secondary to the House of Rumor, which we have already described. When Chaucer had accomplished the not inconsiderable feat of inventing this marvelous structure, his imagination, so far as we know, was exhausted, and he moved on to the composition of a new poem.

III Anelida and Arcite

Probably the work that Chaucer attempted immediately after the *House of Fame* was the *Compleynt of faire Anelida and fals*

Arcite (date doubtful; perhaps 1374). This begins with an "Invocation" to Mars and to the Muse Polymya to help in telling the story of the love of Anelida for the false Arcite. Theseus returns from the war against the Amazons with his wife, Hippolyta. While riding toward his country home, he tells how in Thebes the beautiful queen, Anelida, loves the double-dealing knight, Arcite, who poses as a devoted lover, but actually is as false as he can be. When Anelida learns that she has been deserted by him for another lady, she nearly goes out of her mind for sorrow. To let Arcite know of her grief she sends him an elaborate complaint, chiding him for his duplicity. Half a dozen lines after the conclusion of the complaint, the poem breaks off.

Anelida and Arcite is of some interest in tracing Chaucer's development as a literary artist, but it is of rather little value as literature. Based on Boccaccio's *Teseide,* it is a thin story, but it shows Chaucer's increasing mastery of versification; in fact, the progress shown since the *House of Fame* is remarkable. The seven-line rime royal stanza is a difficult form to master, but Chaucer uses it confidently, as he does the longer stanzas of the *Compleynt.* This was probably not his first attempt to write the seven-line stanza, for he used it in several minor poems that may have been written considerably earlier than this one. Of all of Chaucer's poems of any length, *Anelida and Arcite* has the most formal structure, and probably therein lies the chief reason for its being unfinished. Chaucer's genius lay not in formal structure but in a seemingly natural and conversational tone. Passages in the high style are comparatively rare in Chaucer's works, and they usually quickly give way to his easier manner. When he next used the *Teseide* as a source, he was a more accomplished poet, and the splendid *Knight's Tale* was the result of his labors.

IV *The* Parliament of Fowls

The *Parliament of Fowls* (*c.* 1382) continues from *Anelida* the use of the rime royal stanza. Chaucer was to use this stanza often; whether all the works written in it, including those in the *Canterbury Tales,* should be grouped in the same period of his poetical activity is a matter for debate.

The poem begins with reflections on the art of love, which is learned with great difficulty. Then there are reflections on books, from which comes all good learning. One of the books that

Chaucer had recently read is Cicero's *Dream of Scipio*, which he briefly summarizes. After he had read the book, he had fallen asleep and had dreamed of Scipio, who took him to a walled park, over the gate of which were two inscriptions. One proclaimed that this was the way to the well of grace and all happiness; the other that this was the way to the sphere of danger and disdain. Chaucer hesitates to enter, but Scipio shoves him through the gateway and says that, even though Chaucer is dull, he will find matter to write about within the walls.

Once inside the park Chaucer sees a great variety of trees, flowers, birds, and animals in a garden upon a river's brim. A melody of ravishing sweetness issues from many musical instruments; the air is temperate. Cupid lies under a tree sharpening his arrows, and several personifications dance before a temple. In the temple are to be seen other personifications.

Finally Chaucer comes upon the Goddess of Nature sitting on a lawn. As it is St. Valentine's Day, she is surrounded by all kinds of birds, who have assembled to choose their mates. Birds of prey sit highest; below them are fowls that eat worms; lowest of all are the waterfowl. Chaucer enumerates many of the kinds of birds present. Nature sits with a beautiful formel (female) eagle upon her hand and announces that the royal tercel (male) eagle is to make the first choice of a mate. It is, however, necessary that the female chosen consent to be his love.

The royal tercel explains that he wishes the formel on Nature's hand, whom he loves and to whom he promises to be true. He claims that since no one loves her as well as he, it is only right for him to have her. But another tercel eagle of lower kind disputes the choice. He loves her better than the first one does, he says, and has served her longer; he, too, will serve her faithfully. A third tercel eagle admits that he has not loved her long, but, for all that, his love is intense and he deserves her.

The argument continues for hours. The other fowls, impatient to choose their mates and be on their way, object to its length. The goose says that he will give his opinion of the matter; the cuckoo says that he will speak for the wormfowls; and the turtle dove volunteers to give the verdict of the seedfowls. A tercelet interrupts to suggest that the matter be decided by battle, to which proposition the tercels readily agree, but no bloodshed ensues.

The waterfowls lay their heads together, and the goose, their spokesman, says that if the tercels cannot have the formel, let them take someone else. The gentle fowls sneer at such a coarse idea, and the turtle says that she believes in lifelong fidelity. The cuckoo says that he does not care who chooses whom, so long as he can have his own mate in peace.

At this point Nature takes a hand and says that the choice shall be left to the formel, who blushingly decides that she will have none of her suitors for at least a year. Upon hearing this decision, the other birds choose their mates, sing a very pretty little hymn, and fly away.

For generations the *Parliament of Fowls* was a battleground for symbolists. The classes of birds in the poem seemed to represent something more than mere birds; and the three male birds of prey looked like three royal or at least noble suitors for the hand of a fair lady. Could Chaucer, then, the question was asked, have meant the various classes of birds to symbolize the different classes of society and the three fowls of ravine, three historical personages who all wished to marry the same lady?

The symbolists found it easy enough to work out interpretations for the groups of birds—of course, there was not universal agreement as to what the groups meant. The royal eagle was almost universally thought to be King Richard II, but there the agreement ended. When it came to assigning specific names to the other two tercels, there were many and grave differences of opinion.

The numerous opinions resulted from the failure of the scholars to decide whom the formel represented. Many asserted that she was Anne of Bohemia, who became the queen of Richard II, but there were those who insisted that she was Marie of France, and still others who thought that she was Philippa of Lancaster. There was even a theory that the poem celebrated Chaucer's own marriage, but the idea of Chaucer depicting himself as a royal eagle ready and eager for bloody battle has not met with wide acceptance since there is nothing in his works to indicate that he was anything but the gentlest of men. Some of those who held that the formel was Anne of Bohemia believed that the males were Richard II, Charles VI of France, and Frederick of Meissen; the adherents of Philippa of Lancaster chose Richard, William of Hainault, and John of Blois; and the enthusiasts for Marie of France contended that the royal tercel was Richard, the second tercel was William of Bavaria, and for the third they chose several candidates.

The interpretative efforts always ignominiously collapsed when the end of the *Parliament of Fowls* was contemplated. This work, according to the symbolists, is a poetic compliment to a pair of royal lovers. The fallacy in this theory is that if it was meant to be a complimentary poem, it is probably the most insulting one on record. The formel, instead of accepting the royal eagle as her lover—as would be proper in a work intended to flatter royal personages—is so lukewarm about her suitors that she asks for a year's delay before choosing a mate. Certainly this could not be very elevating to the ego of whoever the royal eagle was meant to be.

Of late the tendency has been to judge the poem simply as a generalized treatise on love, without personal applications; in other words, it is a *demande d'amours* in celebration of St. Valentine's Day. In the large part of the work devoted to the views on love proffered by the different classes of fowls, Chaucer is sometimes thought to be satirizing the different classes of society.

There is a distinct possibility that by the classes of birds Chaucer was satirizing the procedures of the English Parliament. The name of the poem assists this interpretation, and we must remember that Chaucer had once been a member of that body.

When we have said all we can against identifying the groups and individual birds with classes of society and historical personages, the feeling still persists that Chaucer was doing more than writing a generalized St. Valentine's Day poem, but no interpretation thus far advanced has won wide acceptance. When Chaucer wrote the frankly occasional *Book of the Duchess*, he left no doubt as to whom he meant by the man in black and the lady White. With this precedent in mind, we can justifiably think that if the *Parliament of Fowls* was occasional, Chaucer would have let his readers know what the occasion was. When a medieval poet was dealing in allegory or symbolism, he rarely left any doubt about what he was referring to. The *Roman de la Rose* provides a good example of the method. Nor was the method restricted to French poetry, as the allegory is clear enough in Langland's *The Vision of Piers Plowman*.

V *The* Legend of Good Women

In the *Legend of Good Women* (*c.* 1386) Chaucer for the first time uses the heroic couplet—two rhyming iambic pentameter lines. This metrical form was his own invention; he uses it with splendid effect in his later works; and, because of his mastery of it and its employment by succeeding writers, it is considered one of the greatest of the English meters.

The *Prologue* to the *Legend of Good Women* begins with Chaucer's famous tribute to the daisy, the flower he loves so dearly that it, and it alone, can draw him away from his books in the month of May. One evening he speeds home from his contemplation of the daisy in the fields, falls asleep in a little arbor, and dreams that he is in a fair meadow. The little birds sing that they defy the fowler and bless St. Valentine, upon whose day they choose their mates.

A lark announces the arrival of the God of Love, richly clad in embroidered green silk and wearing a crown of roses and lilies. In his hands are two fiery darts. He conducts a queen, Alceste, also dressed in green, but bedecked with a white crown made of many flowers. She resembles the daisy crowned with white petals. After her and the God of Love there come nineteen ladies in royal dress, and after them a tremendous multitude of ladies—all of them true to their loves.

When they come to the daisy, they kneel around it and then dance around it, singing a ballade to Alceste. When the song is concluded, they sit down upon the green and fall silent. Chaucer, who is under a slope, is seen by the God of Love, who demands to know who he is. Upon Chaucer's answering "It am I," the God of Love says that the presence of a worm would be as welcome as that of the poet, who by his translation of the *Roman de la Rose* and by his composition of *Troilus and Criseyde* has caused people to withdraw from the God of Love. Why could he not write of true women instead of untrue ones? Chaucer has sixty books in his library, and in them there is abundant material about good women. Chaucer, says the God of Love, will repent of his reprehensible behavior.

Alceste seeks to placate the angry God of Love and to soothe his ruffled feelings. In the god's court, she says, are many unfaithful people, and it may be that Chaucer has been falsely accused. Perhaps he translated the *Rose* and wrote about Criseyde in all innocence; in his other works he had displayed no like malice. A god or a king should be like a lion and disdain to injure anything as insignificant as a fly; therefore, the God of Love should not avenge himself on Chaucer. When Chaucer was young, he was a lover and had furthered the God of Love's law with his poems; a renegade now, perhaps, but formerly he had taught ignorant folk how to serve the God of Love. Alceste catalogs Chaucer's works and requests the God of Love not to hurt Chaucer, who will again write poems about true women.

The God of Love assents to Alceste's request for clemency, and Chaucer avers that his intentions had always been to further love. Thereupon Alceste says that Chaucer will do penance for his past ills by writing year by year a glorious legend of good women true in love. The God of Love, placated, gives a brief summary of the story of Alceste, who had turned into a daisy, and tells Chaucer that he is to write about her.

Chaucer begins his legends with Cleopatra, and continues with Thisbe, Dido, Hysipyle, Medea, Lucrece, Ariadne, Philomela, Phyllis, and Hypermnestra, the last unfinished.

The *Legend* was probably Chaucer's last lengthy poem before he began the composition of the *Canterbury Tales;* it was also his last to use the dream framework and the last written under the influence of French courtly poetry. The poem actually has two prologues, both customarily printed in modern editions of the poet's works. It is upon these prologues that scholars justifiably center their interest, rather than upon the stories that they preface. They are as charming and graceful as anything that Chaucer composed while under the French influence. Why they are under the French influence poses a question; they were written after *Troilus and Criseyde*, great to a large extent because it is largely free from the courtly influence of France. If, however, Chaucer had been commanded by Anne of Bohemia to write a defense of good women, a possibility treated below, the very nature of the subject would have compelled him to abandon his new manner and to revert to his earlier one.

What is usually designated at the F text of the *Prologue* (also called the B) exists in a number of manuscripts, but the G text (also called the A) in only one. At first glance very similar, the two prologues are actually quite different. Immediately the question arises as to which was the earlier and which the revision, but this seemingly simple query cannot be answered with any degree of finality. Scholarly opinion is fairly evenly divided as to the priority of the two versions, but there seem to be more reasons for believing F (B) was written first than there are for G (A). We might think that a comparison of similar but somewhat different lines in the two prologues would indicate the clear literary supremacy of the revised version; but such a test proves remarkably little. First a passage in the F text strikes us as definitely better than its counterpart in G, but a later passage in the G text proves clearly superior to the corresponding lines in F. Not only will our comparison of parallel passages completely confuse us as to which should be labeled the earlier and which the later, but it will also cause us to wonder about Chaucer and his method of writing. The inescapable conclusion is that he often altered passages for the worse rather than the better. At the very least, our examination will drive home the fact that our literary taste is sometimes at variance with Chaucer's.

In the celebrated opening passage Chaucer pays his reverence to his "sixty bokes olde and newe" (G, 273)—and whoever owed a deeper debt to books or made such charming use of them? It is true, as many have said, that Chaucer was a keen observer of humanity, but the thing that made him a great poet was the use he made of what he read. And so he, here, quite aptly indicates how vital books are to him. But important as books are, the power of the May morning is too much for him; it draws him out into the light of day to render his homage to his beloved flower, the daisy.

The account of Chaucer's love for the daisy is one of the best things he wrote, and it has won him a reputation of being a nature poet. But, though Chaucer might have been genuinely fond of this flower, we should note that what he says about it derives directly from numerous other poets, mainly French. There was in France an elaborate cult of the daisy, or marguerite, and many poems, especially by Machaut, Froissart, and Deschamps, glorified it. Courtiers, indeed, were supposed to be divided into two factions that vied in celebrating the virtues of the flower as against those of the leaf. How much of this marguerite-worship there was in England is difficult to decide; but if the affectation was popular in France, it is reasonable to believe that it was also popular in English courtly circles.

In the *Legend* Chaucer tells us more about himself than that he was a lover of flowers. We learn that he had a private library of sixty books, an extremely large collection for his era. Actually his library might have included several hundred works, since a single volume might contain a variety of titles. In the *Wife of Bath's Tale*, the fifth husband's anthology of stories about wicked wives contained at least half a dozen separate works, and it would be surprising if Chaucer's personal library lacked this collection. Much has been written about the high prices of books in Chaucer's time. It is true that those profusely illustrated were expensive, as a book would be today if it were abundantly hand-illustrated by a good artist; but a plain text, without decorations and simply bound, would not have cost much. Chaucer's sixty books were probably well within his means.

Not only does Chaucer tell us the size of his library, but he gives us a bibliography of his own writings (F, 417-30; G, 405-20). The mention of "the love of Palamon and Arcite / Of Thebes" (F, 420-21) might testify that some version of the *Knight's Tale* was in circulation at a time earlier than that of the composition of the *Canterbury Tales*. There have been theories that the *Knight's Tale* as we have it is a revision of an original "love of Palamon and Arcite," but we have no facts. When Chaucer says that "the storye is knowen lyte" (F, 421), he is probably saying that there is a general lack of knowledge about the tale, not necessarily that his own tale has had a restricted circulation or none at all. We should not be surprised to find Chaucer listing "the lyf also of Seynt Cecile" (F, 426), for the *Second Nun's Tale* has all the earmarks of an early work.

When we come to "Origenes upon the Maudeleyne" (F, 428), we assume that he is talking about a translation of *De Maria Magdalena*, attributed to Origen. Chaucer's translation has been lost, as has been "the Wreched Engendrynge of Mankynde," mentioned only in the G text (414). This translation of Pope Innocent III's gloomy *De Contemptu Mundi sive Miseria Conditionis Humanae* is thought by some to have been rendered into prose and perhaps was to be told by the Man of Law, who mentions it; there are passages from it in both the *Man of Law's*

Introduction and *Tale*. That only the G text of the *Prologue* of the *Legend* mentions the translation might confirm it as the later one, since Chaucer must have done the translation after the F text was completed and before the G text was composed.

The passage in the F text:

> *Goo now thy wey, this penaunce ys but lyte.*
> *And whan this book ys maad, yive it the quene,*
> *On my byhalf, at Eltham or at Sheene,* (F, 495-97)

has frequently been interpreted to mean that Queen Anne assigned Chaucer the task of glorifying women faithful in love as penance for writing about the lack of fidelity in *Troilus and Criseyde* and the *Romaunt of the Rose*. The fact that this passage is missing from the G text is taken to indicate that Queen Anne had died before the G text was composed. As she died on June 7, 1394, this would place the revision of the *Prologue*, if the G text, in the middle of the period when he composed the *Canterbury Tales*—or even later, if we accept at face value what Chaucer says about himself in *Lenvoy de Chaucer a Scogan*, treated in "The Envoys." Scholars believe that the F text of the *Prologue* was probably composed about 1386. If, then, Chaucer's interest in the *Legend of Good Women* persisted from 1386 to 1394, we have a most unusual situation: Chaucer was actively concerned with this poem over a longer span of years than he was with any other of his works, with the possible exception of the *Canterbury Tales*.

Much has been said about the actual tales of the *Legend*, and little of it has been complimentary. To begin with, we cannot state with any finality how many tales Chaucer intended to write. Various texts of the Retractions to the *Canterbury Tales* mention both nineteen and twenty-five as the number of stories in the completed work. We might assume that the *Legend* tales the Man of Law lists in his *Introduction* have been completed. He cites sixteen, but only eight of them are in the *Legend* as we have it and eight are missing; moreover, two tales, *Cleopatra* and *Philomela*, are in the *Legend* but not in the Man of Law's list. Before such confusion we hardly have the heart to formulate a theory to bring order. All we can say is that the Man of Law's statement and Chaucer's performance as we can see it do not agree. It might be added that no one has volunteered the theory that Chaucer finished the *Legend* but that some parts have been lost. The consensus is that we have all Chaucer wrote of it.

The general opinion is that Chaucer, writing on an assigned subject, never really put his heart into his task, quickly tired of it, and abandoned it. Critics say that he became more and more perfunctory and brief as he went along, but a consideration of the poem as a whole may raise a question about this. For one thing, we do not know, we only suppose, that Chaucer was writing on assignment, although Alceste's command (F, 479-95; G, 469-85) to write a legend "yer by yere" about good women certainly makes it look as though the poem was commanded by Queen Anne. Lowes has pointed out that if the work was begun in 1386 and discontinued in 1394, it spanned nine years, and there are nine legends, one for each year.[3] Perhaps the Queen whimsically commanded that Chaucer write one legend each year as long as he lived.

Against the theory that Chaucer wrote the *Legend* because of a royal edict must be placed the fact that a series of stories seems to have strongly appealed to him. Besides the *Legend,* both the *Monk's Tale* and the *Canterbury Tales* are series.

The fact that Chaucer saw fit to give the *Prologue* an extensive and careful revision might provide a clue toward his feeling for the poem. So often he failed to make the trifling changes needed to adapt his poems to their intended purposes that we get the idea he was a somewhat careless worker. Therefore, when we see that he lavished tender care on the *Prologue* to the *Legend of Good Women,* we are driven to the conclusion that this poem, instead of being a bore to him, was actually one of his favorites. The list of the tales in the *Man of Law's Introduction* emphasizes Chaucer's interest in the project; he would hardly have epitomized the one work that was unbearably tedious to him. The detailed description given by the Man of Law is a certain sign of Chaucer's interest; and as there is little doubt that the *Man of Law's Tale* came late in Chaucer's writing career, this interest was enduring.

It must be admitted that in the *Legend of Phyllis,* the last completed tale of the *Legend,* Chaucer says:

But, for I am agroted herebyforn
To wryte of hem that be in love forsworn,
And ek to haste me in my legende,
(Which to performe God me grace sende!)
Therfore I passe shortly in this wyse.

(LGW, *F*, 2454-58)

The word *agroted* means "surfeited," and therefore Chaucer is definitely saying that the subject of treachery in love has palled upon him. And in the *Philomela,* which precedes the *Phyllis,* he says, speaking of Tereus:

But, shortly of this story for to passe,
For I am wery of hym for to telle. (*F*, 2257-58)

If the subject matter of his poem really filled him with repugnance, why did he work at the *Phyllis* until it was longer than six of the other legends? A man who could put eight books of the *Aeneid* into less than forty lines of verse could have written a shorter story about Phyllis had he wanted.

The word "good" in the title of the poem makes the unwary modern reader believe that Chaucer intended to write about women of virtue, but Chaucer had no such idea in mind. He asserted clearly enough that he was going to write about women who were "good" in love; and, for the most part, the women in the tales are just so. Of course, it is possible to quibble with Chaucer and say that it was fear of being led as a prisoner through Rome rather than love for Antony that caused Cleopatra to commit suicide and that the story of Medea is more one of passionate revenge than of wifely fidelity. But hairsplitting of this kind does not refute Chaucer's claim to be writing, in the main, about faithful women.

The individual tales have a great deal more literary merit than is generally accorded them. But if we say that they are not up to the standard of Chaucer's best work, we should then go on to admit that, in comparison with the works of most of his contemporaries, they are very good indeed. John Gower, however, when dealing with the same subjects could outdo Chaucer, as in his story of Medea. The charge that the tales grow shorter toward the end of the series is untrue. The *Ariadne* (No. VI) is second in length only to the *Dido* (No. III), the longest; and the *Phyllis* (No. VIII) is third in length.

Chaucer's occasional bursts of humor in the tales have been cited as showing his lack of sincerity. But this is to object to Chaucer because he is Chaucer. With him, as with the friend of Samuel Johnson who tried to be a philosopher, cheerfulness always broke through.

CHAPTER 4

The Minor Poems

IN comparison with the longer narrative poems, most of Chaucer's minor poems arouse comparatively little interest in the modern reader. Many of them seem formal exercises in technique rather than deeply felt experience. This judgment is perhaps unfair, as Chaucer was working in the style of his day, and it is the style rather than his execution to which we take exception. The minor poems that we assume were written late in his career and are, for the most part, occasional poems, contain more to interest us than the early minor ones.

I An ABC

An ABC, a free translation of Guillaume de Deguilleville's *Pèlerinage de la Vie Humaine*, is a prayer to the Virgin Mary. Each of its twenty-three stanzas begins with a different letter of the alphabet—"J," "V," and "W" are omitted. According to Speght, it was composed for the Duchess Blanche of Lancaster at her own request, to be used as a private prayer. As Blanche died in 1369, we can confidently date this as a very early work.

Although the poem shows nothing of Chaucer's temperament and disposition, aside from his willingness to oblige a great lady, it does show that at an early period in his career he was an adept versifier. The eight-line stanza that he used was handled with considerable skill—more skill than he displayed in the octosyllabic couplet of the *Book of the Duchess*. One of Chaucer's great achievements was his development of the iambic decasyllabic line, in which most of his later works were composed. It is therefore worth noting that the decasyllabic line of *An ABC*, which was, so far as we know, as early as anything he wrote, is done in a very creditable manner.

[78]

II *The Complaints*

In Chaucer's time a popular poetic form in England and especially in France was the complaint, a series of verses in which someone lamented some woe. A common cause of disquietude among medieval poets was unrequited love for a fair but unfeeling lady. This is the theme of *A Complaint unto Pity* and *A Complaint to his Lady*, as it is of the *Complaynt d'Amours*, which is of doubtful authorship. In all three of these there is a first-person speaker, but we cannot say for certain whether Chaucer was sobbing out his own soul or merely writing in the prevailing mode. Some critics see in these works and in some of the longer poems evidence that Chaucer was the victim of a grand but unrequited passion for a stony-hearted lady. Others have difficulty imagining Chaucer playing such a role and classify the poems as pure fiction.

In *A Complaint unto Pity* the speaker, bemoaning the cruelty and tyranny of love, searches for Pity that she might avenge him on Cruelty. But when he finds the object of his unremitting search she is dead and buried in a heart. Since Pity is dead the speaker is "slayn"; but he posts a bill detailing what he would have said to her, had she been alive. The bill, an elaborate song full of personifications, is to the effect that the speaker has been cruelly treated, and now that Pity is dead there is no remedy for him.

A Complaint to his Lady is in much the same vein. The speaker so despairs of achieving love that death seems inevitable; the more he loves "Faire Rewthelees," the more she causes him to smart. She is his foe, but he loves her nevertheless: When he should sleep he wakes; when he should dance, he quakes. In spite of her cruelty, she is one of the worthiest creatures alive, and he would rather serve her than do anything else. The poem concludes with a request for mercy.

The *Complaynt d'Amours* is the utterance of a wretched speaker on St. Valentine's Day, when fowls choose their mates. He, too, is in love with a woman who slays him with her cruelty: she always likes the opposite of what pleases him. All he can look forward to is death, yet, although she is the root of all his ills, one word from her would cure him; although she revels in her disdainful treatment of the speaker, he will continue to serve her with a love that is always fresh and new; although she slays him, he will persevere in his love.

These poems are interesting because of the verse. They were the first in English written in the seven-line rime royal stanza. The experiments with *terza rima* indicate Chaucer's early interest in the works of Dante. His instincts served him well in using *terza rima*, for he never tried it in a major poem. Dante, for whom Chaucer had great admiration, used it with superb results, but it has not proved to be well adapted to the English language.

Whether the three complaints that have been discussed are autobiographical or not, the *Complaint of Chaucer to his Purse* undoubtedly is. Chaucer requests his lady dear, his purse, which is very light, to become heavy again. The concluding envoy asks the King, the conqueror of Brutus Albion, to heed the supplication. Whether this should be labeled a complaint or merely a begging poem is a ticklish question. It does, however, belong to a general type of supplications much in style then, for French examples are fairly plentiful. From the envoy we can date the work as having been composed between September 30, 1399, when Henry IV was declared king by Parliament, and October 3, when Chaucer received an additional pension of forty marks. It might, however, have been written earlier for presentation to Richard II and not delivered to him.

This poem should not necessarily be taken to indicate that Chaucer's finances were particularly desperate when he wrote it. All the money that Chaucer received from his childhood until his death, with the exception of the income from the North Petherton forestership, stemmed from the Crown. From the beginning his salary for services rendered had been supplemented by sundry grants and pensions, and one of the surest and most common ways to get grants and pensions was to ask for them. So in this poem we undoubtedly have nothing more than a routine request for money, but a request much more cleverly phrased than the usual one.

One is tempted to include among the complaints *Chaucers Wordes unto Adam, His Owne Scriveyn,* although it lacks the proper label. If Chaucer really complains anywhere in his entire works, it is in these verses. Chaucer scolds Adam for the careless way in which he copies such works as *Boece* and *Troilus and Criseyde,* and is undoubtedly justified in doing so. But beneath such harsh words as his wish that Adam's head may become scabby unless he is more careful, there is a gleam of his customary good humor.

According to Speght, the *Complaint of Mars,* one of the most elaborate of the minor poems, celebrates the affair between John Holland (Lord Huntington) and Isabel, Duchess of York. Whether, however, the work is anything more than a treatment of an astronomical conjunction of the planets Venus and Mars is questionable. While this is perhaps a fragile theme on which to construct a poem, it was strong enough to allow Chaucer to display the cleverness and ingenuity desired in a complaint.

The *Complaint of Mars* begins with a warning to lovers to flee because the sun, the candle of jealousy, is rising. The speaker then tells how Mars had departed from Venus in the morning: Venus had accepted Mars as her lover, and taught him his lesson, and forbade him to indulge in jealousy, cruelty, boasting, or tyranny. Having bridled him, Venus was in bliss, and the two of them were happy until Mars entered his next palace. Venus remained alone suffering woe while he was away, but their joy was renewed when they met again. Phoebus, however, invaded their house, and Venus was again thrown into woe. Mars hastily armed himself and bade Venus flee, lest Phoebus should espy her. Venus fled to Mercury; when Mars, grown feeble, followed her, he found he could not catch up with her.

Mars makes an elaborate complaint about their separation and his lady's fright. Why did God make love, if it is such a transitory thing? And why are lovers always in such misadventure? It seems as if He has an enmity for lovers and delights to catch them as a fisherman catches fish with a hook; the lover, like the fish, may escape, but he will be wounded. Knights and ladies should pity the lover and complain to Venus, the friend and patroness of lovers.

Because of Shirley's statement that the original of the *Complaint of Venus* was written by Otes de Granson for the Isabel mentioned above, the *Venus* and the *Mars* have been considered companion pieces. There seems little reason to believe, however, that there was ever any connection intended between the two. It is even difficult to see what Venus has to do with the poem, or series of odes, as the work may be classified. Many critics believe that the various parts of the *Venus* were originally unrelated fragments that came together into their present form more or less by accident.

The speaker of the poem is a female who remembers, when she is in heaviness, the many good qualities of the good knight who is her lover. So well has Nature formed him that she is his for ever, and, notwithstanding his manifold virtues, he loves her dearly. It is, the speaker says, a noble thing that men should suffer for love and be jealous, but jealousy causes women to languish in penance. It ought to be enough that love has sent her such a high grace as the man who loves her, but jealousy causes her to languish in penance. The envoy, addressed to a princess, indicates that Chaucer is advanced in age and that he has endured a great penance in translating word by word this work from "Graunson, flour of hem that make in Fraunce."

Although the material of the poem is fairly uninteresting, features of the work are worthy of notice. For one thing, Chaucer indicates in line 76 that he is in advanced age. If we can believe his statement, the poem is a late one, although its tone and versification indicate that it is rather early. The compliment to Granson as the "flour of hem that make in Fraunce" could, of course, have been rendered late in Chaucer's poetic career, but it would be more logical to assume that he had rendered it early, when he was completely under the influence of French poets.

III *The Ballades*

The ballade was a verse form popular in France, and, in writing the seven ballades attributed to him, Chaucer was definitely under French influence. One of the features of the form is the rhymes that continue from stanza to stanza; another feature usually found, but not always, is a concluding envoy. Some scholars believe that at times Chaucer added envoys to earlier ballades or substituted new ones for old ones to give them an occasional turn. Although more of the minor poems are in the ballade form than in any other, Chaucer's seven make a scanty showing in comparison with the more than twelve hundred composed by his French contemporary, Eustache Deschamps.

To Rosemounde, in eight-line stanzas, is perhaps Chaucer's earliest extant poem in this form. It is a compliment to a highborn lady who is beautiful, merry, and jocund. Although the speaker insists that he loves the subject of the verses, it is a little difficult to believe this is true. No one who can say that he weeps many a brewing vat (*tyne,* l. 9) full and wallows in love like a large fish, a pike, in gelatin can be taken as completely serious in his declaration of passion. We hope that Rosemounde, whoever she was, had a sense of humor.

Womanly Noblesse, in a nine-line stanza not unusual with Chaucer in ballades, and with the customary envoy, has had its authenticity questioned by a few critics. But though the work lacks the sparkle we consider distinctive of Chaucer, most scholars are content to attribute the work to him.

It begins with a review of a lady's beauty and virtues, for which the speaker loves her dearly; he is in subjection to her and conforms his will to her ordinance. He requests her to pity him, not to heed his ignorance, and to be aware that he keeps in mind her beauty and steadfast governance.

Fortune, in eight-line stanzas with an envoy, illustrates how the ballade was used for a philosophical subject; in this case, it is combined with a request to three people in authority for favor and reward. It begins with a Plaintiff saying that the wretched world's weal and woe are governed by Fortune. She may cause one to lose his time and labor, but, nevertheless, the speaker defies her. Reason tells who is friend and who foe, and Fortune has no terror for the one who has mastery over himself; she could not, for instance, torture Socrates. Fortune asks why the Plaintiff rails if he is out of Fortune's control. She has, she says, taught the Plaintiff to see clearly; moreover, the Plaintiff was well treated at a time when others were being ill treated. The Plaintiff replies that he will keep to his friends, and Fortune's friends can go reside in the crowd. Fortune says that the Plaintiff complains because Fortune has given some of her riches to the Plaintiff and now will withdraw them. But why should the Plaintiff object to Fortune's fluctuations? The concluding envoy, addressed to princes, asks that they should relieve the Plaintiff's wants.

Based primarily on Boethius's *Consolation of Philosophy,* it is probably an occasional poem, although we do not know what the occasion was. There is a difference of opinion about the date of the work, but the reference to the three princes could mean that Chaucer was addressing the dukes of Lancaster, York, and Gloucester, who in 1390, controlled the King's gift giving. One of the theories about Chaucer, as was said earlier, is that he was not in great favor with Gloucester's party. This group may have forced him out of his official positions and caused him some financial hardship. There is, therefore, a possibility that in this poem Chaucer was suing to the Gloucester party for the restoration of lost privileges.

The ballade *Truth*, subtitled in some copies the *Balade de Bon Conseyl*, occurs in twenty-two manuscripts and establishes itself as the most popular of the minor poems. Derived in general from Boethius, it is of a nature that would commend itself to the general reading public: The good counsel is to avoid the court, which it goes without saying is corrupt; to be content with little; to avoid strife; and, above all, to follow truth. This is the sort of forward-looking optimism that brought Robert Browning into such great popularity in his own time. The Vache to whom the envoy is addressed (and the envoy, it may be said, occurs in but one of the twenty-two manuscript copies of the poem) for a long time puzzled scholars, the word having been taken to be the French for "cow." But current opinion is that it is a reference to Sir Philip de la Vache, the son-in-law of Chaucer's friend Sir Lewis Clifford. Vache's fortunes were in eclipse from 1386 to 1389 because of the opposition to him of the Gloucester party. The poem is thus frequently interpreted as an encouragement from Chaucer to a younger friend to bear his adversity with as good grace as possible.

Gentilesse, a *Moral Balade of Chaucier*, is another ballade without an envoy. Its main idea, derived from Boethius, Dante, and Jean de Meun's part of the *Roman de la Rose*, says that true gentility is a matter of one's personal behavior rather than of inheritance. This is markedly similar to part of the lecture that the old wife gives to the knight in the *Wife of Bath's Tale*. There is nothing at all revolutionary in this idea, it being one that pagans and Christians alike subscribed to. Chaucer may have been pointing to specific people in the last line of each stanza, perhaps Richard II, who discarded his gentilesse in his last years as king.

In *Lak of Stedfastnesse* Chaucer definitely points the moral at King Richard II. The world, says Chaucer, is in a sad state because of lack of constancy. People love dissension; they do their neighbors wrong; they have turned away from the right; and they have embraced fickleness instead of truth. King Richard, if he desires, can wean the people from their evil ways by conducting himself as a king should. It is possible that this is a late poem, written after Richard had given himself over to the tyranny that finally led to his deposition.

The ballade *Against Women Unconstant*, which lacks an envoy, is classed among the poems of doubtful authorship. A complaint against a fickle woman who is constantly shifting from one love to another, the work has a bolder, more peremptory tone than Chaucer's usual lover's laments. But, in spite of this, many authorities believe it to be by Chaucer.

A *Balade of Complaint*, also classed among the poems of doubtful authorship, has little to recommend it and little to cause us to attribute it to Chaucer. It contains the familiar statement that the lady whom the speaker loves is a compound of bounty and beauty; although she almost causes his death by her unkindness, he will continue to serve her. He begs her to accept this poor little ditty as a token of his esteem.

IV *The Envoys*

The envoys, which differ from the ballades in not having interlocking rhymes between the stanzas, are few in number but interesting in content. *Lenvoy de Chaucer a Scogan* consists of six stanzas playfully rebuking Henry Scogan, a young poet and disciple of Chaucer's, for having offended the God of Love by giving up the pursuit of his chosen lady. The envoy contains a request to Scogan, who is apparently in favor at court, to aid his friend Chaucer, who is apparently out of favor.

Because of the mention of the deluge in stanza two, the work has been dated 1393, the year of an extremely rainy autumn. If this dating is correct, the poem is puzzling; for Chaucer, in scolding Scogan for his lack of fidelity to his lady, seems to indicate that Scogan was approximately Chaucer's age. Yet in 1393 Scogan was only thirty-two years old, but Chaucer was fifty years of age, assuming he was born in 1343. And the age of fifty hardly calls for the description that Chaucer gives of himself: "hoor and rounde of shap" (1. 31). True it is that one can be round of shape at any age, but the connotation of *hoor*, or hoary, is definitely that of rather advanced age. In addition, in the sixth stanza Chaucer plainly indicates that he has given up the writing of poetry, indeed, that he had given it up a long time before he wrote this particular set of verses. In other words, he is apparently saying that he had completed his career as a poet by the first years of the 1390's. This would mean that he had composed the *Canterbury Tales* in the spare time between 1387 and 1391, or thereabouts. That he did so is hard to believe.

Lenvoy de Chaucer a Bukton, probably address to either Sir Peter or Sir Robert Bukton, is humorous counsel against marrying. A conventional piece of fun, its like found in all ages, the reader should not infer from it that Chaucer himself had an unhappy marriage. It is the sportive sort of thing that is addressed to prospective bridegrooms by even those whose marital life leaves nothing to be desired. From the reference to the Wife of Bath, we may conclude that it is a late piece.

V   The Former Age

The Former Age, deriving from Boethius, Ovid, the *Roman de la Rose,* and perhaps Virgil, may be an occasional poem, but we do not know what the occasion was. The subject, the perfection that reigned throughout the world at the dawn of time when mankind was young and uncorrupted, has, however, a perennial appeal for poets and philosophers. For this reason Chaucer was probably not prompted to write the work for a special purpose. It has been suggested, however, that he may have written it when he contemplated the last tyrannical years of Richard II.

VI   Merciles Beaute

Merciles Beaute, a triple rondel, is classed among the poems of doubtful authorship, but there seems no good reason to deny it to Chaucer. The light-hearted treatment of love is in Chaucer's most characteristic vein. The theme, a hardhearted lady whose beauty has completely overwhelmed the poet and who has spurned his advances, is conventional. The poet goes on to say that he, having escaped from the prison of love, is sincerely thankful for his deliverance. Although he groans because of the pangs of unrequited love, he tells us with a twinkle in his eye that the role of rejected lover probably suits him better than that of the accepted.

The verse form of *Merciles Beaute* is probably the most elaborate and formal that Chaucer employed in all of his works. But, if we accept what Alceste says to the God of Love in the *Legend of Good Women,* he wrote many such poems:

> *He made . . .*
> *. . . many an ympne for your halydayes,*
> *That highten balades, roundels, virelayes;*　　(F, 417-23;
> 　　　　　　　　　　　　　　　　　　G, 405-11).

VII　Proverbs

These verses are placed among the poems of doubtful author-ship, and there we should be content to let them remain. They have little to recommend them.

CHAPTER 5

The Translations

I *The* Consolation of Philosophy

ONE of the great philosophical works of antiquity was *De Consolatione Philosophiae*, or, in English, the *Consolation of Philosophy*, by Anicius Manlius Severinus Boethius, a distinguished Roman statesman who died in prison about 524 A.D. Based largely on Plato and Seneca, the *Consolation* was philosophy cloaked in fancy and imagination. An important link between classical philosophy and the thought of the Middle Ages, it had tremendous influence on the writers of England and the Continent, and was translated by or for, King Alfred; by Chaucer; and by or for Queen Elizabeth I. It was rendered, therefore, into the colloquial English of the Old, Middle, and Modern periods for or by three of the great people of the English nation. It would be difficult to name any other work that has been so distinguished.

The *Consolation of Philosophy* consists of alternating passages of prose and verse. It begins with Boethius, who has been unjustly imprisoned by the Emperor Theodoric, lamenting the unkindness of Fortune. When he had tried to purify the government, he had been charged with treason, and at his trial men whom he had tried to protect had given false testimony against him. As he despairs in his prison, there appears before him the lady Philosophy, a majestic creature of constantly fluctuating size. She has come to console him because he has always been one of her ardent disciples. Her first task is to discover what sort of remedies should be applied to Boethius's mind to cure him of the depression under which he labors. He agrees that the universe is ruled by God, the source of all things; but when she learns that he has forgotten what he himself is and how the universe is ruled, she is ready to apply remedies to him.

In Book 2 she enumerates the many blessings that Boethius has experienced. He has had friends, wealth, honors, and has been especially fortunate in his relatives: His father-in-law is an excellent and virtuous man, and his own sons have been consuls. She then shows that the gifts of Fortune are to be despised, even though Boethius is lamenting their loss. For one thing, Fortune is inconstant, giving and taking away her gifts unexpectedly and unreasonably; her followers are in constant fear because they can never depend upon her to continue dispensing her gifts. There is also the consideration that the things which Fortune gives do not produce true happiness. Wealth may be lost, good repute may be besmirched, honors may be torn away and turned to dishonors, power may be lost. If bad men may possess all of these things to an even greater extent than the good possess them, they cannot be truly good; what a bad man can have more of than a good man cannot be anything but bad.

Men desire riches, honors, glories, powers, pleasures. But riches make their possessor uneasy (for fear they will be lost) and dependent upon others to protect them. Honors are frequently heaped upon the basest of men. Power is always limited —no one but God has infinite power—and therefore it is a source of unhappiness rather than of happiness, because anything that is limited cannot be counted truly good. Fame, gained through the false opinion of the crowd, is by its very nature of short duration and cannot delight a wise man. Furthermore, fame is never universal because it is always limited in time and space. Good Fortune, the bestower of these gifts, is thus a deceiver, and men often learn virtue as a result of Fortune's disfavor. Thus it can be seen that the general opinion of Fortune and her merits is a mistaken one.

In Book 3 Philosophy promises to lead Boethius to the true happiness, consisting of a union of all good things. It is very different from the false felicity provided by Fortune. Such happiness lies in God, who is a combination of all good things. Philosophy points out that possession of only one good thing, such as wealth, cannot produce happiness; a person must have all of the elements of happiness or he will be unhappy, and only God can have all of the elements. The efforts of men to gain all the elements of happiness almost always lead to unhappiness. The obscure rich man is unhappy because he does not have fame;

the impoverished famous man is unhappy because he is poor, and so it goes.

In Book 4 Boethius wants to know why, if God is good, evils exist; why virtue suffers and vice is rewarded. Philosophy explains that virtue is always rewarded and vice punished. This must be so if God is the highest good, which he is admitted to be. The good man will lack his reward only when he ceases to be good. The evil man becomes beastly and therefore unhappy. And, says Philosophy, wicked men are happier when they are punished then when they are unpunished, and the doer of an injustice is more unhappy than the person to whom the injustice is done.

Philosophy then takes up the matter of Providence and Fate. The essence of this discussion is that Providence is the general overseer and designer of all things, and that Fate executes what Providence has decided upon. Everything that is subject to Fate is also subject to Providence, but some things below Providence are above Fate. Fate is what sets things in motion. It might be likened to a man carrying out with his body the ideas that his mind has conceived. Since Providence is under the direction of God, there is no such thing as blind Fate.

Book 5 is about God's foreknowledge and man's free will. Real chance does not exist, as all things have causes; what we regard as chance is simply an unexpected result from something we do. If a man digs in his garden to prepare a seed bed and uncovers a hoard of gold, it is not chance, because the gold already existed. It is simply that the man was not digging specifically for gold, so the result of his digging was unexpected. Philosophy shows that God does not cause things to happen by foreknowing them. This is a very important point, and it is argued at length. God is a foreknowing spectator of events rather than a causer of them; therefore free will is in no way shackled, as it would be if God's foreknowledge caused things to happen.

There are two kinds of necessity, simple and conditional. Simple necessity is a necessary fact such as "all men are mortal"; conditional necessity is the existence of something we know exists; if a man knew that another man was walking, that man must be walking. Knowing a fact does not cause it to occur, but what is known is necessarily true. The conclusion of the book is that God is the foreknowing spectator of everything.

Apparently Chaucer's interest in the *Consolation* was aroused in the year 1380, or thereabouts, close to the period when he composed *Troilus and Criseyde;* and there seems to be evidence in the lines to Adam Scriveyn that the *Troilus* was written and the *Consolation* translated at about the same time. We find few or no references to Boethius in the early poems, but great use is made of him in *Troilus and Criseyde,* in some of the *Canterbury Tales,* and even in some of the later minor poems.

To the person who, through much reading of it, has become familiar with the easy flow of Chaucer's verse, the translation of Boethius comes as somewhat of a surprise; Chaucer towered above his contemporaries as a poet, but we must admit after reading the *Consolation* that as a writer of prose he was not distinguished. The chief reason for this is that in a language poetry always develops before prose; the period when prose would be cultivated as an art was a long way off. Moreover, that Chaucer was not adept at prose should occasion no wonder, as major poets generally do not write prose with great ease. Wordsworth admitted that he wrote it with difficulty, and the majestic organ tones of Milton's verse are quite lacking from his prose. Chaucer, however, did write one charming piece of prose, the prefatory matter to *A Treatise on the Astrolabe,* which will be dealt with later.

Chaucer's intention was to render the *Consolation* into English as accurately as possible rather than to produce an independent work of art. This intention is responsible for the numerous glosses inserted into the body of the text, glosses that probably came from Nicholas Trivet's commentary on Boethius. What Chaucer primarily wanted in his translation was clarity, and, therefore, he never hesitated to interrupt the flow of the original when he felt that explanation was in order. Probably it was this same desire to present Boethius's meaning with as little distortion as possible that caused him to render the meters of the original into prose instead of verse. It would be natural to assume that a poet as gifted as Chaucer would translate the metrical parts of his text into verse, but he evidently felt that what he was working on would be for his contemporaries a philosophical textbook rather than a work of art. His method of meticulously following his original in order to bring out all of its shades of meaning differed from his method when he embarked upon the composition of a poem based on a previously existing work; in the latter situation he felt under no obligation to reproduce his source exactly. In the *Knight's Tale* he drastically compressed his original and in *Troilus and Criseyde* he expanded it; in each instance, by showing a commendable independence, he vastly improved upon the poem that had inspired him.

Although the modern reader is tempted to avoid reading the *Consolation* and to give all of his attention to the gayer works, an adequate knowledge of it will clarify many a passage of Chaucer's poems that might otherwise remain obscure. It is not feasible to give here the complete influence of the *Consolation of Philosophy* on Chaucer's works; Bernard L. Jefferson[1] says that there are 1041 lines scattered through thirty-one of Chaucer's works which show the influence of Boethius. But we can show some of the influence in a sampling of the main themes.

Offhand one might think that the long complaint of the man in black against Fortune in the *Book of the Duchess* is derived from Boethius, since Fortune is one of the subjects that Boethius treats at length in the *Consolation*. The *Book of the Duchess,* however, was apparently composed before Chaucer became acquainted with the *Consolation*. The remarks on Fortune in the *Duchess* are for the most part medieval commonplaces and are derived, where a definite source is indicated, quite largely from the *Roman de la Rose;* but this work, however, was influenced by Boethius.

Many of the so-called minor poems show a strong influence of the *Consolation of Philosophy. The Former Age* derives very directly from *Consolation,* Book 2, meter 5. Even the title, which is used instead of the more usual "golden age," comes from this passage of Boethius. The whole essence of Chaucer's poem springs from this meter, although some details are taken from other sources, such as Ovid's *Metamorphoses.*

Lak of Stedfastnesse develops a main idea of Book 1 of the *Consolation,* that of man's giving himself up to selfish pursuits. These pursuits are, as Philosophy brings out, not the things that produce true happiness. The ballade *Truth* is the positive side of the matter that is expressed negatively in *Lak of Stedfastnesse.* Whereas the *Lak of Stedfastnesse* deplores the fact that there has been a general falling off from all the virtues that may collectively be called "truth," *Truth* contains the positive idea that "trouthe thee shal delivere," or save. The idea of fleeing from the crowd is implicit in much of the first book of the *Consolation*, where Philosophy points out how little felicity there is to be gained from anything that the crowd can bestow upon a virtuous man. The ballade *Fortune* is a summing up of almost everything that Boethius said about Fortune in Book 2 and elsewhere in the *Consolation*. The ballade *Gentilesse* derives very directly from *Consolation*, Book 3, prose 6 and meter 6. The theme is that gentility is a matter of individual virtue and cannot be inherited. The old hag in the *Wife of Bath's Tale* delivers identical sentiments to her reluctant husband (CT, III, 1109-76).

The *House of Fame* owes a great debt to Boethius. The appearance of Lady Fame, who is the main character of the second book, is probably modeled upon Lady Philosophy in her continual changing of size. The general conception of Fame, who Chaucer says is Fortune's sister, is remarkably similar to the characterization of Fortune in the *Consolation of Philosophy* in that she is utterly whimsical in her bestowing of rewards and punishments. Philosophy, in enumerating the things that really do not produce happiness, gives a long discussion of the unreliability of fame in this connection. The idea that the eagle in the *House of Fame* develops of the tendency of things to seek their place, for fire to rise and for heavy things to sink (739-64), occurs a number of times in the *Consolation*. Boethius uses it to show that as everything seeks its place, so man seeks happiness, his real home (*Consolation*, Book 3, meter 9 and prose 11).

The *Knight's Tale* contains about sixteen reminiscences of the *Consolation*, of which several are lengthy. Arcite moans that gaining his freedom lost him the sight of Emelye (I, 1251-67); this is the theme of *Consolation*, Book 3, prose 2, that one good alone does not make for happiness. The lament of Palamon in prison, enviously thinking of the opportunity the liberated Arcite has to win Emelye (I, 1303-15), is similar to the well-developed section of the *Consolation* that asks why God allows the innocent to suffer (*Consolation*, Book 1, meter 5 and Book 4, prose 1). Chaucer explains at some length the arrival of Theseus at the battle in the woods between Palamon and Arcite (I, 1670-73); he is here following Boethius's development of the idea that our desires are ruled by the sight above—God (*Con-*

solation, Book 4, prose 6). Perhaps the major part of the *Consolation* showing Boethian influence is Theseus's long speech (I, 2987-3040) explaining how God brings all things about, even death, and so Arcite's death is not to be lamented. This passage is derived from *Consolation,* Book 4, prose 6 and meter 6.

The *Physician's Tale* deals with the gifts of Fortune, a subject treated at great length by Boethius in the entire first half of the *Consolation;* that these gifts cause death, mentioned in the *Introduction to the Pardoner's Tale* (VI, 295-300) is from *Consolation,* Book 3, prose 8.

The *Monk's Tale* is practically from beginning to end a treatise on the mutability of Fortune that is developed so thoroughly in *Consolation,* Book 2, prose 1.

The *Nun's Priest's Tale* contains a number of minor influences of the *Consolation,* such as the widow's "hertes suffisaunce" (VII, 2839), derived from *Consolation,* Book 2, prose 4; the idea that Fortune governs all in common (VII, 2999-3000) from *Consolation,* Book 2, prose 2; the fact that destiny cannot be avoided (VII, 3338) from *Consolation,* Book 5, prose 3; and the allusion to Nero's burning of Rome (VII, 3370-74) from *Consolation,* Book 5, prose 3. The major influence is seen in the debate on free will (VII, 3234-50), an important subject of Book 5 of the *Consolation.*

The *Manciple's Tale* contains a passage about the bird in the beautiful cage that will flee to the forest if it gets the chance to do so (IX, 163-74), based on *Consolation,* Book 3, meter 3. This passage, like the similar one in the *Squire's Tale* (V, 609-20), was perhaps influenced by the *Roman de la Rose.* The *Manciple's Tale* also contains a passage in almost the same form as that in the *General Prologue* about the word being cousin to the deed (IX, 207-08 and I, 741-42), a point made in *Consolation,* Book 3, prose 12.

Troilus and Criseyde, so largely concerned with questions of fate in its relation to human happiness, makes great use of Boethian thought. The poem is filled with allusions to the fleeting nature of earthly joys: the first three books of the poem develop the idea of joy until suddenly, at the beginning of Book 3, Fortune's wheel turns and there is no more joy for either Troilus or Criseyde. Examples of references to felicity occur in III, 813-36, from *Consolation,* Book 2, prose 4; in III, 1691-92, from *Con-*

solation, Book 3, prose 2; in IV, 835-36, from *Consolation*, Book 2, prose 4; and in V, 732, from *Consolation*, Book 2, prose 4.

Fate and Fortune run all through *Troilus and Criseyde*. Troilus, for example, complains (I, 837-40) against Fortune, whom he considers his enemy because she teases free men and bondsmen with her cruel wheel (*Consolation*, Book 1, prose 4; Book 2, proses 1 and 2 and meter 1). Pandarus, in reply (I, 841-54), uses the Boethian argument that if her wheel ceases to turn, she ceases to be Fortune. If she casts someone down, she also elevates him (*Consolation*, Book 2, proses 1, 2, and 3). In the episode about the rainstorm that keeps Criseyde at Pandarus's house for the night (III, 617-22), Fortune and Fate are the causers of the storm (*Consolation*, Book 4, prose 6, and Book 5, meter 1). The opening of Book 4 (lines 1-7) is on the deceit and scorn of Fortune. Men may, however, by making a virtue of necessity, be lords of Fortune (IV, 1587-89, from *Consolation*, Book 2, prose 4, and Book 4, prose 7).

The idea of necessity is enunciated by Troilus (IV, 958-59) when he says that all that comes, comes by necessity (from *Consolation*, Book 5, prose 2). This is continued (IV, 960-66) with the idea that God's purveyance, or foresight, sees all that will happen, and therefore God has foreseen that Troilus and Criseyde will be separated (*Consolation*, Book 5, prose 2). Troilus indulges in a long argument (IV, 974-1078) about free will and its place in the world (from *Consolation*, Book 5, prose 3). The fifth book begins (V, 1-3) with the idea that God himself does not execute his decrees, but has Fate to do it for him (from *Consolation*, Book 2, meter 3).

Examples such as these above could be greatly multiplied, but these will undoubtedly serve to indicate the great debt that Chaucer owed the *Consolation of Philosophy*.

II *The* Romaunt of the Rose

No other work of literature, not even the *Consolation of Philosophy*, influenced Chaucer as deeply as did the *Roman de la Rose*, by Guillaume de Lorris and Jean de Meun, or Meung, or Clopinel, as he was variously called. Whereas the *Consolation* was influential in Chaucer's later years, the *Roman* was his inspiration from the time he wrote his first poems until he finally laid down his pen. The first part of the *Roman,* that by de Lorris, is a highly conventionalized dream allegory of a lover in search of his love, symbolized by a rose growing on a bush. The lover enters a garden inhabited by various personifications and makes valiant efforts to achieve the rose, but this section of the poem ends before he is crowned with success. Although Chaucer could have been influenced in the dream settings he used for his early works by a number of other French poems, it is likely that every time he fell asleep to dream the substance of a poem he was being primarily influenced by de Lorris's part of the *Roman*.

By far the larger part of the poem is by Jean de Meun, who maintains the allegorical machinery of de Lorris but sets off on a course of his own. What his intention was in this writing is a matter of doubt, but what he succeeded in doing was to write an encyclopedia. He takes practically all knowledge for his province and deals with it masterfully; there is nothing that interests him that he does not introduce into his poem. A notable distinction between his part of the poem and de Lorris's is his cynicism regarding women. Where de Lorris was tenderly sentimental toward the fair sex, de Meun is bitterly satirical against what he considers an unfair sex.

It would be difficult, if not impossible, to give a complete list of Chaucer's borrowings from the *Roman de la Rose*. We can point to some parts of his works that certainly are derived from the French poem and to a large number that possibly come directly from it. The basic machinery of having a narrator tell in the form of a dream the substance of such poems as the *Book of the Duchess,* the *House of Fame,* the *Parliament of Fowls,* and the *Legend of Good Women* is certainly similar to the scheme of of the *Roman de la Rose.* As the device, however, was a commonplace of other French poems with which Chaucer was undoubtedly familiar, we cannot attribute a definite influence for this method to his favorite poem, the *Roman.*

But we do not have to read far into the *Roman* to establish a definite influence, for Chaucer made repeated use of its opening lines:

> *Full many a man hath cried amain*
> *That dreams and visions are but vain*
> *Imaginings and lies, but I*

> *Believe that they may truthfully*
> *Forecast the future; and full clear*
> *And plain this matter doth appear*
> *By that famed dream of Scipio,*
> *Whereof Macrobius long ago*
> *The story wrote, and stoutly he*
> *Affirmeth dreams for verity.*   (Ellis trans., 3-12) [2]

These lines certainly influenced Chaucer when he wrote the opening lines of the *House of Fame* (1-65), *Troilus and Criseyde* (V, 358 ff.), and the *Nun's Priest's Tale* (VII, 2891 ff.). The mention of "Macrobeus" in the *Book of the Duchess* (284) and in the *Nun's Priest's Tale* (VII, 3123) and the reference to him in the *House of Fame* (524) may have been suggested by this passage in the *Roman de la Rose*. It is almost certain that Chaucer actually read Macrobius' *Somnium Scipiones*, a commentary on Cicero's dream of Scipio, although in what form we do not know. It seems logical, however, that his initial knowledge of Macrobius stems from his study of the *Roman*.

The *Physician's Tale* and the Monk's stories about Nero (VII, 2463-2630) and Croesus (VII, 2727-65) are the only complete works that are usually attributed to Chaucer's borrowings from the *Roman*. The *Physician's Tale* comes from lines 5908 ff. (of the Ellis translation), Nero from 6533 ff., and Croesus from 6844 ff. It is not unlikely that the *Roman* influenced Chaucer's treatment of the Monk's account of Samson, especially the part that moralizes about the lack of wisdom in being too talkative about one's affairs (Ellis, 17,490-504).

The Prioress's table manners are a close rendering of a passage in the *Roman* (Ellis, 14,117-40):

> *"Tis well she take especial care*
> *That in the sauce her fingers ne'er*
> *She dip beyond the joint, nor soil*
> *Her lips with garlick, sops, or oil,*
> *Nor heap up gobbets and then charge*
> *Her mouth with pieces overlarge,*
> *And only with the finger point*
> *Should touch the bit she'd fair anoint*
> *With sauce, white, yellow, brown, or green*
> *And lift it towards her mouth between*
> *Finger and thumb with care and skill,*

That she no sauce or morsel spill
About her breast-cloth.
                    Then her cup
She should gracefully lift up
Towards her mouth that not a gout
By any chance doth fall about
Her vesture, or for glutton rude,
By such unseemly habitude,
Might she be deemed.
                    Nor should she set
Lips to her cup while food is yet
Within her mouth.
                    And first should she
Her upper lip wipe delicately,
Lest, having drunk, a grease-formed groat
Were seen upon the wine to float.

Even such a bit of homely wisdom as the following from the
Manciple's Tale derives from the *Roman de la Rose:*

Taak any bryd, and put it in a cage,
And do al thyn entente and thy corage
To fostre it tendrely with mete and drynke
Of alle deyntees that thou kanst bithynke,
And keep it al so clenly as thou may,
Although his cage of gold be never so gay,
Yet hath this brid, by twenty thousand foold,
Levere in a forest, that is rude and coold,
Goon ete wormes and swich wrecchednesse.
For evere this brid wol doon his bisynesse
To escape out of his cage, yif he may.
His libertee this brid desireth ay.   (IX, 163-74)

The source of this is:

The bird which from the wood is lured,
Captured, and in gay cage immured,
Tended with gentle love and care,
And fed with choice and dainty fare,
With pleasant song our ear enchants,
But yet one thing doth lack, it pants
Once more to flit among the boughs
And branches which so well it knows

> *And where 'twould once more gladly be.*
> *In vain you nurse it tenderly,*
> *Ever it pineth to regain*
> *That liberty whereof 'tis fain.* (Ellis, 14,653-66)

The *Roman de la Rose* and Chaucer's works both abound in names of mythological beings. Perhaps Chaucer's first acquaintance with these personages came through the *Roman*. Such a thing is, of course, hypothetical, and there can be no doubt that before Chaucer was very old he had read the works of Ovid, the *Aeneid*, and other pieces of literature that mention such beings.

In the words of the Knight, "It were al to longe for to devyse" the whole story of the influence on the *Roman* on Chaucer. The samples above may perhaps give some hint how Chaucer used the poem, but an exhaustive comparison with the originals of the passages in Chaucer's works that derive from the *Roman* would take more space than can be afforded here.

It must not be thought that Chaucer was alone in being influenced by the *Roman de la Rose*. It was a source of inspiration for scores of Continental poets, especially the French. It also influenced English poets writing in the courtly tradition: John Gower frequently drew upon it. But the *Roman's* influence was naturally less in England than in the land of its birth.

That Chaucer was influenced by the *Roman de la Rose* is not in question, but everything else concerning his connection with the poem is. He mentions in the *Prologue* to the *Legend of Good Women* that he translated the *Roman* or, rather, the God of Love accuses him of having done so; and Eustache Deschamps' finely turned poetical compliment says that Chaucer was famous in France as the translator of the *Roman*. In the light of these statements, there would be no problem if we had a complete translation in good Chaucerian English, but what we actually have is a series of three fragments of translation totaling 7996 lines from a total of about 22,600 lines in the original. The first fragment, A (ll. 1-1704), stops less than midway through de Lorris' contribution to the poem; fragment B (ll. 1705-5810) finishes de Lorris' part and begins on Jean de Meun's; and Fragment C (ll. 5811-1696) is wholly de Meun's.

In the *Prologue* to the *Legend of Good Women,* the angry God of Love rebukes Chaucer with:

Yt is my relyke, digne and delytable,
And thow my foo, and al my folk werreyest,
And of myn olde servauntes thow mysseyest,
And hynderest hem with thy translacioun,
And lettest folk from hire devocioun,
To serve me, and holdest it folye
To serve Love. Thou maist yt nat denye,
For in pleyn text, withouten nede of glose,
Thou hast translated the Romaunce of the Rose,
That is an heresye ayeins my lawe,
And makest wise folk fro me withdrawe.   (F, 321-31)

A statement of this sort certainly indicates that the translation was more than a few fragments, as, of course, does Deschamps' poem. In other words, we have bits and pieces where we should have a complete poem.

An additional difficulty—and a great one—is that nowhere in the extant English fragments is there the bitter satire on women that is so notable in some parts of Jean de Meun's contribution to the poem and which the God of Love finds so reprehensible. Nothing at all, in fact, in the extant fragments could be objected to by even the most ardent partisan of women. We are thus driven to the conclusion that Chaucer's translation of the *Roman de la Rose* has been either wholly or partially lost.

Modern Chaucer scholars have done little to help us clarify just which of the extant fragments Chaucer translated. A fairly popular present-day position is that there is not much doubt of Chaucer's authorship of Fragment A; Fragment C could possibly be by Chaucer, although there are doubts; and Fragment B is almost certainly not by him, as it is in a Northern dialect that Chaucer did not use. Thomas Lounsbury, a Chaucer scholar whose opinions command a great deal of respect, after a highly detailed examination of all three fragments, concluded that there was no valid reason for denying any of them to Chaucer, but his opinion has not gained widespread acceptance.[3] On the other hand, another scholar denies all three fragments to Chaucer; still another contends that Fragments B and C form one fragment instead of two, and the combined fragment is not by Chaucer. In the face of such conflicting opinions, it is difficult for the lay reader to decide what the truth of the matter is.

If Chaucer at one time translated the entire *Roman de la Rose* and if the existing Fragments B and C are not by him, we are faced with several first-rate literary mysteries. The first is how a literary monument of this magnitude and importance—for a Chaucerian translation of the *Roman* would have been important in fourteenth-century England—could have vanished with the exception of one short fragment. It is true that Chaucer's *Book of the Lion*, his *Origen on the Magdalene*, his *Wretched Engendering of Mankind*, and some early poems have vanished; but they must have been lesser works than a complete translation of the *Roman* would have been.

The God of Love's statement in the *Legend of Good Women* would lead us to believe that the work was fairly well known at the time that Chaucer was writing the *Prologue* to the *Legend*. It would be reasonable to assume that it existed in copies that were in general circulation. The God's remark would have been utterly pointless if it had referred to a work about which the public was ignorant. The second mystery is why two other poets of a skill similar to Chaucer's would duplicate part of his work—always assuming that Chaucer translated the whole of the poem. The third mystery is how most of Chaucer's work came to be discarded and the work of two other poets came to be joined to the one short fragment that was preserved. Anyone who can solve these mysteries will be justified in considering himself a literary detective of no mean ability.

III   A Treatise on the Astrolabe

The least read of all of Chaucer's works is *A Treatise on the Astrolabe* (1391), a work derived almost entirely from Messhala's *Compositio et Operatio Astrolabii* and from John of Scarobosco's *De Sphaera;* but there are also sections of the work for which sources have not yet been found. Perhaps it is incorrect to classify this piece of writing with the translations, but it is so derivative that it hardly merits being considered an original composition. Not without reason does it rest in comparative obscurity. Few people now living have ever seen astrolabes, although they do exist in some museums. When we add to the scarcity of astrolabes the fact that Chaucer's treatise consists only of mathematics and astronomy, we can account for its lack of popular appeal without the slightest difficulty.

And yet there is much to attract our attention to this work. It is, for instance, the first how-to-do-it book by a major English writer. It must not, however, be thought to be the first how-to-do-it book in the English language; the *Anglo-Saxon Leechdoms,* centuries older than Chaucer, contains a mass of instructions in medical and agricultural matters. But Chaucer's book differs from all the others in being a highly personal work: it is addressed to "Lyte Lowys my sone," whereas the rest of Chaucer's works are for that impersonal body known as the reading public. There is a glow of warmth connected with this work, written as it was for one specific small boy, that is missing in those addressed to the world at large. The short introduction, the only piece of Chaucer's prose that is neither translated nor adapted from some other work, has a smoothness and power that are lacking when he is presenting someone else's ideas.

Who little Lewis was has been the object of considerable speculation. Chaucer plainly says in the third and fourth words of the work that Lewis was his son, but scholars, reluctant to accept so plain a statement at face value, have sought to prove that he was anything but what Chaucer said he was. The aforementioned theories, that he was Sir Lewis Clifford's son and Chaucer's godson, or that he was the illegitimate son of Chaucer and Cecilia Chaumpaigne, have lost favor. Modern scholars have reluctantly come around to the belief that little Lewis was probably what Chaucer said he was—his son.

Sister M. Madeleva has charmingly developed the idea that in this stern and forbidding piece of work we find Chaucer's warmest and most personal writing,[4] and anyone who reads her essay must agree with her. Here is one piece addressed to an individual, and the terms of address are tender and loving indeed. But when Sister Madeleva insists that *A Treatise on the Astrolabe* is such a model of clarity that the ten-year-old Lewis eagerly read it and perfectly comprehended it, we must pause to wonder if what she says is true. We must never lose sight of the fact that the work is unfinished; and the question arises: whose enthusiasm for it died first, Chaucer's or little Lewis's? Unless small boys have changed most remarkably since Chaucer's time, the *Astrolabe* should have made "a-nyght ful ofte" little Lewis's "hed to ake in his studye."

The work has one significance not to be overlooked. It shows a mathematical and scientific interest that is frequently associated only with so-called "practical" people. Too often we think of the poet as the sort of woolly-headed dreamer that Chaucer sometimes represented himself as being, not as the man of attainment that he actually was.

IV   The Equatorie of the Planetis

There is in existence another scientific work which may be by Chaucer. It is *The Equatorie of the Planetis,* a treatise on the construction and the use of an astronomical instrument called the equatorium, a companion piece to the astrolabe; it may even be a necessary complement to it. So closely are the two instruments related that some who have read this treatise have thought that it was the missing part of Chaucer's *A Treatise on the Astrolabe.* The work has never yet been included in a volume of Chaucer's works, as for centuries it was not associated with Chaucer, but was attributed to Simon Bredon, an astronomer of Merton College, Oxford. It is, however, now available in a fine edition (Derek Price, *The Equatorie of the Planetis,* Cambridge, 1955).

The directions for constructing the device are amazingly clear and detailed, and a person moderately skilled in the use of tools would still have no trouble in following them. The part of the treatise on how to use the instrument becomes involved with mathematics that might daunt the ordinary citizen, but for a trained mathematician it presents no difficulties. Incidentally, one of the uses of the equatorium is the casting of horoscopes. Yet even if the work is ever proved beyond the shadow of a doubt to be Chaucer's, it will never be widely read. Its importance is once again to indicate the range and depth of Chaucer's interests.

Scholarly attention was focussed on the work when it was discovered that the word "Chaucer," written on the inside margin of a page of the vellum manuscript, had been almost completely covered in the process of binding. When the binding cords were cut, the word plainly appeared. The discovery of Chaucer's name caused Price to compare the manuscript, which he considers an author's holograph (Chapter XI, "Ascription to Chaucer," pp. 149-66), with other supposed Chaucer holographs. Price believes that the manuscript is an author's holograph rather than a scribal copy because it is filled with erasures, scrapings, and corrections such as would result from a translator's revising his work as he progressed. We do not, it may be said, know what the original was, but it has been conjectured that it was in Latin, and possibly by Simon Bredon. The great difficulty in comparing this manuscript with a Chaucer holograph is that we are not certain that we have any, although a number of pieces of manuscript are thought to be in Chaucer's own hand. Nevertheless, for a variety of reasons, which are set forth in Chapter XI, Price believes, while cautiously admitting that the ascription must remain tentative, that the work is really by Chaucer, in Chaucer's handwriting.

CHAPTER 6

Troilus and Criseyde

IN *Troilus and Criseyde* Chaucer produced not only the finest piece of literature that he was to write, but the masterpiece of the whole Middle English period.

In *Troilus and Criseyde* Chaucer tells us that Troilus, a young Trojan prince and a great scorner of love, goes to a temple festival where he sees the beautiful young widow Criseyde. He is instantly stricken by love, but shame at his former scorn of it makes him conceal his affliction from his fellows. He spends much time moping in his room, becoming positively ill from the strength of his love. Once, while he is almost despairing of life, he is visited by a friend, Pandarus, who wrings from him the admission that he is suffering from an unrequited passion. Pandarus offers to help him in his affair, no matter who the lady may be. When Troilus, almost swooning from the intensity of his feeling, tells that he loves Criseyde, Pandarus says to be of good heart; she is his niece, and he will see that all is well with Troilus.

Pandarus visits Criseyde and, with mysterious hints that she is about to be visited by rare good fortune, stimulates her curiosity to a high pitch. Finally he tells her that Troilus loves her, a piece of information that she does not at all relish. She rebukes him for proposing that she, a widow, should become involved in an affair. When Pandarus has departed from her house, she calmly thinks over the wisdom or foolishness of falling in love, considers what the advantages would be and what the disadvantages. She finally decides that a very discreet love, in which she would not become deeply involved, could do no harm. When Pandarus tells Troilus that all will be well, Troilus writes a letter to Criseyde.

The next morning Pandarus delivers Troilus's letter to Criseyde and cajoles her into writing an answer to it. This he speedily delivers to Troilus, who broods upon it, but finally takes all in it for the best. Pandarus then arranges with Troilus's brother, Deiphebus, to hold a gathering at his house to pretend to consult upon a legal matter of Criseyde's.

The gathering is attended by a group of Troilus's and Criseyde's relatives and acquaintances. Troilus feigns illness and takes to bed in a darkened room, where he is visited by all and sundry, including Criseyde, with whom he has his first interview. Intensity of emotion almost robs him of the power of speech, but he declares his love.

Matters run quietly for a while, until Pandarus invites Criseyde to have dinner at his house. She, somewhat suspicious, but assured that Troilus is out of town, attends; Troilus is carefully hidden away in an inner room. A fearful storm makes it necessary for Criseyde to remain in Pandarus's house all night; and, when the attendants of Pandarus and Criseyde are asleep, Pandarus introduces Troilus into Criseyde's room. The proximity of Criseyde causes Troilus to faint, but he is revived. Pandarus then leaves the two to spend the night together.

For a time after this the two live in bliss. Finally Antenor, one of the more important Trojan warriors, is captured by the Greeks, and a Trojan parliament agrees to exchange Criseyde and Antenor; the seer Calchas, Criseyde's father, wants to get her out of the city before the downfall he foretells. Troilus is stricken at the idea of separation, but he cannot oppose the exchange, for speaking out would break the bond of secrecy that is so important in a courtly love affair.

The lovers are immediately plunged into the depths of woe, but Criseyde promises to return to Troy at the end of ten days. Pandarus advocates Troilus's abducting Criseyde and fleeing from the city, but this course is unthinkable to Troilus because it also would violate secrecy. When the exchange takes place at last, Troilus himself conducts Criseyde to the Greek side and turns her over to the Greek Diomede. Diomede, a very different sort of person from Troilus, immediately plans his conquest of Criseyde.

During the ten days' wait for Criseyde, Pandarus and Troilus attend a house party at the home of Sarpedon, but Troilus is so distraught that he goes home before the party is over. Criseyde, on her part, mourns the separation as keenly as does Troilus; but, on the tenth day of her stay in the Greek camp, Diomede visits her and declares his love and his own worthiness.

Day follows day without the return of Criseyde to Troy, and Criseyde gradually becomes more and more receptive to Diomede's suit. She gives him a horse, a brooch, and a device made from her sleeve. She is conscience-stricken at betraying Troilus, but eventually she accepts Diomede as her lover.

Troilus, who watches for her return as the days pass, finally goes to his sister Cassandra, the seeress, for an interpretation of a dream that he has had. Cassandra tells him that the dream means that his lady, whoever she may be, has become the love of Diomede. This interpretation greatly angers Troilus, who still has complete faith in Criseyde. Troilus and Criseyde exchange letters, and Criseyde insists that she will return to Troy. But when a coat captured from Diomede is displayed in Troy, Troilus finds on the collar the brooch that Criseyde had given to Diomede—a brooch that Troilus had formerly given to Criseyde.

Convinced of Criseyde's perfidy and not caring whether he lives or dies, Troilus attempts to kill Diomede in battle, but before he can he is slain by Achilles. His spirit ascends to the eighth sphere, and after surveying this little earth from this vantage he comes to hold all earthly concerns as vanities in comparison with the felicity of heaven. He then condemns the blind lust that motivates human conduct.

Chaucer concludes with six stanzas urging young, fresh folk to repair from mundane affairs and turn their visages to God. With an address to Gower and Strode and a prayer to Jesus, the poem ends.

To understand the magnitude of Chaucer's achievement, one should know the chief source of the poem, Boccaccio's *Filostrato*.[1] Although the main story of this work is similar to that of *Troilus and Criseyde*, Chaucer's modifications of the original make his work great where Boccaccio's is merely good. Chaucer improved upon the dialogue and overlaid the entire poem with philosophical and moralistic reflections, but more, it was in the development of the characters that he really excelled. His Troilus is quite similar to Boccaccio's Troilo—strong, brave, generous, noble; and, it might be added, the least colorful of the three central characters. Troilo was a mighty warrior, second only to the peerless Hector, and, as a prince of the royal family, he was wealthy and influential.

Boccaccio's Pandaro was Criseida's cousin, a young fellow not very strikingly portrayed. Chaucer's Pandarus, on the other hand, is one of the great literary inventions of all time. Good-hearted, curious, energetic, he has been transformed by Chaucer from Criseida's cousin to Criseyde's uncle. The natural inference from this change is that Chaucer intended him to be a generation older than Troilus and Criseyde. Chaucer, however, never tells us a thing about Pandarus' age, and there are several cogent arguments against assuming that he was elderly. When he first bounces into Troilus's bedroom, we get the impression that he and Troilus are comrades; and, though a firm friendship between men of dissimilar ages is by no means impossible, companionship between those of similar ages is far more common. Had Chaucer wished us to assume a difference in ages, we might expect that he would have said so, but he remains obdurately silent throughout the whole poem about the ages of all his characters.

Some critics of the poem have found Pandarus repulsive on the grounds that he is a lecherous ancient who finds vicarious pleasure in a love affair that he, incapacitated by age, could not enjoy himself. But this is to misread the poem completely. When Criseyde jestingly asks him how it is that he is tired of the company of women, there is certainly no hint in what she says that he is too old to enjoy love. That he runs, never walks, that he always leaps into a room, is also out of character with an elderly person.

Certainly Pandarus is not credulous; he sees the world realistically, neither brighter nor darker than it is. This lack of illusion and disillusion has caused him to be labeled cynical by some of his critics. Some readers feel that his realistic view of life is a characteristic of age, but this is not necessarily so; some people are realists in their teens and some are starry-eyed idealists until old age cuts them down.

The transformation of Boccaccio's Criseida to Chaucer's Criseyde was a great, though subtle, one. Criseida was a simple, amorous widow who became Troilo's lover without undue urging, and her capitulation to Diomede was swift. Of this relatively uncomplicated character Chaucer made one of the most complex of literary inventions. We never know exactly what Criseyde thinks, for Chaucer has carefully seen to it that we do not. And therein lies much of her charm; she, like the Mona Lisa, remains an eternal puzzle.

As with Pandarus, we do not know her age. Chaucer tantaliz-ingly tells us that the matter is not treated in his source. Scholars have varied widely in their estimates of how old she was. Many assume that she was about the same age as Troilus, but there are those who believe she was much older. The critics who believe that she was in full maturity look upon Troilus as a young boy infatuated with an older woman. But the only possible justifica-tion of this theory is that there is not a single statement in the poem to refute it. True it is that she is a widow, but certainly there is no set age for widows. Criseyde herself says that she is young (II, 752). That Diomede decides upon a conquest of her as soon as he sees her also argues for her youth, for it is difficult to imagine that he became suddenly enamored of a full-blown matron.

To the reader who comes to *Troilus and Criseyde* without some knowledge of the conventions of courtly love, the actions of the characters are at times puzzling, if not positively unbelievable. Their behavior is so entirely at variance with modern customs that the present-day reader tends to wonder why some simple, direct course of action could not be pursued instead of the tor-tuous and involved course in the poem. The characters, however, strictly adhere to the rules of the game of courtly love, and it is only at the end of the poem, when Criseyde is false to Troilus, that there is any violation of the code.

The essence of courtly love was secrecy. At all hazards, the affair had to be kept from the eyes and the ears of the world. It was vital that the lady's honor remain unspotted; and, as in all other ages, it remained unspotted so long as no one knew what she was doing. The high crime lay, not in immorality as such, but in being found out. The insistence throughout *Troilus and Cri-seyde* that Criseyde's honor be kept safe has almost the effect of a chorus, so often is it repeated.

A man and a woman who embarked on a courtly love affair could each have a confidant to act as a go-between, but no one else was supposed to know about the matter. The Troilus and Criseyde story has only one go-between for the two lovers, namely, Pandarus.

In courtly love the man was a servant to the woman, and, theo-retically, subject to her every whim. But that the object of the whole affair was sexual gratification might argue that the man was in a position of dominance. This is not true in theory; he was supposed to remain in subjugation to the woman.

A feature of courtly love that often baffles the modern person is that it was not supposed to lead to marriage. So far as we know, there was a long period in which Troilus and Criseyde could have been married had they wanted to be, but the thought never crossed their minds. There was a considerable argument during the medieval period as to whether it was moral for lovers to be married. The stricter theorists held that love in marriage was equivalent to adultery. Chaucer, however, apparently did not share this view, for he states in the *Franklin's Tale:*

> . . . *he hath bothe his lady and his love;*
> *His lady, certes, and his wyf also,*
> *The which that lawe of love acordeth to.* (CT, V, 796-98)

While it is true that Chaucer here takes the position that lovers may marry, he still finds it necessary to explain the fact. In the *Knight's Tale* both Palamon and Arcite wish to marry Emelye, but their objective crystalized only after Theseus had stated that the winner of the tournament would be allowed to marry her. Until that time—and it was a good many years since they had first seen her and had fallen in love with her—the cousins had been content merely to serve their lady. The irony of their service is brought out by Theseus when he interrupts the duel in the woodland to say that Emelye had not the slightest idea they were in love with her and, hence, no knowledge that they were serving her. It is noteworthy that in the *Book of the Duchess*, a tribute to the love of John of Gaunt for his wife Blanche of Lancaster, marriage is never mentioned. Thus in the four works in which courtly love is an important element—the *Book of the Duchess*, the *Knight's Tale*, the *Franklin's Tale*, and *Troilus and Criseyde*—two admit the possibility of marriage between lovers and two do not. An analysis of the four poems will show that marriage or the lack of it is vital to three of them, the *Knight's Tale*, the *Franklin's Tale*, and *Troilus and Criseyde*. Were this otherwise in any one of the three, the stories would not be possible; in other words, marriage or the lack of it had a highly important place in the development of the various plots.

[110]

Marriage would have supplied such a simple solution to the problem that eventually confronts Troilus and Criseyde that the modern reader is exasperated because the characters do not resort to it. But by the rules of this particular game, they could not, and the matter is never even discussed. When Troilus and Pandarus canvass the possibilities of Troilus's abducting Criseyde before she is traded to the Greeks for Antenor, the word marriage never enters the conversation. And from Troilus's point of view abduction is as impossible as marriage; either one would break the vital seal of secrecy. People would learn that Troilus and Criseyde were lovers and so Criseyde's honor would be besmirched. This matter of secrecy is something that puzzles modern scholars. How, they ask, was it possible, in the crowded life of the Middle Ages which was totally lacking in any real privacy, to conduct a secret love affair? And in some of the most famous examples of courtly love—Launcelot's love for Guinevere and Tristram's for Iseult in *Le Morte D'Arthur*—there was little or no secrecy. In the latter case King Mark was constantly aware of Tristram's love for his wife, and everyone in the court knew of Launcelot's love for Guinevere.

At any rate, the code called for a secrecy that rendered Troilus powerless to act when action was urgently needed. He could not even speak out in the parliament of the Trojans against the exchange of Criseyde. It was this aspect of courtly love that made a discreet go-between a necessity. In assuming this role, Pandarus is impaled on the horns of a dilemma. As Criseyde's uncle he must keep her honor clean by seeing that she does not get involved in a love affair.

When, however, Pandarus bounded into Troilus's bedroom and tried to pry the secret of Troilus's love from him, he promised to be his second in the affair no matter whom it might concern. Once having made that promise, he could never honorably withdraw from it. So he eventually finds himself with the duty of keeping Criseyde out of a love affair and with the equally binding duty of getting her into one. His final choice—to aid Troilus —causes him a great deal of soul-searching. He is of the opinion that future ages would use his name to indicate a procurer, and it must be admitted that Pandarus was right in his prophecy.

A number of critics of *Troilus and Criseyde* have had little respect for Troilus. This is largely because they consider him a

weakling, basing their opinion on the fact that he is given to retiring to his room to weep, banging his head on the wall, sighing
repeatedly, losing his color, and falling into illness from the intensity of his love. These extravagant acts were, however, not
peculiar to him; they were routine in courtly love. Chaucer by no
means makes Troilus out as lacking in masculinity; he specifically
tells us that Troilus is so highly esteemed as a warrior that he is
considered to be Hector the Second. It would be difficult to pay a
greater compliment to his manhood than this. Troilus's prowess as
a man of arms was one reason why Criseyde fell in love with him.

The truth of the matter is that the behavior for which we now
might scorn him was quite in line with courtly tradition. In the
Knight's Tale Palamon weeps a good part of the time he is in
prison. The banished Arcite falls into such a serious illness for
several years that his appearance becomes completely changed
from what it was, so changed that the gods decide he would be
unrecognized by those who formerly knew him. Aurelius, in the
Franklin's Tale, becomes so ill for Dorigen that he cannot even
get out of bed for two years. Pandarus himself becomes so indis-
posed from the pangs of love that at times he retires from the
public view into his private chamber. In the horrid burlesque on
courtly love in the *Merchant's Tale,* the squire Damyan takes to
his bed with lovesickness. In *Le Morte D'Arthur,* Tristram runs
mad in the woods for a year because of his longing for the Lady
Iseult. It is while he is totally dazed and irresponsible from the
intensity of his woe that he makes the mistake of marrying Iseult
of the Fair Hands. In the *Romaunt of the Rose* there are several
descriptions of what the lover must endure (cf. the Chaucerian
translation, lines 2395-2418; 2553-96). He is now hot, now cold;
sometimes as still as a tree and as dumb as a stone, and sometimes sighing and weeping. At night in bed he is now up, now
down, at times wallowing in anger at his lady's disdain and again
soothed by dreams of her kindness.

Troilus and Criseyde, however, is more than a poem of courtly
love, no matter how important the concepts of that system were.
The poem is greatly concerned with the role of fate in the course
of human lives. We would probably be mistaken to assume that
Chaucer sat down to write with the intention of producing a
theological treatise on fate and determinism; but the situation in
which he set the young lovers was one in which they were caught

up by forces beyond their control. The sorry ending of the action was inevitable from the beginning, and this sense of unavoidable calamity has been an essential part of the Troy story since Homer's first telling of it. In Chaucer's version of the tale, the whole essential action hinges on the fact that Calchas had forseen the inevitable destruction of the city.

In treating the subject of fate in *Troilus and Criseyde* Chaucer was not, of course, dealing with a subject alien to his interests. His highly admired master Boethius deals with the subject at length, and Chaucer himself was to return to the theme in the *Knight's Tale* and again, with a lighter touch, in the *Nun's Priest's Tale*. In the latter work he has the Nun's Priest say that he cannot solve the matter of what theological system we live by, as greater authorities than he have debated the question for a thousand years without arriving at an acceptable answer. *Troilus and Criseyde*, however, is based on the premise that fate rules the world. It should not, however, be assumed that, because Chaucer uses fate in this poem, he was necessarily convinced of its supremacy. Probably he, like any person who has thought deeply on the matter, never finally made up his mind about how the world is run.

Some critics have felt that Chaucer lost interest in the poem when Criseyde succumbed to the wiles of Diomede. This is a doubtful conclusion, for it is difficult to imagine Chaucer continuing to work on a poem in which he had lost interest. Certainly the psychological insight into the characters of the various actors in the last book is masterly—too masterly to be the work of an uninterested author. The cynical Diomede's decision, made as soon as he sees Criseyde, to effect a conquest of her is a marvelous contrast to the behavior of the love-stricken Troilus of Book I. It takes Chaucer a long time to produce a foil for Troilus, but when he does bring him onto the stage he is, although only a minor character, perfectly delineated. Whereas Troilus repairs to his bedroom to weep at the thought of his own unworthiness, Diomede calmly appraises the situation and decides that Criseyde must have time to let what is evidently a very warm love cool to the point where she may be receptive to a new approach. When he does speak, his performance is a splendid piece of acting. When he makes his declaration, insisting that he is a complete beginner in the art of love, his voice quakes with the intensity of his emotion. But he manages to drive home the fact he is a king's son and every bit as good as any Trojan.

Criseyde's great crime is that she acts like a woman instead of what she was supposed to be—a character in a drama of courtly love. To play her role correctly, she is bound by all the conventions to one single, inevitable course of action: absolute fidelity to Troilus as long as they both shall live. But the circumstances in which she finds herself are too much for her. A long time earlier she had run over in her mind the reasons for and against falling in love with Troilus; now she does the same thing about entering an affair with Diomede. All practical considerations are in favor of it; after all, she realizes that her parting from Troilus is final. He may still nourish hope that the two will be reunited, but she knows that they never will be. So at last she gives in to Diomede's importunities. But only in agony of spirit does she succumb, as is attested by her heartrending soliloquy to the effect that she knows she will be an object of contempt throughout the ages to come because of her falsity to Troilus, who had served her faithfully and had preserved her honor. Since there is no better way and since it is too late to rue, she at least hopes that she will be true to Diomede (V, 1054-84).

Some readers have held Criseyde to be cold and calculating because she tried to make realistic appraisals of the situations in which she found herself; but Chaucer, with his practical knowledge of humanity, knew what a reasonably intelligent human being would do when placed in such situations. The all-for-love-and-the-world-well-lost attitude has popular appeal in ephemeral literature, but Chaucer was telling how a real woman thinks and acts.

Criseyde's tragedy is brought about by Chaucer's attempt to combine two entirely different traditions: the courtly and the realistic—and the two systems are irreconcilable. If she attempts to live in accordance with either system, she does violence to the other one. The *Knight's Tale*, written in the tradition of courtly love, does not involve the realistic, and so the characters work out their destinies without enduring the psychological stresses experienced by Criseyde. They suffer, but their suffering is of a different kind. The Wife of Bath lives entirely by a realistic code, and she is able to look back on her life with satisfaction and exclaim:

> But, Lord Crist! whan that it remembreth me
> Upon my yowthe, and on my jolitee,
> It tikleth me aboute myn herte roote.
> Unto this day it dooth myn herte boote
> That I have had my world as in my tyme. (III, 469-73)

Criseyde, trying to live in two worlds, becomes an object of pity to some, of contempt to others.

We regret Criseyde's fall from fidelity, as Chaucer himself did. We perhaps regret it less than Chaucer, for the system of courtly love is so alien to us as to require us to make a conscious effort to understand it. When Pandarus, finally convinced of Criseyde's betrayal of Troilus, says, "I hate, ywys, Cryseyde" (V, 1732), he is expressing a medieval judgment. The ethics involved in his judgment are those of the courtly system: her immorality with Troilus he considered entirely laudable, but that with Diomede entirely reprehensible. The Scottish Chaucerians (a group of late fifteenth- and early sixteenth-century Scottish poets who held Chaucer in great esteem) who imitated and even continued the Criseyde story, were in complete agreement with Pandarus on this matter.

One thing that strikes a jarring note is Criseyde's answer to Troilus's letter (V, 1590-1631). She rebukes him for thinking only of his own pleasure and adds the lie that she is tarrying in the Greek camp to let the wicked gossip about her relations with him die down. She says that much more of it was known in Troy than she had realized. "Come I wole," she promises, knowing full well that she will never return to Troy and to Troilus. She has added untruth to infidelity.

When, soon after he receives the letter, Troilus learns from the brooch on Diomede's captured coat that Criseyde has been false to him, the story speeds to its end. When Troilus tries to kill Diomede in battle, he dies at the hands of Achilles. His spirit ascends to the eighth sphere, from where he looks with contempt on the petty concerns of "this litel spot of erthe."

Lines V, 1328-34, sum up the end of Troilus's worldly love and joy, but no matter how one strains the facts, one cannot see how Troilus met his death as a result of loving Criseyde. Troilus' death is simply one of the incidents of war and is not even related to his rival, Diomede, but the stanza does indicate that earthly love is a matter of the "false worldes brotelnesse."

[115]

Some critics find the passage from V, 1835, to the end of the poem out of harmony with all that has gone before. Actually, it is not. Chaucer is saying that a far worthier thing than a purely human love is a love of Christ. One might be constrained to say that there can be little argument over this matter, but why stitch it onto the end of a great poem about human love—pagan love, at that? The answer to this question is that Chaucer has been devoting his energies to writing about a matter which the Church considered sinful, extramarital love emphasizing physical pleasure. The whole code of courtly love was, of course, anti-Christian and utterly abhorrent to the Church, as it made a religion of love wherein a human woman was worshipped. But there were many laudable features about the concepts of courtly love, and the system had a refining and civilizing influence on western Europe.

Much has been written about Chaucer as a pious son of the Church. He is, however, such an objective writer that it is difficult to prove much about his religious views. But at the conclusion of *Troilus and Criseyde* he takes a firm position on the side of orthodoxy. In other words, he is writing his retraction, as he did at the end of the *Canterbury Tales*.

A first reading of *Troilus and Criseyde* is a fascinating experience, but it is only on a second or a third reading that we begin to appreciate Chaucer's art. One thing that we should notice is Chaucer's economy. The poem is a long one, but it includes a very small number of characters. Criseyde has her attendants and there are the people at the conference at Deiphebus's house, where Troilus and Criseyde first meet, but our eyes are focused throughout on the three main actors of the drama: Troilus, Criseyde, and Pandarus. Even Diomede, important as he is in the working out of the story, is kept in a secondary position. By having only the three main characters constantly in our sight, Chaucer can look into their minds and souls in a way that had never before been attempted. He keeps our attention focused on the mental working of the characters and not simply on their physical actions. The physical action of the poem is, of course, essential, but it is secondary to the psychological action—and this was Chaucer's great innovation. Never before had the minds and souls of characters in a poem been more important than what they did physically. If we compare this poem with something like the *Tale of*

[116]

Gamelyn, which in some manner found its way into manuscripts of the *Canterbury Tales,* we can see the great difference in method; *Gamelyn* is violent action from first to last, with not a single glimpse into the mental working of the characters.

Although the poem is long, every word counts. There are no needless digressions, no descriptions just for the sake of describing, no padding. No sooner does Troilus see Criseyde than he falls in love with her. Then comes the establishing of relations between Troilus and Criseyde; this part of the poem is extensive, but there is always something happening. As soon as Troilus and Criseyde are mutually in love and are reveling in their happiness, Chaucer speeds on toward their parting; and once the parting is affected, he drives on to Criseyde's defection and Troilus's disillusion and death. There are no dead passages; there is no waste wordage.

One feature of *Troilus and Criseyde* that has baffled critics is the source from which Chaucer maintains he was drawing his story—his author Lollius. Chaucer's pose throughout the poem is that of a mere translator, a pose highly useful when he does not want to convey information. If he does not want to reveal something he simply says that there is nothing about the matter in his original. Because Chaucer was actually drawing on Boccaccio, some have thought that Lollius was a nickname that Chaucer had given to the Italian poet. George Lyman Kittredge, however, evolved a more logical explanation.[2] He believed that when Chaucer referred to Lollius in the *House of Fame,* he actually believed that there had been a writer of that name who had dealt with the Troy story. By the time he wrote *Troilus and Criseyde* he had become convinced, however, that there was no such person, but he continued using Lollius as his source in a humorous effort to gain authority for his work. Attributing the work to an ancient authority on the story of Troy would tend to lend more credence to the tale than if he had attributed it to one of his own contemporaries.

CHAPTER 7

The Canterbury Tales

I *Fragment I*

ACCORDING to the most widely held theory, Chaucer began the composition of the *Canterbury Tales* in 1387. Why he chose the form that he did—a number of tales told by traveling pilgrims—has aroused much speculation. As it is one of the high crimes of scholarship to attribute originality to any author, especially a great one, source hunters have diligently combed all literature extant in Chaucer's time for a similar plan. The closest one they have found is the *Novelle* of Sercambi; this is, however, not too similar, for in it the travelers roamed around most of Italy, and Sercambi himself told all of the tales. It is fairly well agreed that Chaucer was not familiar with the *Decameron* of Boccaccio. There is nothing in Chaucer's works that shows a direct influence of those tales.

When Chaucer embarked on the project of the *Canterbury Tales* he was thoroughly familiar with the principle of the frame-story or group of tales. He had already written the *Legend of Good Women* and had probably set down a good part of what is now the *Monk's Tale*. The *Canterbury Tales* was projected on a far larger scale than either of these two works, but they serve to show that Chaucer was apparently fond of the idea of a series of tales.

People have wondered whether Chaucer actually went on a pilgrimage to Canterbury. It is believed that also in 1387 Chaucer's wife Philippa died, and he might have made a pilgrimage to Canterbury because of her death. It is difficult to see why her death would have caused him to render thanks to St. Thomas à Becket. The idea of using pilgrims en route to Canterbury, then, might have arisen from what was said earlier in this book, namely that he was undoubtedly familiar with Canterbury and the road to it. He frequently went to the Continent on Crown business, and the normal route from London to France was through Canterbury and on to Dover and thence across the Channel to Calais. As the Pilgrims' Way was rough, lonely, and dangerous, we may assume that he would travel in company when he could find it, and the most readily available company would usually be bands of pilgrims.[1]

It is generally assumed that Chaucer spent the thirteen years between 1387 and his death in 1400 in unremitting toil on his great project. This assumption, however, may be unwarranted. We know that he had a considerable body of work already written before he embarked on the *Tales*, material that he inserted into its fabric and attributed to various pilgrims. A more logical assumption would be that he stopped work on the project a considerable time before he died. In *Lenvoy de Chaucer a Scogan*, which was discussed in Chapter IV, Chaucer refers to himself as one of "hem that ben hoor and rounde of shap" and says:

> *Ne thynke I never of slep to wake my muse,*
> *That rusteth in my shethe stille in pees.*
> *While I was yong, I put hir forth in prees;*
> *But al shal passe that men prose or ryme;*
> *Take every man hys turn, as for his tyme.*   (Scogan, 38-42)

When he so charmingly mixes his metaphor by having his muse rust in its sheath he is plainly saying that he has given up the writing of poetry. When he wrote *Scogan* we do not know, but if we can trust what he says in it, the *Canterbury Tales* are unfinished because Chaucer abandoned work on them and not because death cut him down as he busily toiled to complete them.

The *General Prologue* to the *Canterbury Tales* is probably more admired and more often commented upon than any other piece of literature of its length in the English language. At first glance, this is not much short of miraculous, as it consists of little more than apparently unsystematic descriptions of about thirty ill-assorted people and a plan for a trip. But unsystematic as Chaucer may seem, never have people been more memorably described.

Although marvelous literary art, the *General Prologue* is in essence so simple that a summary of it sounds utterly prosaic. Chaucer says that one April evening he, a pilgrim to Canterbury to visit the shrine of St. Thomas à Becket, resorted to the Tabard Inn in the London suburb of Southwark and was there joined by a band of "wel nyne and twenty" other Pilgrims to the Saint's shrine. The group is made up of a Knight and his attendant Squire (who was his son) and Yeoman, a Prioress and another Nun who was her chaplain, three Priests (only one of whom ever appears in the subsequent story), a Monk, a Friar, a Merchant, a Clerk of Oxford, a Sergeant of the Law, a Franklin, a Haberdasher, a Carpenter, a Weaver, a Dyer, a Tapestry Maker (which last five characters are hereafter referred to as the Gildsmen), a Cook, a Shipman, a Doctor, a Wife of Bath, a Parson, a Plowman, a Reeve, a Miller, a Summoner, a Pardoner, and a Manciple. Chaucer describes and characterizes the various personages and then has the Host of the Inn propose a plan for recreation on the trip to Canterbury: Each Pilgrim will tell two tales on the way to that city and two more on the way home to London; the Host will go along on the pilgrimage to act as judge of the tales so that he can award the prize of a free dinner at the Tabard Inn to the teller of the best tale. Anyone who rebels at the Host's authority is to defray the entire expenses of the expedition.

Chaucer begins the *Prologue* in high style, setting the time and the occasion: April and a pilgrimage to Canterbury. By the end of the first eighteen lines, however, he has descended from his lofty manner to his usual comfortable style. At first, plain rain water is "swich licour," and the breeze is "Zephirus"; but at the end of the passage the reference is to those who have been helped by the saint "whan that they were seeke"—good straightforward English with no frills attached. Nowadays we are apt to think of a pilgrimage to a saint's shrine as a solemn religious occasion. But in the Middle Ages such matters were treated more lightly. The fact of the matter is that when Chaucer's Pilgrims departed from the Tabard Inn in Southwark, the age of great veneration for St. Thomas was a thing of the past. People in large numbers still made the pilgrimage, but the old fervor that had originally elevated Thomas to the status of a saint, in spite of the efforts of the Church to prevent it, had largely died out. Chaucer says that he himself was making the pilgrimage with "ful devout corage," but with the exception of Chaucer's own mention of the saint, the only other references to him in the whole of the *Canterbury Tales* are the Host's calling him "the blisful martir" (I, 770) and the statement that the cavalcade was halted at "the wateryng of Seint Thomas" (I, 826). St. Thomas may have been in the minds of the Pilgrims, but he certainly was not often on their tongues.

It has been said that the Pilgrims represent a complete cross section of the English society of Chaucer's day. This is hardly the truth; it would be better to say that they represent a cross section of middle-class society. Members of the nobility are absent, as are the serfs and villeins who composed almost three-fourths of the population. The Plowman, who is at the bottom of the social stratum represented on the pilgrimage, is probably a freeman of moderate means; he has sufficient wealth to take a fairly extensive trip in the company of a group of people who are in the main represented as living well, even luxuriously. Chaucer also omitted any representatives of the powerful victualing trades. There are no civil servants, with the exception of Chaucer, and no one to represent the many branches of artistry that flourished in the Middle Ages.

The band of Pilgrims is made up of a number of groups and also of people unattached to others. The Knight, with the Squire and the Yeoman; the Prioress, with her attendant nun and either three priests or a single one; the Pardoner and the Summoner; the Franklin and the Man of Law; the Gildsmen and their Cook; the Parson and the Plowman are all groups. The Monk, the Friar, the Merchant, the Manciple, the Clerk of Oxford, the Shipman, the Wife of Bath, and the rest are single travelers. An odd feature of the pilgrimage is that no member of a group ever has anything to do with any other member of the same group, even so far as to say a word to him. And equally remarkable is the general truculence that prevails between groups and single individuals. Open quarrels such as those between the Miller and the Reeve, the Friar and the Summoner, the Cook and the Host, and the Pardoner and the Host are readily noted; but there is also friction between the Wife of Bath and the Friar, the Wife of Bath and the Clerk, the Shipman and the Parson, and so on. It is, of course, this almost universal animosity that raises the *Canterbury Tales* from a mere anthology of tales to the status of one of the great human comedies of all times.

Chaucer makes his Pilgrims outstanding; they are not ordinary people. The Knight is "a verray, parfit gentil knyght," who in thirty-six lines is five times described as being "worthy" or as possessing "worthynesse." The Squire is described in the terms of a perfect gentleman; the Prioress is head of her nunnery; the Monk is "a manly man, to been an abbot able"; the Friar is a "worthy man," as is the Merchant; the Sergeant of the Law is "ful riche of excellence"; the Franklin is "Seint Julian . . . in his contree," "knyght of the shire," "a shirreve," and a "contour;/was nowhere swich a worthy vavasour"; and the Wife of Bath "of clooth-makyng she hadde swich a haunt,/She passed hem of Ypres and of Gaunt"; the Gildsmen are worthy to be burgesses and aldermen. In like manner all the rest of the Pilgrims are distinguished, even those who are unsympathetic to the reader and presumably to Chaucer also. The Manciple is a shrewd swindler, but he has the intelligence to cheat a band of highly trained men; the Reeve, a thief of agricultural produce, is such a clever accountant that no one can prove him to be in the wrong; the Miller, who steals grain, is proficient at his trade—all of them, in fact, excelled at their callings. Chaucer says of the character who is most generally execrated in modern times, the Pardoner, "but of his craft, fro Berwyk into Ware,/Ne was ther swich another pardoner."

Much has been made of the fact that Chaucer never pronounces moral judgments. He, the detached observer of human comedy and tragedy, is content to record what he sees before him, never crying out against the abuses of the day; and critics wring their hands at his almost complete neglect of the stirring events of his times. The Black Death and the Peasants' Revolt are accorded bare mention in his works, and nowhere does he say a word about the Statute of Laborers or the enclosure of common lands, with its attendant dispossession of the peasants. War he merely hints at, and about the political upheavals of the times he is silent.

The criticism that Chaucer was indifferent to the abuses of his times is misdirected because it fails to perceive the extraordinary effectiveness of how Chaucer allows the reader to form his own conclusions. Being the genius that he is universally admitted to be, he realized that a shrill outcrying against abuses was not the best way to direct attention to what was wrong with the world. Chaucer was an aristocratic poet who addressed the "judicious" that Shakespeare felt to be few but far worthier of attention than the more numerous "general." Understatement is frequently more effective with such an audience than overstatement.

[122]

When Chaucer presented his Knight as perfect, the more acute among his original audience must have made the comparison between this paragon of virtue and the very imperfect knights of Chaucer's own times; for chivalry was in a rapid decline. Such knights as Chaucer's might have existed in his day, but they were probably rare. The poor Parson of a town is a model for men of religion for all time. Unless practically all of the authors contemporary with Chaucer were completely wrong in what they had to say, parsons were an ignorant, lustful, slothful lot; *The Vision of Piers Plowman* is especially bitter against unworthy priests.[2] Certainly the discerning reader of Chaucer's time could make the comparison between the ideal and the actual. Chaucer's Parson has been thought to be a Lollard follower of Wycliffe, and the Shipman accuses him of being such an one, but it is doubtful if this is what Chaucer wanted him to be considered. The accusation is not developed, and, as is brought out later, the Parson does not object to the Host's swearing in his own *Prologue*. Chaucer apparently wanted the Parson to be a sympathetic character, and by the time he wrote the *Canterbury Tales* the earlier popular enthusiasm for Lollardry had greatly declined.

The Parson's brother, the Plowman, is also an ideal character, against whom no word of criticism can be directed. But here again the ideal was in strong contrast to the real. The actual peasant was not a jolly fellow compacted of all the virtues that he is sometimes made out to be. In sober truth he was a fairly brutal creature—because he never had a chance to be anything else. But if there was one thing upon which practically everyone in England agreed, it was in resisting the payment of tithes. Chaucer, however, says of his Plowman: "His tithes payde he ful faire and wel,/Bothe of his propre swynk and his catel" (I, 539-40). Tithes may have been paid, as the penalties for nonpayment were severe, but the payment was rarely "ful faire and wel." The clergy's claim to the peasant's second-best beast upon his death was justified on the grounds that at some time or other the peasant had probably cheated in the payment of what the Church considered its due.

The method Chaucer uses to describe such a character as the Monk is more effective than a stream of invective would be. Surely the people of the fourteenth century knew what a monk was originally meant to be like. The significance of Chaucer's picture of a luxury-loving, hard-riding, sportsman-businessman who neither studied nor labored with his hands nor remained within his cloister would not be lost upon them. And neither would his portrait of the Friar, a proud, avaricious, wenching flatterer of the wealthy, who avoided the sick and the poor and who was a giver of easy penance "ther as he wiste to have a good pitaunce." Readers would contrast the activities of this friar with the ideal activities that St. Dominic and St. Francis had envisioned—dedication to poverty, obedience, chastity, and good works among the diseased and the destitute—and see the point that Chaucer was quietly making.

And so through the rest of the *Prologue* we would find that although Chaucer has in the main given what at first glance seem to be very admiring portraits of the various Pilgrims, he has sprinkled his admiration with cutting irony. The Manciple and the Pardoner are both "gentil," but at the same time they are dishonest rascals. The Miller and the Reeve are excellent at their callings, but they are also bold-faced thieves. The Franklin was a notable public servant, but he was also consistently guilty of the cardinal sin of gluttony, as a great part of what Chaucer says about him bears upon his eating habits. The Prioress is an imitator of court manners and a devout lover of small animals rather than human beings.[3] The Shipman was a splendid skipper, but also a murderous pirate.

After Chaucer has described the Pilgrims he offers his first disclaimer (I, 725-42). He explains that he is not to blame for the improper tales he will have to tell; he says that if someone tells an improper tale, the reporter has the solemn duty of reproducing the tale exactly as he heard it. This is a very neat excuse for including salacious stories in the *Canterbury Tales*, although, of course, they add greatly to the realism of the whole work by fitting tales to tellers. The Miller, the Reeve, the Summoner, and the Shipman are of a type from which coarseness might be expected; this is not necessarily true of the Merchant, but, as is discussed later, the *Merchant's Tale* was undoubtedly not originally written for the Merchant.

After the disclaimer, Chaucer has the Host propose the plan for entertainment on the pilgrimage. If we accept Chaucer's statement that he joined twenty-nine other Pilgrims at the Tabard Inn, the total number of stories would have been one hundred and twenty. Of this number, only twenty were completed, and there is an additional tale by the Canon's Yeoman, who was not an original member of the band. Why such a grand project was allowed to die so far from completion we can only guess. And it must always be sincerely regretted that the project did fail, because the stories we assume to be of late composition show a heightened sense of drama in comparison with the earlier stories. The "marriage group," the tales the Friar and the Summoner tell against each other, and the Canon's Yeoman's interruption show increasing rather than diminishing poetical powers in Chaucer. This fact makes the abandonment of the *Tales* all the more puzzling. If Chaucer's powers had been waning, we could understand why he might have thought it wise to terminate his poetical career—but he was progressing from excellence to greater excellence.

It can hardly be that the magnitude of the project overwhelmed him. Many another man has written far more than Chaucer either did or projected, and Chaucer himself was not one to shirk a task merely because it was large. Anyone who had translated the *Roman de la Rose* was unlikely to be appalled at the size of a piece of work, and we have Chaucer's word that he translated it. About all we can conclude is that Chaucer wearied of the *Canterbury Tales* and gave them up because he felt no compelling reason to finish them. If the portrait of Chaucer in Hoccleve's *Regiment of Princes*, which dates from 1412, is a reliable indicator of his general condition in the latter years of his life, we may conclude that he was not in very robust health. There is, therefore, the possibility that he gave up the *Tales* because of illness.

He had, however, left unfinished the *Legend of Good Women*, the *House of Fame*, the *Cook's Tale*, and the *Squire's Tale*. As for the *Squire's Tale*, Chaucer may have intended to return to it, but never did so. The epilogue, "Heere folwen the wordes of the Frankeleyn," in which the Franklin praises the Squire for his story, is noncommital and could adequately serve if the story had been completed. Or possibly we are to understand that the Franklin had had enough of the Squire's romancing and had interrupted him in the telling of his story.[4] This theory would make the Franklin a fairly rude old man, for all his blandishing words. One would think, however, that if Chaucer meant there to be an interruption by the Franklin, he would have made it clearer than he did. The reader is in absolutely no doubt that *Sir Thopas* and the

Monk's Tale were purposely cut off in mid-career by members of the group—and for good reason. They had served their artistic purposes and more of them would have been boring.

When Chaucer had the Knight win the draw to tell the first tale, he was motivated by social, artistic, and practical considerations. It was eminently fitting that the Pilgrim of highest social standing should begin the proceedings. And the *Knight's Tale,* a dignified story of courtly love, was a far more appropriate opening for the project than a ribald tale would have been.

Of all the tales in verse, the *Knight's Tale* is on the highest plane. But there was also a practical reason for placing it first. As we know from the *Legend of Good Women* (G, 408-09), at a period presumably earlier than that of the composition of the *Canterbury Tales,* Chaucer had written "al the love of Palamon and Arcite / Of Thebes, thogh the storye is knowen lite." The expression "is knowen lite" is open to several interpretations. One, stated before, is that the story of Palamon and Arcite was, in general, not well known to the public.

Another interpretation is that Chaucer's version had not been put into circulation. If, however, his working of the tale was unpublished, it is a little difficult to see why he mentioned it at all in the *Legend of Good Women,* as there would be small point in enumerating works reposing in his desk drawer. If, on the other hand, he had circulated it, his incorporating it in the *Canterbury Tales* would be odd; for, so far as we know, the *Tales* included no previously published material. Many scholars assume that Chaucer reworked an early version of the *Knight's Tale* for inclusion in the *Canterbury Tales.* But there is really no valid reason to believe that the tale is not now in the form in which Chaucer originally composed it.

The Knight tells about Theseus, who, escorting home to Athens his new wife Hippolyta and her sister Emelye from the expedition to conquer the Amazons, is met by a group of widows who tearfully beg his aid in the burial of their husbands, slain in the war against Thebes. Theseus turns around and goes to Thebes, where he defeats Creon, tyrant of the city. When the field is being ransacked after the battle, two wounded cousins, members of the royal house of Thebes, are found unconscious in the heap of slain. These young men, Palamon and Arcite, are condemned to life imprisonment in Athens.

One morning in May, Palamon, from his prison, sees Emelye in a garden and is instantly stricken with love for her. When Palamon says that he does not know whether she is a woman or a goddess, Arcite looks at her and is also instantly stricken. Then ensues a long wordy battle as to which one has the right to love her. Finally Arcite is freed through the good offices of his and Theseus's friend, Pirithous, and is banished from Athens upon pain of death.

At Thebes his love-longing causes him to become so ill that when he recovers his strength he is no longer recognizable to his former acquaintances. At a god's suggestion he returns to Athens, where he gains employment in Emelye's household and is eventually promoted to a place in Theseus's retinue.

Palamon effects his escape from prison one May day and hides in a woods outside the city. To those woods comes Arcite all alone and makes his observance to the May. In Palamon's hearing he delivers a soliloquy in which he discloses his identity and declares his continuing love for Emelye. Upon being confronted by the enraged Palamon, he agrees to bring arms the next day so that the two can settle the matter of loving Emelye by battle.

As they are fighting up to their ankles in blood, Theseus, out hunting deer, with Hippolyta and Emelye in his train, suddenly arrives upon the scene and stops the battle. Upon learning who the combatants are he sentences them to instant death, but, moved by the women's pleas for clemency, he says that in a year the young men, each attended by a band of a hundred knights, will decide the matter by a formal battle.

There is a detailed description of the lists (arenas for combat), upon the walls of which are temples to Venus, Mars, and Diana. In due course the young knights and their bands arrive, Lygurge of Thrace being on Palamon's side and Emetreus of India on Arcite's. Before the battle Palamon prays at the shrine of Venus that he may gain possession of Emelye and Arcite at the shrine of Mars for victory in the battle, a victory that would automatically gain him possession of Emelye. Emelye prays at the shrine of Diana that she will not have to marry either of them, but if she must marry, she wishes to fall to the lot of the one who most loves her.

Arcite wins the battle, but when he is parading before the ladies immediately after, a fury, sent by Saturn so that Venus could keep her promise to her knight, frightens Arcite's horse. Arcite is thrown and fatally injured and is buried in a most elaborate series of ceremonies. Some years later, Palamon, on a diplomatic mission from Thebes to Athens, is awarded Emelye's hand in marriage by Theseus. The two live in love and prosperity for the rest of their lives.

Chaucer derived the *Knight's Tale* from Boccaccio's *Teseide*, but the differences between the two works are perhaps more noteworthy than the correspondences. For one thing, the *Teseide* has twelve books and nearly ten thousand lines; Chaucer condensed this mass of material to four books and to less than a quarter of the number of lines, of which only about seven hundred show even a loose resemblance to the source. Certainly Chaucer used the *Teseide*, but he used it as a starting point for the creation of an original work of art rather than a translation, adaptation, or paraphrase.

Although the *Knight's Tale* is set in the heroic age of Greece, it is actually a medieval tale of courtly love. So completely is it medieval that only one chariot, the indispensable conveyance in classical warfare, ever crosses the stage—and that one is pulled by four white bulls. Instead of riding in chariots, the warriors of the *Knight's Tale* are mounted on horses, like good medieval knights taking part in one of the tournaments that Chaucer helped to stage at Smithfield.

It is generally assumed that Chaucer composed the *Knight's Tale* in one form or another at about the time he wrote *Troilus and Criseyde*. If he actually did this, it is remarkable, for in *Troilus and Criseyde* he created two of the notable characters of all literature, Pandarus and Criseyde. With these two vivid creations in mind, we cannot help asking ourselves how, at the same period, he could have written as extensive a work as the *Knight's Tale* and have embodied in it such completely unindividualized characters. Even the man in black and his lost lady in the *Book of the Duchess*, presumably his first extensive work, have more of reality about them than do either Palamon or Arcite. Theseus is but a name and Emelye a compliant shadow. It is true that we learn something of the workings of Theseus's mind from what he says, but he never assumes the life that makes Criseyde and Pandarus such memorable characters. Only the subordinate char-

acters Emetreus and Lygurge give the impression of being real
people.

We are almost driven to the conclusion that Chaucer definitely
subordinated the characters for a purpose. It could hardly be
that he wanted simply to give an extensive exposition of courtly
love. Instead, it would seem that in this poem he was interested
in showing what determines human behavior and the outcome of
human lives. Almost at the beginning of the work, Arcite, mis-
taking Palamon's outcry upon seeing Emelye for the first time
for a bewailing of his imprisonment, says:

> *For Goddes love, taak al in pacience*
> *Oure prisoun, for it may noon oother be.*
> *Fortune hath yeven us this adversitee.*
> *Som wikke aspect or disposicioun*
> *Of Saturne, by som constellacioun,*
> *Hath yeven us this, although we hadde it sworn;*
> *So stood the hevene whan that we were born.*
> *We moste endure it; this is the short and playn.*   (I, 1084-91)

In his reply Palamon says:

> *And if so be my destynee be shapen*
> *By eterne word to dyen in prisoun. . . .*   (I, 1108-09)

Later, part of Arcite's lament at being freed from prison is:

> *Allas, why pleynen folk so in commune*
> *On purveiaunce of God, or of Fortune,*
> *That yeveth hem ful ofte in many a gyse*
> *Wel bettre than they kan hemself devyse?*   (I, 1251-54)

He continues:

> *. . . O crueel goddes that governe*
> *This world with byndyng of youre word eterne,*
> *And writen in the table of atthamaunt*
> *Youre parlement and youre eterne graunt,*
> *What is mankynde moore unto you holde*
> *Than is the sheep that rouketh in the folde?*
>
> *.   .   .   .   .*

What governance is in this prescience,
That giltelees tormenteth innocence?   (*I, 1303-8; 1313-14*)

When Chaucer is in process of bringing Theseus, who is out in the country to hunt deer, to the scene of the battle between Palamon and Arcite, he takes a whole paragraph to explain the coincidence (I, 1663-72); the passage includes the following line: "Al is this reuled by the sighte above" (I, 1672).

Examples such as the above show how Chaucer indicates throughout the work that the forces which shape human destiny are outside the individual. A major episode in the poem, the prayers of Palamon and Arcite at the shrines on the walls of the lists, would at first glance indicate that the two young knights were directing their petitions to pagan deities, but closer examination shows that the deities have been transformed into planets. In other words, Palamon and Arcite are under astrological influence; this is again true when Arcite, under the influence of Saturn, is thrown from his horse and killed. Theseus, at the end of the poem (I, 2987-3066), gives a long speech that also indicates belief in outside forces that shape human lives.

Few will dispute that the *Knight's Tale* is the finest metrical romance in English. It is, however, so different from the conventional romances that a comparison is hardly fair. The others are little more than records of action. Although there is action in the *Knight's Tale*, there is much more that is not in the ordinary romance. Nor were the authors of the other romances, for the most part, interested in what makes man act the way he does; it is enough for them that he acts.

When the Knight finished his tale, the Pilgrims all approved his effort and the Host was of the opinion that matters were going aright. To keep things on the same plane he called on the Monk for the second tale, for the Monk, presumably a man of education and taste, might be expected to tell a refined story. But here Chaucer showed fine artistic sense; he brought the literary level crashing down from the romance of the Knight, who "nevere yet no vileynye ne sayde / In al his lyf unto no maner wight," to the crude tale of the drunken lout, the Miller, who "was a janglere and a goliardeys, / And that was moost of synne and harlotries." The Miller, the coarsest and roughest member of the pilgrimage, insists upon telling his story, or else he will sever connections with the company and go his separate way. He announces: "I kan a noble tale for the nones, / With which I wol now quite the Knyghtes tale" (I, 3126-37). His story of low life is in sharp contrast to the *Knight's Tale,* but it also resembles it in a dreadful way. The *Knight's Tale* is the story of two young men in love with one woman, and so is the *Miller's Tale*—if one can call the emotions of Hende Nicholas and Absolon love. The *Miller's Tale* becomes in effect a parody on the *Knight's Tale.*

The story concerns an elderly rich lout, a carpenter, who takes lodgers into his home. One of the lodgers is Nicholas, a former student at Oxford, who does not seem to have an occupation. He is a musician, an astronomer, and a lover. The object of his affections is the eighteen-year-old wife of his host; she is a neat, pretty, amorous creature named Alison. Nicholas attempts to seduce her; her sole reaction to his proposal is that they will have to be careful, as her husband is jealous. A rival for her love is Absolon, a village dandy, a jack-of-all-trades who is adept at singing, dancing, and playacting.

Nicholas locks himself into his room and refuses to answer knocks upon the door. When the old carpenter has had the door broken down, Nicholas is found in a supposed trance; when he regains consciousness, he tells the carpenter that a huge flood is imminent—the greatest flood since Noah's. This matter, he insists, must be kept secret from everyone. The carpenter, Alison, and Nicholas will save their lives by sleeping in three kneading tubs hung to the roof of the house. The carpenter must remain far separated from his wife and maintain complete silence.

The three repair to their tubs that night, and, as soon as the carpenter has fallen asleep, Nicholas and Alison go to a bedroom. They have not been there long when the lovelorn Absolon appears and requests a kiss from Alison, who sportively puts out of the window a part of her body not usually kissed. Absolon, in the dark, kisses it and becomes enraged at the deception that has been played upon him.

He borrows a red-hot plow coulter from a blacksmith and returns to the bedroom window, where he says that he has a ring of his mother's to give Alison if she will kiss him. Nicholas, who had been convulsed with merriment at Absolon's discomfiture, takes Alison's place at the window. Absolon promptly applies the glowing coulter to Nicholas, who screams, "Help! water!" The carpenter in the attic, hearing the cry and deciding that the flood prophesied by Nicholas has come, cuts the cords that hold up his kneading tub. He falls to the floor and breaks his arm.

It is as if Chaucer, having presented the courtly lovers who were content to serve their lady year after year without her even knowing of their existence, decided to show that this was not all there was to be said on the subject of love, that there was an earthly aspect in contrast to the idealistic. Arcite, upon being freed from prison, falls ill when deprived of the sight of his lady —truly noble, if impractical, behavior. But Nicholas roughly seizes the object of his affections and suggests that the two of them immediately repair to bed—perhaps effective wooing, but hardly on a high aesthetic plane.

The Miller's announcement that his tale will relate how a clerk deceived a carpenter immediately arouses the ire of that carpenter, the Reeve, who on moralistic grounds asserts that the Miller should not defame wives. It is noteworthy that the other carpenter, one of the five Gildsmen, has no word of objection to offer. Indeed, this episode suggests that Chaucer is indicating a previous acquaintance between the Reeve and the Miller, and a cordial dislike between them, as the Miller leads the group out of town with his bagpipes and the Reeve always rides at the very tail end of the procession, as far from the Miller as he can get and still remain in the company. Millers and reeves, however, naturally disliked each other, as their interests were in conflict. The reeve had to have his grain ground at the miller's mill, where he was certain that part of it was being stolen. Such suspicions, with their resulting accusations, always made for hard feeling.

The *Millers' Tale*, a fusing of two *fabliau*-type stories, is structurally rather weak. The theme of the deception of the carpenter-husband is but loosely connected to the theme of Absolon's revenge. But what the tale lacks in tightness of plot sturcture is amply compensated for in the portraits, which rise to greatness. Hende Nicholas, the idling scholar, interested in astrology and secret love, with his astrolabe, his augrym stones, and his gay harp, is a fine fellow, scented with sweet herbs. Alison, the young wife, is a wonder of descriptive art. Her body is slender and small as a weasel, and who but Chaucer would have hit upon this remarkable simile to describe a woman? For thirty-eight lines Chaucer describes her, and she finally stands before us a living creature, a pretty, well-dressed, active, merry little housewife fairly exuding sex appeal. It is difficult to choose the best line in her description, but probably "And sikerly she hadde a likerous ye" must be accorded the palm. The narrative economy of this line is superb.

Absolon is also wonderfully portrayed. From the openwork design on his shoes to his fan-shaped coiffure he is the perfect picture of a small-town dandy. Even his extraordinary virtuosity in the dance is characteristic of the village lady-killer.

As was said, the story is a combination of two plots, and both involve cruelty. The old carpenter, actually the only decent person in the tale, breaks his arm when he chops the rope and his kneading tub falls to the ground, and Nicholas is severely burned. The inflicting of such pain is rarely a part of the better modern humor, but it definitely was part of medieval fun.

Cruel or not, the tale was enjoyed by everyone except the Reeve; but, as he had registered his disapproval before the story was told, it is hardly surprising that he should withhold his approbation at its conclusion. When the tale is finished, he embarks upon a maundering analysis of the ills and vices of old age, but is cut short by the Host, who has small patience with such preaching. The tale that the Reeve tells is as improper as that of the Miller—a churl's tale—but it is not so funny. Again Chaucer starts his story with fine portraits. The portrait of Symkyn the miller, a small-town bully, contains so many of the characteristics of Robin the Miller of the pilgrimage that we wonder if Chaucer is giving us pictures of actual people. The "riche gnof" (I, 3188) of the *Miller's Tale* much resembles the carpenter-Reeve of the pilgrimage: he is old, well-to-do, and perhaps has a skittish young wife whose virtue is not beyond suspicion. At any rate, the particulars dealing with Symkyn's wife, the daughter of the parson of the town, are so individualized that they could easily point to some actual person.

Chaucer does not indicate such universal approval of the *Reeve's Tale* as of the *Miller's Tale*, but the story mightily appealed to the Cook, Roger or Hodge of Ware, who was eager to keep the ball rolling by telling another tale of the same kind. The Reeve tells of a miller of Trumpington, not far from Cambridge, who is visited by two university students, John and Aleyn, with grain to grind. Suspicious of the miller's honesty, they de-

[133]

cide to watch him closely to prevent his stealing any of their grain. The miller, however, lets loose their horse, which runs away to the fens. While the students are capturing their horse, the miller steals some of their meal and has his wife bake it into a large cake. When the students finally catch their mount, night has fallen; the miller agrees to provide food and a night's lodging for them.

At supper the miller becomes drunk and finally goes to bed with his wife, who is also far from sober. At the foot of their bed stands a cradle with their baby. Their daughter and the students also retire. While the miller snores loudly, Aleyn creeps into bed with the miller's daughter, who welcomes him. John, reflecting ruefully upon his aloneness, moves the cradle from the foot of the miller's bed to the foot of his own.

The wife rises to relieve herself, and, upon coming back to the bedroom, gropes until she finds the cradle. She enters the adjacent bed and is warmly received by John. When dawn comes, the daughter tells Aleyn where he can find the cake baked from his stolen meal. He arises and seeks out the bed in which he had begun the night. He finds the bed with no cradle at its foot and creeps into bed with the miller.

Aleyn shakes the miller, supposing him to be John, and tells him of his jolly night's adventure. Instantly the miller and Aleyn engage in a wild fight, which temporarily halts when the miller falls upon his wife, who had been calmly sleeping with John. She, convinced that she had been assaulted by the devil, cries out and immediately procures a club with which she endeavors to hit Aleyn, but only succeeds in knocking her husband unconscious. While he is out of the fight, the students hurriedly dress, take their meal and the cake, and depart for home, having been amply revenged upon the dishonest miller.

The extant fragment of the *Cook's Tale* is not long enough to enable us to tell what direction the plot would have taken had Chaucer completed it, but the cast of characters indicates that it would not have been a morally uplifting tale. The story begins with an account of Perkyn, a reveling apprentice, who is so dishonest and so reluctant to do any honest work that his master turns him out into the world. He seeks shelter with a friend of the same sort whose wife runs a shop for show but who really earns her living as a prostitute. Here the story breaks off.

In so far as we can learn, this would have been an original story. The fact that the Cook is called upon in the *Manciple's Prologue* to tell a story indicates that Chaucer intended to cancel the existing Cook's fragment. With this piece the first group of the *Canterbury Tales* ends.

II *Fragment II*

Fragment II, consisting as it does of only the *Man of Law's Tale*, could stand almost anywhere in the *Canterbury Tales*, as there is nothing at either the beginning or the ending to connect it to any other story. Its position in modern editions of Chaucer's works is a result of its placement in the best manuscripts, but the order of the tales in the manuscripts may not be a matter of great importance. The *Introduction to the Man of Law's Tale* contains several interesting points. One is that it was told on April 18, but the pity of this is that we are not certain which day of the pilgrimage this was; all we know from this piece of evidence is that one day on which the pilgrimage was in progress was April 18. We do not, of course, know how many days the pilgrimage was supposed to take. The trip from London to Canterbury was often made in two days, but we cannot be sure how long Chaucer intended to keep his Pilgrims on the road.

Another matter of interest is the reference to some of Chaucer's works. After a slighting reference to Chaucer's skill as a poet, combined with a compliment to his fruitfulness in the production of verse, the Man of Law says: "In youthe he made of Ceys and Alcione" (II, 57). This sentence has puzzled scholars, for although Chaucer included this story as part of the prologue to the *Book of the Duchess*, they cannot believe that he would refer to that book, concerned as it is with the love of John of Gaunt for the Duchess Blanche, by this introductory episode. They speculate that Chaucer might have written a longer Ceyx and Alcyone which he abbreviated in the *Duchess*. Probably Chaucer, for some reason about which we are ignorant, decided in the *Introduction to the Man of Law's Tale* to emphasize the classical tale rather than the John of Gaunt-Duchess Blanche story, perhaps hesitating to emphasize John's grief for his first duchess after he had married two more duchesses.

But this brings up the question why he saw fit to mention the matter at all. He might have done it because he was embarking on a list of classical lovers—a list he says is contained in "the Seintes Legende of Cupide," or the *Legend of Good Women*. The interesting thing about the list as here given is that it does not correspond with the contents of the *Legend*. Cleopatra and Philomela, who are in the *Legend*, are not mentioned in the *Introduction to the Man of Law's Tale*, and Dianire, Hermyon, Erro, Eleyne, Briseyde, Ladomya, and Penelopee, who are not in the *Legend*, are mentioned here. Alceste is also mentioned, but she is in only the *Prologue* of the *Legend*, and is not treated in a separate tale. It would, therefore, seem that this list, and hence the *Introduction to the Man of Law's Tale*, were written while Chaucer was still at work on the *Legend of Good Women*, or at least had not yet definitely given over the project.

In the *Introduction* Chaucer makes some slighting remarks about the tales of Canacee and of Tyro Appollonius as abominable matters. As John Gower told stories of these two people in the *Confessio Amantis*, a legend grew up about how Chaucer's reference produced such enmity between the two poets, who had formerly been friends, that Gower removed a complimentary mention of Chaucer from the conclusion of the *Confessio Amantis*. This supposed episode is based on no known facts and is a part of the legendary life of Chaucer that formerly grew to such large proportions.

In II, 96, the Man of Law says, "I speke in prose." Actually he does nothing of the sort, and this has inclined scholars to believe that this statement was written to go before the *Tale of Melibee* or, more likely, before the lost or perhaps untranslated *De Contemptu Mundi sive de Miseria Conditionis Humanae* of Pope Innocent III, with which Chaucer was familiar and which he says in the *Legend of Good Women* he had translated (LGW, G, 414-15). Why Chaucer changed from the prose tale to the present verse tale of Custance we cannot say. The *Tale of Melibee*, with its interminable citing of authorities, would have been eminently fitting for the Man of Law; but the tale of Custance does not fit him, or any of the other pilgrims. Moreover, the *Introduction to the Man of Law's Tale*, a spirited condemnation of the hateful harm of poverty, is derived very directly from Innocent's *De Contemptu Mundi*. There is nothing at all in the following tale of Custance about poverty, and this is another reason for believing that Chaucer originally intended to assign some other tale to the Man of Law.

The Man of Law tells that Syrian merchants who go to Rome carry home such a glowing account of the beauty and virtues of the daughter of the Emperor of Rome, Custance, that the Sultan of Syria falls in love with her and negotiates for her hand in marriage. One of the conditions for the marriage is that the Sultan and his followers will be baptized into the Christian faith. This piece of information arouses ire in the breast of the Sultan's mother.

The mother receives the bride and groom at a feast, where the Sultan and his followers are murdered by the mother's orders. Custance is set adrift in a rudderless ship which in time runs aground in Northumberland, England. Custance is kindly received by the chief constable and his wife Hermengyld, and she converts Hermengyld to Christianity. Through the agency of a blind man, the chief constable is also converted.

A young knight who had wooed Hermengyld, but who had been repulsed, slips into her bedroom and stabs her to death as she sleeps, leaving the bloody knife with Custance, who is accused of the murder. At the trial for her life before Alla, King of Northumberland, the wicked knight swears that she is guilty, but an arm and hand appear, break his neck, and knock the eyes out of his head.

Alla marries Custance; and, for a time, all is well except that Donegild, Alla's mother, hates Custance. When the time comes for Custance to bear a child, a messenger is dispatched to tell Alla the news. Donegild gets the messenger drunk and changes his letters to read that Custance has given birth to a horrible fiendish creature. Alla received the news sadly, but says she is to do nothing until he gets home. The messenger is again intercepted by Donegild, who changes the letter to read that the chief constable is to set Custance and her child adrift in her old ship. He does this. In the course of the years Custance arrives back in Rome, having been picked up at sea by a homeward bound naval expedition that had been sent out by the Emperor her father and led by a senator to avenge her on the Sultan's wicked mother. She takes up lodging with the senator who had found her, and she and her son dwell quietly with the senator and his wife.

Alla, who had killed his mother when he had learned of her duplicity concerning Custance, comes to Rome to receive absolution for his crime. At a public gathering he sees his son, who awakens memories in him. Alla goes with the boy to his home. He is reunited with Custance, and Custance is also reunited with her father, the Emperor. Alla and Custance return to England, where they live happily for a year. At the end of the year, Alla dies and Custance returns to Rome, where she spends the rest of her life performing good works. Her son becomes the Emperor Maurice.

The *Man of Law's Tale* is most immediately derived from Nicholas Trivet's *Anglo-Norman Chronicle*, but many of the moralizing passages are from *De Contemptu Mundi*. The story, however, exists in a number of versions in various languages, and the general theme of the maligned wife is to be found in many analogues. The tale as we have it in the *Canterbury Tales* could scarcely be considered one of Chaucer's major works, although it contains some fine passages.

There is nothing to connect the *Man of Law's Epilogue* to the *Man of Law's Tale;* indeed, the *Epilogue* is found after various other tales in some of the manuscripts. The Host describes the tale that preceded the *Epilogue*—whether it was the *Man of Law's Tale* or some other—as "thrifty" (II, 1165), a term properly used to refer to a morally rewarding piece. Certainly the *Man of Law's Tale* fits this description, and the Man of Law is with equal certainty one of the "lerned men in lore" (II, 1168). The Host emphasizes his opinion about the merits of the story with an oath which brings down upon him a reprimand from the Parson, whom he calls upon for a tale. The Host, taking immediate umbrage at the scolding, accuses the Parson of being a Lollard and predicts that the company is about to be treated to a sermon. The Shipman, however, interrupts to say that the Parson will preach no heresy to the Pilgrims; instead, the Shipman himself will tell a tale.

We might expect the *Shipman's Tale* to follow immediately upon such a pronouncement, but in Manly's edition of the text of the *Canterbury Tales* and in all editions that follow Manly's— and this means practically all of the modern editions—the order of the better manuscripts is followed. This order puts a considerable number of tales between the statement of the Shipman and the actual tale that he finally tells. Bradley's *Six-Text Edition of* the *Canterbury Tales* rearranges the manuscript order and puts the *Shipman's Tale* immediately after the *Man of Law's Epilogue.* In the Robinson edition of Chaucer's works and in most other editions, the *Man of Law's Epilogue* ends Fragment II.

III *Fragment III*

The *Wife of Bath's Prologue,* which has nothing to connect it to anything preceding it, begins Fragment III. In it Chaucer creates one of the great comic characters of all literature. But oddly enough, although scholars are unanimous in their praise of the Wife as a literary creation, they often show a certain lack of understanding of her. For instance, Robinson says, "But it might be replied that the Wife is none too feminine." [5] Actually, it would be difficult to find a more completely feminine character in the pages of literature. It is possible that we as individuals may not wholeheartedly approve of her brand of femininity, but femininity she definitely possesses. From an early period in her life she has been intensely interested in love and marriage, particularly their physical aspects. She was first married at the age of twelve, but whether her sexual experiences antedated matrimony we do not know, the "oother compaignye in youthe" (I, 461) not being dated. All told, she had had five husbands and, apparently, a number of lovers, for she says:

> *For God so wys be my savacioun,*
> *I ne loved nevere by no discrecioun,*
> *But evere folwede myn appetit,*
> *Al were he short, or long, or blak, or whit;*
> *I took no kep, so that he liked me,*
> *How poore he was, no eek of what degree.* (III, 621-26)

It may be said that there is nothing in the *Canterbury Tales* to indicate that the Wife was ever guilty of adultery. Chaucer, in his own person, says: "Housbondes at chirche dore she hadde fyve, / Withouten [besides, in addition to] oother compaignye in youthe" (I, 460-61). And she herself admits in the passage quoted above (III, 621-26) to having had lovers, but neither Chaucer nor she says that she had had lovers while she had been married. In fact, she definitely states that when she had feared her fourth husband had had delight in another, she had angered him and made him jealous, but not with her body in a foul manner (III, 485). Thus, so far as we can tell from anything that is actually said, the Wife was properly moral so long as she was married. But her behavior during the periods when she was unmarried might have been open to question.

This in itself is sufficient to indicate an intensely feminine nature, but we must add to this the fact that she confesses to a great desire to be loved—it runs all through her *Prologue* and is the point of her *Tale*. Coupled with this desire is her passion for dominating her husbands. Whatever scholars may believe to the contrary, as the old wife in the *Tale* brings out, this is the paramount feminine quality. Some critics might be disposed to find the Wife's readiness to indulge in fisticuffs with her fifth husband unfeminine. It must be admitted that the female impulse toward physical violence is deplored in certain circles of society, but in others it is accepted as the essence of femininity.

The Wife shows a feminine love of chatter. Her *Prologue* is 856 lines long, just two lines shorter than the *General Prologue* to the entire *Canterbury Tales*. The Wife confesses to a love of gossip— surely not an unfeminine characteristic. She likes pretty clothes, dancing, party-going, seeing and being seen. How could she be more feminine? We should not let the fact that she has passed her physical prime mislead us into thinking that she was necessarily unattractive. A woman does not ordinarily have the marital career of the Wife unless she is a good bit less than repulsive.

After a career of love, both marital and extramarital, she says that she has lost her beauty (III, 475); and, if she has lost it, it stands to reason that she once had it. She, however, looks back upon her career with unalloyed delight (III, 469-73).

The straitlaced may say that the Wife's sentiments are all wrong, that she has arrived at an age when she should repent the carnality of bygone years. But her real regret is that she missed opportunities for more carnality. Thus to say that the Wife is unfeminine because she has impulses of unregenerate mankind— or womankind—is foolish.

There is no doubt that the Wife as a living person might be somewhat overwhelming to a modern person of quiet tastes, but Chaucer was not trying to appeal to such a person. He depicted a woman with a tremendous appeal for a certain class of men of the riotous, violent, unrestrained fourteenth century.

The Wife's *Prologue,* derived from no source that has ever been discovered, it is undoubtedly an original work, although Chaucer has incorporated into it passages from a large number of authors. To label the Wife's long speech a confessional would be wrong, as the term "confessional" connotes the admission of some sort of sin, misdemeanor, or at least misbehavior. But there is nothing apologetic about what the Wife has to say. She subjugated five husbands and she is proud of it; she loved perhaps not wisely, but according to her opinion very well. Never does she indicate that her husbands were right and she was wrong. Her explanation of how she brought her first three good, old, and rich husbands to heel is filled with amusement. Her fourth husband irritated her by having a paramour, but she evened scores with him:

> . . . I made folk swich cheere
> That in his owene grece I made hym frye
> For angre, and for verray jalousye.
> By God! in erthe I was his purgatorie,
> For which I hope his soule be in glorie.
> For, God it woot, he sat ful ofte and song,
> Whan that his shoo ful bitterly hym wrong.
> Ther was no wight, save God and he, that wiste,
> In many wise, how soore I hym twiste.   (III, 486-94)

She certainly gives no indication that she regretted her treatment of him; it was what he deserved. And her fifth, and favorite, husband she beguiled into marriage and then finally conquered. In her dealings with him, the only error she admits is the signing over of her property to him; this bit of dotage allowed him to get the upper hand of her for a time. All in all, she had had an active life, and she looks back upon it with the certainty that she had always been in the right.

Those who find the Wife's frank recital of the intimacies of her various marriages unrealistic do not properly take into consideration either her character or the occasion upon which she reveals them. The good Wife is not from a high level of society in which reticence about intimate affairs is considered good taste. Probably never at any time in her life would she have shrunk from disclosing the details of her amorous adventures to anyone who cared to listen. What is more, she is on a journey, and there is nothing like traveling to make a person disclose all of his private affairs to perfect strangers.

The interruptions of the Wife by the Pardoner and by the Friar show a developing dramatic sense of the realistic on Chaucer's part. There are some who believe that the Pardoner's interruption is motivated by a desire to parade a virility that he does not possess; but the Friar, who has simply become restive during the Wife's bombardment of words, says that it has been a long preamble to a tale. This speech provides an excellent opportunity to start the Friar-Summoner quarrel, which comes to full flower after the *Wife of Bath's Tale* is completed.

The *Wife of Bath's Tale*, which has never been traced to any one source, belongs to a common type of story of the Transformed Hag or the Loathsome Lady. The essence of it is that a beautiful girl has been bewitched into a frightful-looking old woman and can be transformed into her proper form only by a display of love, frequently a kiss, from a young and handsome man. The Wife sets her tale in the days of King Arthur when bewitchings were commonplace; in her first paragraph she evens scores with the Friar for his objection to her *Prologue* by explaining that the only danger that could now come to women wandering in the country was that of being dishonored by friars, whom she likens to incubi, or devils who have sexual intercourse with women.

The Wife goes on to tell about a knight who is condemned to death for raping a young girl, but King Arthur's wife saves his life on the condition that he will tell in a year what it is that women most desire. The knight travels through the land, receiving many answers to the question he has to answer. When the year is almost spent he sees a group of ladies dancing beside a wood. He goes to the place where he has seen them, but he finds no one except an exceedingly ugly old woman. She learns his problem and promises to provide a satisfactory answer if he will fulfill the first request that she makes of him. The knight agrees and they go to court. There the hag supplies the answer to the question: Women most desire to have sovereignty over their husbands as well as over their lovers.

When the answer is accepted by the ladies of the court, the hag requests marriage of the knight, who is appalled at the idea. But she says that she will have him, even though she is foul, old, and poor. The knight marries her and they go to bed, where he wallows in anguish. The wife says that if there is anything amiss she will see that it is amended; but the knight says that such is impossible, because she is so loathsome, old, and comes from such a low family.

The old wife then delivers a long lecture to the knight about true gentility, old age, poverty, and beauty. She finally asks him whether he would rather have her old, ugly, and always faithful, or young, beautiful, and take his chance on her virtue. It is odd how people misread the hag's proposition. One writer, for example, says, "She informs him that he can have her young and lovely and faithless, or old and ugly and true." [6] What she actually says is that, if he wants her young and beautiful, he can take his "aventure," or chance, with her. When he cannot decide which he wants, he lets her decide. In triumph she announces that she has achieved sovereignty over him and tells him to cast up the bed curtain. He does so, and sees that she has been transformed into a beautiful young lady, whom he eagerly embraces. The two live the rest of their lives in perfect joy.

In no other instance in the *Canterbury Tales* do we find a story as well adapted to the teller as the Wife's. Her tale perfectly expresses her lifelong ideal of love between man and wife, between her husbands and her, at least, combined with female domination.

Chaucer, with his dramatic sense functioning as well in these tales as anywhere in the entire works, had already laid the groundwork for the next two stories in the brief spat between the Friar and the Summoner at the conclusion of the *Wife of Bath's Prologue*. At the conclusion of the Wife's tale, the Friar begins his *Prologue* in which he again objects to the Wife's contribution to the proceedings. The Wife had been dealing with a matter of religion: sovereignty in the family; and she had been utterly heretical in her views, as the Bible very definitely states that woman is to be subject to her husband. All the members of the clergy on the pilgrimage would shudder to hear her bold denial of Holy Writ. The Clerk later delivers an elaborate rebuttal of the Wife's opinions, but at this point the Friar dourly directs the Wife to leave doctrinal matters to the clergy. He then announces that he is going to tell a story about a summoner. Friars and summoners were natural enemies; the first being mendicants, the others being possessioners, they were rivals in extorting money from the same source—the common people. The Host begs for a more polite tale than the Friar threatens to tell, but the Summoner says to let him alone; he will even scores in due time.

The *Friar's Tale*, for which no definite source is known, is a bitter satire on the grasping nature of summoners, who were highly unpopular in Chaucer's time. They were ecclesiastical jackals whose appearance on a scene never boded anything but misfortune for someone. The Friar's summoner is traveling through the land to find someone from whom he can extract money. He is joined by a gay yeoman dressed in green who at first says that he is a bailiff. The two swear eternal brotherhood, and the summoner asks the bailiff for some tricks to get money from people. The bailiff explains that he takes anything that is given to him. The summoner says that he will take anything that is not too heavy or too hot. Finally the bailiff admits that he is a devil, and there ensues a discussion on the nature of devils.

The two come to a cart stuck in the mud at the edge of a town. The carter, in seeking to urge his horses to free the cart from the mire, says that the fiend can have them. The devil, however, explains that he cannot take the horses because the carter had no real desire to give them away. In a moment the carter indicates the truth of the devil's diagnosis of the situation by blessing his team. At this point the two arrive at the home of a poor old woman whom the summoner intends to victimize. He holds over her head the threat of a summons to the archdeacon's court unless he can have her new pan, since she owes him money from the time he paid her fine when she was found guilty of adultery. In a rage she says that he lies and adds that the devil can have the summoner and the new pan also.

The devil asks her whether she really means what she has just said. She replies that she does if the summoner does not repent. Upon the summoner's saying that he has no intention of repenting, the devil seizes the summoner and the pan and goes off to hell, where summoners have their heritage.

Chaucer shows splendid skill in the characterizations of the various persons in this tale, and his storytelling ability is as good here as it is at any place in his works. The basis of the story is the legal matter of intention, which is of vital importance in the making of contracts and in giving gifts. The yeoman-devil explains that he can accept only those things that are offered to him in complete sincerity; he could not, for instance, accept the team of horses when the cart was stuck in the mud because the carter was not making a genuine offer. But the case is different when the old woman offers the summoner, along with her new pan. The only difficulty from a legal point of view is that the old woman did not have title to the summoner and therefore could not convey him to the devil.

The Summoner, in his *Prologue*, wrathfully displays genuine bad taste, descending to the use of obscenity. It may be that the Summoner is expressing Chaucer's own opinions, for friars were probably the most disliked element of fourteenth-century English society. The story, mentioned earlier, of Chaucer's having been fined 2s. for beating a Franciscan friar in Fleet Street may or may not be true; but the chances are that it is. It is quite possible that we can get Chaucer's general attitude toward friars from this anecdote. Certainly his portrait of the Friar in the *General Prologue* is cuttingly satiric; the Friar is depicted as a thoroughgoing hypocrite who has completely departed from the original idealism that motivated the founders of the various orders of friars.

The Summoner tells of a friar in the marshy country of Holderness in Yorkshire who, intent upon begging, arrives at the home of a sick man named Thomas. The friar greets Thomas and his wife and explains to her that he will have to examine Thomas's conscience. The wife is all in favor of this, as Thomas has been very irritable of late. When the wife says that her child has recently died, the friar replies that he saw it in a vision, as the child was borne to bliss. The friar explains how efficacious friars' prayers are and also what abstemious lives the friars live. The friar then indicates that he would welcome a gift of money from Thomas.

Thomas says that he has not had any good from all the money he has given to friars, but the friar explains that his own particular convent specializes in highly effective prayers. The friar then embarks on a sermon against ire and seeks to confess Thomas and to get some money from him. Thomas, in a rage, says that he will make a gift that must be equally divided among the brothers of the convent, and the friar willingly swears that it will be divided. Thomas then directs the friar to place his hand on his buttocks; when the friar's hand is there, Thomas breaks wind.

In a fearful rage the friar departs from Thomas's house to visit a neighboring lord, who asks the cause of the friar's great displeasure. Both the lord and his lady, upon hearing the friar's story, decide that Thomas is possessed by the devil. Jankyn, a page, who overheard the tale, explains how the noise and the odor of the burst of gas can be equally distributed among the thirteen brothers of the convent. Each one of twelve is to put his nose at the end of a spoke of a cartwheel while Thomas breaks wind above the nave, or center, of the wheel. The friar who had won this prize is to put his nose directly below the nave so that he, as a man of great worthiness, can get the first fruits of the gift. The lord and his lady agree that Jankyn spoke with great wisdom.

The *Summoner's Tale* is a devastating expose of the greediness and worldliness of the friars. Such touches as the friar's having a servant to carry a bag for contributions so that he, himself, will not pollute his hands by touching money and then his scratching the donors' names off the record tablets as soon as he is out of sight are shrewd—and undoubtedly merited—criticisms of the friars' customary dishonesty in their dealings with the laity. Not only were friars dishonest, they were immoral, and nowhere does Chaucer write lines more suggestive of a leacherous nature than:

> *The frere ariseth up ful curteisly,*
> *And hire embraceth in his armes narwe,*
> *And kiste hire sweete, and chirketh as a sparwe*
> *With his lyppes . . . . (III, 1802-05)*

Unfortunately the *Summoner's Tale* ends this group of tales, or fragment. The tight connection of the stories within the group, the interruptions, and the general ill-feeling among the tellers of these tales produce a dramatic effect without parallel in the *Canterbury Tales*.

IV Fragment IV

Fragment IV, beginning with the *Clerk's Tale*, continues the theme that the Wife of Bath had introduced—sovereignty in marriage. When the Host calls on the Clerk to tell a merry and not too learned tale, he says that he will relate a story he learned at Padua from Petrarch. Although he says that Petrarch taught him the story, he immediately afterwards indicates he had learned it from a written version, an inconsistency on Chaucer's part probably explained on the ground that the *Clerk's Tale* is an early work partly revised for the *Canterbury Tales*. Moreover, the Clerk of the *Clerk's Prologue* and the Clerk of the *General Pro-*

logue are not consistently portrayed. The Clerk of the *Clerk's Prologue* is a foreign traveler who apparently has entrée into exalted literary circles in foreign lands. The Clerk in the *General Prologue* is no such fellow; he is a poverty-stricken scholar who, spending what he can get from his friends on books and learning, has difficulty in making ends meet. We certainly cannot picture him, dressed in his threadbare "overeste courtepy," gracing an Italian literary salon.

Some scholars have pictured the Clerk as still attending the university—a college boy, in fact—and as the youngest member of the entire band of Pilgrims. It seems more likely that Chaucer thought of him as the perpetual scholar, one who had long ago finished his formal schooling but who could not bring himself to desert learning for a more remunerative occupation. Chaucer's concluding remark about him in the *General Prologue*—"And gladly wolde he lerne and gladly teche"—hardly suggests an undergraduate. Another item in Chaucer's description of the Clerk is frequently misinterpreted. Many commentators indicate that the Clerk already possessed twenty volumes of Aristotle's works; Chaucer merely says that the Clerk would rather have such a library than such worldly things as rich robes, fiddles, or psalteries. In other words, they are his ambition. The fact that he wants them bound in black or red is an indicative statement. Such luxurious bindings were usually far beyond the means of indigent students. One thing Chaucer may have had in mind when he says this about the bindings is that the typical academic has total disregard for money—other people's money, that is— where books and study are concerned.

The statement that the Clerk had learned his tale from Petrarch was for a long time taken to mean Chaucer was saying he himself had known the Italian poet in Italy. But much as it grieves us to do so, we must abandon the enthralling idea that the greatest living poet of England was on familiar terms with the greatest living poet of Italy. The best critical opinion now holds that Chaucer never met Petrarch.

In his tale the Clerk tells about Walter, marquis of Saluzzo in Italy. A popular ruler, his one fault is that he is unmarried and so has no heir to inherit his noble title. The people request that he remedy the situation; he agrees to do so, stipulating that they accept the lady of his choice without argument. His choice is

Grisilde, the beautiful and virtuous daughter of a poor old peasant who lives in a hovel in a village not far from Walter's palace. When Walter proposes marriage to her he insists that Grisilde must always obey him implicitly, never indicating in any way that his will is contrary to hers.

The marriage is at first very successful, and the populace love Grisilde for her goodness; news of her manifold virtues even spreads to foreign parts. Soon she bears a daughter. Walter, desiring to test her fidelity, tells her that the people are murmuring at her low birth, especially since the birth of the daughter. In the dead of night the baby is turned over to an ugly sergeant of dubious reputation, presumably to be destroyed. The sergeant, however, secretly conveys the child to Walter's sister, the Countess of Panico, who rears it carefully. Grisilde utters no word of sorrow or reproach when the child is taken from her or at any later time. Four years later she gives birth to a son, who at the age of two is also taken away from her in the same way as the daughter had been. And still Grisilde does not rebel. But the people begin to talk among themselves about Walter's cruel murder of his own children.

When the daughter is twelve years old Walter, still not convinced of Grisilde's steadfastness, has papal bulls forged announcing his divorce from Grisilde, who is of too low birth to produce a suitable heir to his lands. He will have to marry a highborn lady. And still Grisilde offers no objection. He sends her home to her old father, leaving her in possession of only enough clothes to make the journey decently.

He then sends for his daughter and son; and, when they are due to arrive, he sends for Grisilde. He explains to her that she will have to keep house for him, as she knows what he likes, and the new bride is too young for the work. He even asks her to praise the beauty of the supposed new wife. At long last Grisilde is emboldened to make a remark to the effect that she hopes he will treat the new wife more gently than he has treated her, for the new one is more delicate than she. Walter, in a fit of generosity, announces that she is still married to him and that the new wife and her brother are actually her own children. She swoons, but recovers and lives happily with Walter. Her children have prosperous and happy careers.

The *Clerk's Tale* presents convincing evidence that Chaucer was unacquainted with Boccaccio's *Decameron.* The story of Grisilde related by the Clerk has its origin in the tenth tale of the tenth day of the *Decameron,* but Chaucer apparently did not know it in Boccaccio's prose. Rather he was probably familiar with Petrarch's verse reworking of it in a French translation, as it seems clear that Chaucer did not work directly from Petrarch.

Although Boccaccio originated the tale as we have it, it belongs to a general group of obedience stories, and more specifically to stories based on tests of fidelity of wives to their husbands. Folklorists contend that they see a fairy-tale origin for the story, but they have considerable difficulty in proving their contention.

The *Clerk's Tale,* telling of the total surrender of sovereignty by a woman to her husband, is undoubtedly the one poem in all of Chaucer's works that most irritates modern sensibilities. The feeling is that both Grisilde and Walter are lacking in realism. Even the Clerk admits that Grisildes are hard to come by: "It were ful hard to fynde now-a-days / In al a toun Grisildis thre or two" (IV, 1164-65).

But instead of considering Grisilde a model for women to imitate, says the Clerk, we should look at this whole matter from a religious point of view, and, taking our cue from Grisilde, be patient when God tries us. God already knows all our weaknesses but will test us anyway, although what His purpose is in doing so may not be too clear. The three stanzas from IV, 1142 to 1162, are thus an attempt to convert a tale of callous brutality into something resembling a religious allegory. Chaucer is doing something similar to what he did at the end of *Troilus and Criseyde:* attempting to moralize a tale not particularly concerned with morals. Certainly the moralizing is in perfect keeping with the Clerk's character, for Chaucer tells us in the *General Prologue* that whatever he said was "ful of hy sentence" (I, 306) and that he would "gladly teche" (I, 308). This passage, filled as it is with the most exalted sentence, or significance, gives the Clerk an excellent opportunity to teach.

But if we consider the circumstances, we are driven to the conclusion that the attempt to moralize is somewhat unsuccessful. The Wife of Bath in her *Prologue* and in her *Tale* preached the doctrine of female supremacy. This was, as has been said, a heretical matter; the curse of Eve in *Genesis* puts woman into a position subordinate to man, and certainly no member of the clergy and practically none of the laity during the Middle Ages would dispute such a self-evident proposition as that the man is the absolute monarch of the household. The Clerk, biding his time during the telling of the Friar's and the Summoner's tales, refutes the Wife of Bath with a tale of male supremacy. Then for Chaucer to have the Clerk say that the story does not have this point at all, that the heroine is not supposed to be a model for women to imitate in their earthly relationships, is an unnecessary weakening of the tale.

To indicate that women more often act as the Wife of Bath does —and by inference that it would be better if they behaved themselves as Grisilde does—the Clerk delivers the *Envoy*. In some unfortunate way the title *Lenvoy de Chaucer* got connected with this very clever poem and has occasioned a great deal of debate. One body of critics says that Chaucer in his own person steps forward and delivers the *Envoy*. A more unlikely procedure would be hard to imagine! For Chaucer—the good-natured approver of everybody and the retiring and naïve recorder of the events of the pilgrimage—to intrude himself without a word of introduction except a marginal gloss, to berate one of his characters, and then to leave the scene without a word of comment about his strange behavior, is unthinkable! There is absolutely no reason to believe that anyone but the Clerk is to be understood as delivering lines 1170-76 and the ensuing *Envoy*.

The *Merchant's Prologue* is attached to the *Clerk's Tale* by means of a reference to Grisilde. The Merchant says that although his two months of marriage have been a terrible experience, his tale will not concern his own woes. Having made this clear, he straightway embarks on his tale, which was probably written originally for one of the Pilgrims in holy orders, as is attested by the mention of "thise fooles that been seculeer" (IV, 1251). Whether the reference is to the secular clergy or to the laity is not clear.

The Merchant begins his tale with an encomium on marriage by January, who ardently desires to have a wife. Finally he marries May, a young woman with whom his page Damyan becomes so infatuated that he takes to his bed with lovesickness. He and May exchange letters, and when January loses his eyesight, they decide to meet in a locked garden to which January and May often resort. May provides a key for Damyan.

[150]

Upon the assigned day Damyan arrives at the garden before January and May and keeps profoundly silent when they get there. May signals him to climb a certain fruit tree. At this point Pluto and Proserpine appear and discuss the matter of May's approaching adultery. Pluto says that he is so against the cuckolding of January that he intends to restore his eyesight when the event occurs. Proserpine says that she will provide May with the wit to get out of the scrape with an undamaged reputation.

May tells January that she longs for some of the pears that she sees growing on one of the trees in the garden. January must help her to climb the tree, and then he must encircle its trunk with his arms so that there will be no danger of her slipping away to engage in illicit amours. As May and Damyan make love in the tree, Pluto, true to his promise, restores January's eyesight. January raises a terrible clamor when he sees what is happening, but May, provided with wit by Proserpine, assures him that she had only been performing her wifely duty, for she had been told that if she struggled with a man in a tree January's eyesight would be restored. When January insists that her struggling had a very immoral tinge, she convinces him that his newly functioning eyesight is not yet to be completely trusted. He accepts her explanation and is extremely happy with her.

Why Chaucer wrote the *Merchant's Tale* will ever remain a mystery. This savagely cynical work is by far the darkest piece in his entire works. Except for Justinus, who appears only briefly in an advisory capacity, no character has anything admirable about him. January is a worn-out lecher who wants a wife chiefly for sexual purposes. May is a characterless adultress, and Damyan a faithless servant.

In spite of this, however, January is marvelously depicted; in fact, he is as well drawn as any character in the *Canterbury Tales*. Having lived as a libertine for over sixty years, he suddenly decides that he must marry at the earliest possible moment. Whom he will marry, he has no idea; but whoever she is, she must be beautiful, tender, and not over twenty years of age. Instead of quietly going about the business of choosing a suitable bride, as a sensible man would, he holds a conference of relatives and friends to be advised upon the feasibility of his project, and, as is usually the case, takes the advice that accords with his desires. While the hunting out of the bride goes on, he spends a large amount of time gloating in "heigh fantasye and curious bisy-nesse" (IV, 1577) on the joys that marriage will bring. He is seriously concerned because he does not see how he can receive such pleasure on earth and go to heaven, too, since it is not given to man to have two perfect blisses.

At the wedding feast he sits reveling in the thought of the feats of sexuality he is soon to perform; and, when he arrives at his home, he loads himself with all of the aphrodisiac drinks and other stimulants that he can hold and hurries the wedding guests out of the house so that he can begin his amorous play as soon as possible. His bouts with his wife are apparently eminently satis-factory to him, although the Merchant does not commit himself so far as to give May's opinion of the matter. January is finally grossly duped by his wife and his page, but the trickery and deception cause him but momentary discomfiture. He is in fine spirits when we last see him.

Chaucer, with consummate art, plays a neat trick on the reader here. The highly ironic tone of the praise of marriage at the beginning of the tale and January's dreams of the pleasures he is to experience from being a wedded man point the way to his being betrayed and disillusionment. And betrayed he is—but disillusioned he is not! And so he was right from the beginning: Marriage was to bring him great joy, and that is what it did.

Damyan, a parody of a courtly lover, does not have the de-cency to wait until the honeymoon is over before beginning the seduction of his master's wife. But never did anyone attempt to seduce a more willing victim. It is to be noticed that the ro-mantic May always reads Damyan's love letters in the privy, truly a note of refinement and sentiment, and she avers that she is a gentlewoman and no wench (IV, 2202). Her taking of a wax impression of the key to the walled garden and having a duplicate made is in the best traditions of burglary; she is truly January's love, his lady free (IV, 2138).

The seduction episode of the tale, called the Pear-tree or the Fruit-tree Story, is known in a variety of versions all over Europe. The Pluto-Proserpine element is, however, treated in an unusual manner: These beings are associated, not with the classical sys-tem of mythology, but with fairyland, as Pluto is called the "kyng of Fayerye" (IV, 2227) and Proserpine "a queene of Fayerye" (IV, 2316). This identification of Pluto and Proserpine with fairyland is, however, not peculiar to Chaucer. It is also found in the anonymous romance of *Sir Orfeo*. As either pagan deities or fairies, however, they make some unexpected references: to Solomon (IV, 2242 and elsewhere); to "Jhesus, *filius Syrak*" (IV, 2250), the reputed author of Ecclesiasticus, and to God (IV, 2290 ff.).

The debate between Pluto and Proserpine (IV, 2237-2319) carries us back to the Wife of Bath and her theory of female domination. There is, of course, a close connection between the *Merchant's Tale* and the *Wife of Bath's Prologue,* as Justinus refers to the Wife of Bath (IV, 1685). This reference by a person who dwelt "whilom," or formerly, in Lombardy, to a character on the Canterbury pilgrimage has occasioned a great deal of critical explanation, none of which is highly convincing. But the fact remains that there is a connection between the Merchant's and the Wife of Bath's themes. The debate, then, resolves itself into a contest between man and woman for supremacy, and the woman wins. Pluto gives January his eyesight and lets him see what is going on in the pear tree, but Proserpine gives May the wit to delude him into thinking that she is innocently working a cure for his blindness. The Wife of Bath had already said that a wise wife could always delude a husband (III, 226-34), and January is completely deluded: "Who is glad but he? / He kisseth hire, and clippeth hire ful ofte" (IV, 2412-13), and leads her home in great content.

In spite of the degraded characters and the derisively cynical tone of the *Merchant's Tale,* it is a brilliant piece of work. Not a pleasant story, it is a shrewd satire on courtly love. Why Chaucer interjected this story into the marriage group of tales is not altogether clear, as the other stories of the group—the *Wife of Bath's Tale* and the *Clerk's Tale*—are both on questions of sovereignty. Perhaps Chaucer felt that the matter of a wife's outwitting her husband was close enough to the matter of sovereignty to entitle the *Merchant's Tale* to a place in the marriage group. If this is true, however, the *Shipman's Tale* is just as much entitled to a place in the group, as it too is concerned with a wife who gets the best of her husband in her adultery.

The *Franklin's Tale,* also a member of the marriage group, is taken by some to be a treatise on sovereignty. Although it does briefly take up the question, it is really, as we shall see later, on a different subject. If we accept the view that the *Franklin's Tale* is about family honor, we can readily see how the *Merchant's Tale* fits into the marriage group: It deals with dishonor and untruth and is thus a low-key foil for the more elevated *Franklin's Tale,* which soon follows it. It might be argued that adultery is adultery and that the *Merchant's Tale* and the *Franklin's Tale* both deal with it, but undiluted animality makes the *Merchant's Tale* far lower in tone.

V *Fragment V*

As an immediate contrast to the low *Merchant's Tale* Chaucer presents the pure and romantic *Squire's Tale.* For it there is no single source known, although many of its elements exist otherwise in one form or another, mainly in Oriental tales. The episode of the falcon is very much like that of Anelida in *Anelida and Arcite.* The *Squire's Tale* is the most fanciful of all the *Canterbury Tales,* dealing as it does with love, magic, and matters of fairyland.

The Squire tells that when the Tartar khan, Cambyuskan, is holding a feast to celebrate twenty years on the throne, a strange knight appears with gifts from the King of Arabia and India. The first gift is a steed made of brass that is operated by twisting a secret pin; it will fly through the air to any place in the world and return within twenty-four hours. The second gift is a mirror that shows the truth or falsity of anyone who is reflected on its surface. The third is a ring that enables the wearer to understand and to speak the language of birds. A fourth gift is a sword that will bite through any armor, and any wound it makes can be cured only by passing the flat of the sword over it. The ring and the mirror are for Canacee, the daughter of Cambyuskan.

The morning after the feast Canacee, wearing the ring, takes a walk in a wood. She hears a female falcon in a tree emitting loud moans. The falcon tears herself until she swoons from lack of blood, falls from the tree, and is caught in Canacee's lap. When the falcon revives from her faint, she explains that she was wooed by a tercelet who seemed to be the very well of gentility and the possessor of all virtues. Finally she accepted his love, but he was false and deserted her for a kite. In pity Canacee carries the falcon home and makes her a pretty little cage. After outlining what is to come in the story, the Squire breaks off his tale.

[154]

Whether this tale was originally intended to come immediately after the *Merchant's Tale* is not known, but it is as likely a place for it as any other. It may be that its position was dictated by Chaucer's having intended to present some proper love stories in it as a contrast to the improper *Merchant's Tale*. Certainly the story of the falcon deals with love, and the Squire's summary of what was going to be treated (V, 661-70) indicates that love would be an important feature of what was to follow. The story of Cambalo fighting the two brothers for the hand of Canacee (V, 667-69) is, however, far from clear and scholars have given various explanations for this passage.

As was said earlier, the usual opinion about the unfinished state of the *Squire's Tale* is that Chaucer, temporarily baffled in the development of his intricate story, dropped it, intending to return at some future time to finish it. An alternative view is that the Franklin interrupts the Squire because he is bored by his story and alarmed at the Squire's promise of what is to come. It is probable, however, that Chaucer would have made it clear if interruption had been intended. As matters stand, what the Franklin says could very well come after either a complete or an incomplete tale. The situation seems to be that Chaucer wanted to discontinue the *Squire's Tale*, at least temporarily, to write the *Franklin's Tale*; and, in order to effect some sort of transition from one to the other, he wrote the highly noncommittal "Heere folwen the wordes of the Frankeleyn to the Squier, and the wordes of the Hoost to the Frankeleyn."

In this passage the Franklin laments the lack of gentility of his own son and is answered by the Host's rude, "Straw for youre gentillesse!" (V, 695). This remark by the Host does much to place the Franklin in the social scale. Although he is the owner of land —and perhaps a fairly large amount of—and is officially ranked among the country gentry, he is not of a sufficiently exalted position to merit the courtesy that the Host reserves for the members of the upper class, such as the Knight and the Prioress. The *Franklin's Prologue* reasserts the idea that the Franklin is a plain, uncultured fellow, a "burel man," to whom the niceties of speech are too "queynte"; his spirit feels nought of such matters. From all of this we might expect a rude tale, but what we get is as refined in sentiment and in language as any of the stories in the entire *Canterbury Tales*.

[155]

The Franklin tells how Arveragus, a knight of Brittany, woos the fair lady Dorigen, who finally accepts him as her love and marries him. When they marry, Arveragus promises never to take sovereignty over her, except some for the world's eye; she, in turn, promises that no fault will ever be found in her. After they have lived in great happiness for a time, Arveragus goes to England to gain renown in feats of arms. Dorigen is filled with sorrow at the separation, and what especially afflicts her is the contemplation of the dangerous rocky coast, which has destroyed many a ship and all aboard. In the depths of her woe she is approached by the virtuous squire Aurelius, who has loved her in silence for years. In reply to his suit to become his ladylove, Dorigen says that she has no intention of being anything but a completely faithful wife. She, however, sportively adds that she will become his love if he will remove all the rocks from the coast of Brittany. This reply brings upon Aurelius such a fit of lovesickness that he cannot leave his bed for two years. While he is languishing in bed, Arveragus returns from overseas, and he and Dorigen live in perfect felicity.

Aurelius's brother, casting about in his mind for a remedy for Aurelius's illness, thinks of the students of magic who dwelt in Orleans when he was a student there. He and Aurelius accordingly go to Orleans, where on the outskirts of the city they meet a young clerk to whom they tell the purpose of their visit. He takes them to his house and shows them many illusions, in some of which Aurelius and Dorigen dance together. Finally he and Aurelius agree that he will remove the rocks for a payment of a thousand pounds. The three thereupon go to Brittany, arriving in the frosty Christmas season.

By a combination of astral influences and magic the young clerk makes it appear that all the rocks are away. Aurelius communicates this fact to Dorigen, who is immediately horror-stricken at the situation in which she finds herself. As Arveragus is away from home, she cannot consult him; while she awaits his return she contemplates suicide. Finally he returns, and she breaks the sorry news to him.

Arveragus says that, since she has given her word, she must keep it, but she is to tell no one else about it. Dorigen, in a frenzy, meets Aurelius, who asks her where she is going; she tells him that she is coming to him to keep her bargain, as her husband has commanded her. Aurelius, overwhelmed by Arveragus's generous behavior, releases Dorigen from her compact. She returns to her husband, and they live happily ever after. Aurelius tries to arrange a series of payments to the magician, for it would take all his patrimony to discharge the debt with one payment. The magician, however, learns how the affair has gone and releases Aurelius from paying him.

The tale begins on the theme of courtly love, something we might not have expected from the downright Franklin, if he were anything like his description of himself. The second matter treated is that of sovereignty in the family; here the Franklin opposes the views of both the Wife and the Clerk by advancing the idea that the perfect relationship between man and wife is one of equality and that domination causes love to spread its wings and fly away. This view, while it finds greater sympathy among modern readers than do the extremes expressed by the Wife and the Clerk, is almost as heretical as the Wife's doctrine of female supremacy. But, as the Franklin has the last word on sovereignty, we may not be too far astray in thinking that he expresses Chaucer's own belief. Yet when a decision in the family of Arveragus and Dorigen has to be made, Arveragus makes it. There is no debate on the matter, no effort to achieve equality; Arveragus simply says that Dorigen has made a promise and must keep it, and Dorigen does not for a moment debate the command.

The main theme of the tale is neither courtly love nor family domination, but honor. When Dorigen is told that the rocks have disappeared, she is horrified at the situation in which she finds herself. A cynical modern reader might have difficulty in understanding her mental turmoil. What could be simpler than for her to inform Aurelius that she has no intention of keeping her foolish promise, that she never intended to keep it, because the deed had seemed impossible? Instead of refusing to keep the bargain, she contemplates suicide as her only alternative, and she reviews in her mind all the classical examples of women who had preferred death to dishonor. Nor does Arveragus assume any lighter attitude toward the matter. When she informs him of her rash promise, he views what she has said as a promise-for-a-promise contract from which there is no honorable withdrawal. His attitude is summed up in a single sentence: "Trouthe is the hyeste thyng that man may kepe" (V, 1479). He does not resort to the legal quibble that a promise given without geniune intention on the part of the promiser is not binding. Aurelius had accepted Dorigen's words at face value, and that was enough for Arveragus.

The conclusion of the tale raises the question of whether Arveragus, Aurelius, or the clerk acted with the most generosity, or was "fre," in his behavior. This is another way of simply asking which one had comported himself most honorably.

VI   *Fragment VI*

The Physician, as Chaucer describes him in the *General Prologue*, is well versed in two fields of knowledge—astronomy and the theory of humors. The humors were four in number—phlegm, bile, black bile, and blood—and each was either hot or cold and moist or dry. These humors were responsible for the health of an individual. When they were in balance, the man was well; when they were out of balance, the man was ill. One humor, however, dominated each individual: The predominance of phlegm made a man phlegmatic; of bile, bilious; of black bile, melancholy; and of blood, sanguine. As Walter C. Curry brings out,[7] the Physician's two forms of knowledge were complementary, for it was quite largely the astral influences on the body that produced disease by causing an oversupply of one of the humors; and, as they produced disease, so would they have to be used in the art of curing. To make the "image" necessary for a cure, particular attention had to be paid to the positions of the planets, especially Luna, in relation to the positions of the other planets. In his adherence to these matters, which were considered highly scientific in his day and long after, the Physician naturally, as Chaucer points out, had a certain disregard for the Bible.

The *Physician's Tale*, which begins a group of stories not connected at the beginning with any other fragment, was ultimately derived from Livy's *History*, but Chaucer uses the version of the tale found in the *Roman de la Rose*. This tale was probably composed early in the course of the composition of the *Canterbury Tales*, and whether or not it was originally written for the Physician is unknown. Certainly the general theme has nothing to do with medicine, but it is probably unreasonable to assume that a physician would have to tell a tale about doctoring. The tale fits

its teller as well as it does anyone else, but as a story it ranks as one of the weakest of the *Canterbury Tales*.

The Physician says that Virginius, a knight, has a daughter, Virginia, of marvelous beauty and virtue. When she is twelve years old, she accompanies her mother to a temple, where she is seen by a judge, Apius, the governor of the region. The fiend enters into his heart, and he decides that he has to have the maid. He therefore sends for a wicked churl, Claudius, with whom he conspires to work his will. The churl appears before the judge and charges that Virginius is holding Virginia, Claudius' servant, against the law. Virginius, according to Claudius, had stolen her away at night when she was young, and she is not his daughter at all. Nothing that Virginius can do or say has any effect on the false Apius, who awards her to Claudius. Virginius goes home and explains the situation to Virginia, and then to preserve her virtue unsullied he kills her with a sword. He presents her severed head to Apius. The people rise up and cast Apius into prison, where he commits suicide; Claudius they hang upon a tree. Virginius, who had acted from a virtuous motive, they exile.

The story makes a powerful impression on the Host, who, in "The wordes of the Hoost to the Phisicien and the Pardoner," comments upon it at greater length than upon any other story. Not only is he impressed by the tale, but he is also filled with admiration for the Physician, who, he says, is "a propre man, and lyk a prelat." Then with the quaint oath of "by corpus bones!" he says that he must have a "triacle," a draught of ale, or a merry tale to revive his spirits from the depression into which the Physician's story has cast them. He thereupon calls upon his "beel amy," the Pardoner.

The Pardoner, his *Prologue*, and his *Tale* have probably been the object of more controversy than any other material in the *Canterbury Tales*. The portrait of the Pardoner in the *General Prologue* is highly individualized: his clothing and his manner of wearing it, his hair, his eyes, his face, and his voice are all mentioned in such detail that we are led to believe that Chaucer was presenting the picture of an actual person. Who he was, we do not know. One line of the description, "I trowe he were a geldyng or a mare" (I, 691), has stirred up a vast amount of comment.

Everyone has focused his attention on the word "geldyng," which is fairly understandable, and has completely neglected "mare," which is not understandable in this context. It could be that "mare" is a significant word that might tell us what Chaucer meant the Pardoner to be, if we could only interpret it. Certainly the word merits more than the almost total oversight it has received; it is usually looked upon as the equivalent of "geldyng," but there is a vast difference between a gelding and a mare.

When the Pardoner interrupts the Wife of Bath to say that he is contemplating marriage, she makes no derogatory remarks about any lack of manhood on his part. All she does is tell him to hear the rest of her story (III, 169-79). Some commentators would have it that she directs scornful glances at him, indicating by her looks her disbelief in his virility. But we cannot allow this sort of extension of what Chaucer says. Had he wanted us to believe that the Wife suspected the masculinity of the Pardoner, he would undoubtedly have had her voice her suspicions; she certainly says enough else, and she could have said a few words more had she wanted.

In his *Prologue* the Pardoner says that he will "have a joly wenche in every toun" (VI, 453), and again no one comments on either his virility or lack of it. A real outburst occurs at the end of the tale, when the Host, in a violent anger, says, "I wolde I hadde thy coillons in myn hond" (VI, 952). This sentence has also been taken as an indication of the Pardoner's lack of manhood, but the whole point of it is that the Host very definitely attributes virility to the Pardoner.

There is, however, when all is said and done, a continual reference to sex in everything said concerning the Pardoner. An interesting sidelight to this is given by a continuation of the *Canterbury Tales* known as the *Tale of Beryn*. This work, written but a short time after the *Canterbury Tales*, might be supposed to reflect the manner in which contemporaries interpreted the Pardoner's sexual capabilities, and the author of *Beryn* assumes in his *Prologue* that the Pardoner is as capable as need be. The evidence is possibly of considerable value, as Curry, throughout his treatment of the Pardoner, makes the point that Chaucer's original audience would immediately recognize the Pardoner as a *eunuchus ex nativitate*. It is entirely possible that Chaucer was

hinting time after time that the Pardoner was some sort of sexual deviant, but what sort he does not make as clear as Curry
claims he does. If Chaucer was actually dealing with sexual irreg-
ularity the matter is highly noteworthy, for early English literature is singularly free of the mention of such affairs. At any rate,
although the word "geldyng" continues to plague us, the Pardoner
does not seem to be depicted as a eunuch.

We can all agree, however, that he is a hypocritical swindler.
He tells us as much. Some scholars assume that because he takes a
drink while he broods on what honest thing he will tell, he is
supposed to be drunk when he confesses his rascality in his *Prologue* and when he subsequently tells his tale. Such an inference
is by no means necessary. In an age when the drinking of alco-
holic beverages was universal and the potability of water was
hardly suspected (consider Sir Thopas, whose unusual habit of
imbibing water was allowable only because he had the precedent
of the doughty knight, Sir Percival, VII, 915-16), ale did not
invariably produce intoxication. Even nuns had a daily allowance
of a gallon of it,[8] and Chaucer, as an esquire of the King, would
have had a much larger daily ration than that. When Chaucer
wants his readers to understand that a Pilgrim is drunk, he frankly
says that he is, as he does with the Miller and the Cook.

The belief is unsound that the Pardoner would hide his villainy
unless drink caused him to spill out his story. But besides his
natural inclination to boast of his evil practices,[9] he is on a trip;
and, as was said in connection with the Wife of Bath, a traveler
has a very loose tongue.

The *Pardoner's Tale* has been considered by some scholars to
be a model medieval sermon; actually, however, it is a poor one.
It begins unsystematically with invective against all the tavern
sins, and not until the three rioters are introduced does the work
begin to take on power and unity; from this point on it is genuinely great and has few equals as a short story.

The Pardoner begins his tale by saying that in Flanders there
was a company of young folk who indulged in all sorts of folly
associated with taverns and houses of ill repute. He then embarks
on an elaborate condemnation of gluttony (especially drunkenness), dice playing, and swearing. As three of the young rioters
are drinking in a tavern one morning, they hear the bell that

rings to announce a corpse that is being carried to its grave. Upon inquiry they learn that the dead man had been a fellow of theirs who had been cut down without warning by the thief Death. Thereupon the three decide in their drunken rage to kill Death.

As they go on their search, they meet an old man who is all wrapped up save his face. They speak roughly to him and accuse him of being one of Death's spies. He tells them that, if they want to meet Death, they will find him down a certain crooked way under a tree. They follow the old man's directions and find eight bushels of newly minted gold coins under the tree the old fellow had indicated.

They decide that the gold is theirs, as they have found it. But it cannot be carried to their houses until nightfall, as anyone who saw them transporting it would accuse them of having stolen it. It is therefore necessary for one of them to go to town to get them food and drink, as the vigil will be long, and it is decided that the youngest will go. As soon as he is out of earshot, the other two conspire to murder him upon his return so that the gold will be divided between only two. The young one, thinking of the beauty of the coins, decides to murder the other two and so get all the money for himself. He accordingly gets two bottles of wine, into one of which he puts a powerful poison. When he rejoins his companions, they stab him to death and then drink the poisoned wine and die most horribly. Death is the fruit of covetousness.

The Pardoner, however, then announces that he will sell pardons to the Pilgrims and will confess them of their sins, beginning with the Host, who is most enveloped in sin. The Host reacts violently to this proposal and heaps obscenity upon the Pardoner, who becomes so angry that he cannot speak. The Knight acts as a peacemaker, and the Pilgrims ride forth upon their way.

It is easier to justify the beginning of the tale on practical grounds than on artistic ones. The reprehension of sin is always timely, and if our knowledge of the fourteenth century is at all accurate, we realize that the populace was particularly given to just the sins the Pardoner mentions. Since the three rioters, inflamed by drink, are in a tavern when we first see them, and later their avarice is aroused because they will be able to gamble their hoard of gold to their hearts' content, there is a connection between at least some of the tavern sins mentioned at the opening and the tragic conclusion. There is the further practical point that

[162]

if the Pardoner can prevent his hearers from frittering away their money on amusements, there will be all the more for him to extract from them.

A major problem arises where the Pardoner says:

> . . . And lo, sires, thus I preche.
> And Jhesu Crist, that is oure soules leche,
> So graunte yow his pardoun to receyve,
> For that is best; I wol yow nat deceyve.   (VI, 915-18)

This passage is not particularly remarkable, although many have found it so. If the tale had ended here, we would agree that these lines were a perfect conclusion. All they say is that Christ's pardon is better than a human one—a fairly orthodox statement in Chaucer's age or any other. But then comes the speech in which the Pardoner tries to sell his pardons to the Pilgrims. If he does this with the expectation of getting the Pilgrims to bid for the relics which he has but a short time before said were bogus, the passage becomes truly difficult; it presents the Pardoner as a fool, which he is not. The most logical interpretation is that the Pardoner gives an adaptation of the sales talk he customarily uses in churches; he is merely giving an illustration of his selling technique. He has emphasized the fact that he is a fine salesman, and it is only logical to show the Pilgrims how he works. It was, however, his bad fortune to include the Host in his demonstration of salesmanship, though probably intended as no more than a mild joke. He made the mistake of poking fun at the Host's corpulence —"I rede that oure Hoost heere shal bigynne,/ For he is moost envoluped in synne" (VI, 941-42). But the Host was evidently of the type who jokes about others but cannot be joked about. The obscenity of his reply to the Pardoner passes the bounds of reason and decency, even if the Pardoner had hinted that he customarily ate too much. A frequent explanation of the Host's fury is that he was insulted by the Pardoner's effrontery in trying to entice the Pilgrims into buying admittedly bogus relics. This is hardly convincing: It is usually possible to insult a group of people with perfect impunity, but when the insult becomes personal, tempers flare.

Whether the *Pardoner's Tale* was supposed to be delivered while the Pilgrims were interrupting their trip with a stop for refreshments at an alehouse or were continuing their ride toward

Canterbury has been much discussed. It is perhaps an inconsequential matter, but it is significant as an illustration of how real the *Canterbury Tales* have become to even the most sober-minded academics. The matter does, however, have its interest, for it may afford us a glimpse of how Chaucer envisaged the trip. If all of the tales were delivered as the Pilgrims rode on their way, the trip might have become slightly mechanical; but if Chaucer thought to have his Pilgrims tell stories during breaks for drinks and on other occasions, the whole thing would be pervaded by reality. It is not impossible that, in the original grand vision of a hundred and twenty tales, the Pilgrims would have told their stories at inns at night and at other places where travelers might reasonably stop.

It seems as if Chaucer wanted his readers to imagine the *Pardoner's Tale* as told while the cavalcade was resting. We know that there was a halt for refreshments, as the Host had indicated the presence of a tavern when he said that he was in need of a drink of ale and the Pardoner immediately afterwards says: "But first," quod he "heere at this alestake / I wol bothe drynke, and eten of a cake" (VI, 321-22). Furthermore, the language at the end of the story suggests a group of people temporarily dismounted rather than still on horseback: "Com forth anon, and kneleth heere adoun" (VI, 925) and "Com forth, sire Hoost" (VI, 943). One would suppose that there would be some indication of the need to dismount if the Pilgrims were on horseback when the Pardoner issued these injunctions. Salesmanship in a moving cavalcade would not be so practical as it would be on the ground. And the last line of the *Tale*, "Anon they kiste, and ryden forth hir weye" (VI, 968), reinforces this supposition. The last half of the line, "and ryden forth hir weye," probably should be taken to mean that at this point the Pilgrims all mounted and rode forth. If they were already riding there would be very little point in saying that they rode forth; it would be understood. And those who hold that when the quarrel began the Pilgrims all halted their horses in consternation or amazement betray an ignorance of horsemanship: To think thirty or more people suddenly tightened their reins and brought their horses to a stop because two members of the band were exchanging hard words is extremely unrealistic.

[164]

VII   *Fragment VII*

For the *Shipman's Tale* no exact source is known, although many analogues exist. Chaucer's immediate source was probably a French *fabliau.* That the tale was originally written for the Wife of Bath is evident from the first paragraph and from the last couplet. When Chaucer, after a considerable part of the *Canterbury Tales* had been completed, conceived the idea of the marriage group of tales, he shifted the story from the Wife to the Shipman without troubling to take out the references to "us wives." The fact that the monk in the tale is an outrider, like the Monk on the pilgrimage, is, so far as we know, without deep significance. If, however, the theory that Chaucer was in many instances giving portraits of actual people in the *Canterbury Tales* is to be believed, it may be that he was pointing his finger at a real monk recognizable by his original audience.

The Shipman tells of a rich merchant of St. Denis, France, who has a beautiful and companionable wife to grace his worthy home. A fair young monk, Don John, an outrider, is a frequent and welcome guest in the house. He poses as the merchant's cousin, although he is unrelated to him. Once when the merchant has to go to Bruges on business, he sends to Paris for Don John to come to spend a few days with him and his wife.

On the third day of the visit the merchant repairs to his counting house to go over his accounts. The monk and the wife meet and indulge in some risqué talk about the sexual relations of the merchant and his wife, but the wife insists that her life is devoid of all sorts of pleasures. Her husband is a wretched fellow who is worth nothing in amorous dalliance; in addition, he is stingy with his money. She thereupon negotiates a loan of a hundred francs from the monk, who promises to provide the money while the husband is in Flanders.

Before the husband departs for Bruges, the monk borrows a hundred francs from him, telling him that he needs it to buy cattle for one of the monastic farms. He promises that the loan will be promptly repaid. After the husband has turned the money over to Don John, he departs for Bruges; upon his arrival there, he conducts himself with complete propriety, doing nothing amiss. When the monk gives the money to the wife, she rewards him for his kindness by letting him spend the night with her.

Don John tells the merchant, upon his return home, that he has delivered the money to his wife. The merchant, after a night spent in sport with his wife, rebukes her for not reporting that Don John had repaid the hundred francs to her. She, not daunted at the turn affairs have taken, admits that she has received the money, but that she has spent it and that the only way the husband can regain the value of his money is to receive payments on the installment plan in bed. The merchant, whose affairs are thriving, decides, since there is no other remedy, that such a system of repayment will be acceptable.

The relatively simple and rather vulgar plot of the *Shipman's Tale* is subordinate to the characterizations of the persons in the story. In fact, in this tale more space is devoted to character drawing in proportion to the space devoted to plot than in any other of the *Canterbury Tales*. Although the tale was undoubtedly composed solely for amusement, it could be forced into the marriage group; it could be construed as a treatment of the misorderly shifts to which wives of niggardly husbands resort. We would not offhand, however, think of the Shipman as being vitally concerned with questions of ethics in marriage, although the Wife of Bath, for whom the tale was intended, was.

The tale is more fit to its present teller than it would have been to any other member of the band. For one thing, it is coarse, and the Shipman is by no means a refined fellow; for another thing, shipmen and merchants are natural enemies and the *Shipman's Tale* tells how a merchant was victimized.

The *Prioress's Tale* is generally acknowledged to be one of the gems of the *Canterbury Tales*. Although it is in rime royal, a verse form that Chaucer used most frequently at an earlier period than that of the composition of the *Canterbury Tales*, many scholars believe it to have been composed specifically for the *Tales*. Besides being perfectly fitted to the teller, it is also a very fine story. There are those, however, who do not believe that Chaucer sought to assign a beautifully sentimental little tale to a sentimental woman to achieve artistic unity. They hold that the Prioress is worldly and thus that her sentimental tale is in contrast to her character. Making the tale contrast with her nature is supposed to indicate that she has a rounded character. But to prove the Prioress a worldly character is somewhat of a task. The outstanding thing about her is her gentle nature: "And al was conscience and tendre herte" (I, 150). Mice, little dogs, and fragile children enlist her sympathies. And nowhere in Chaucer is there a more devout and unworldly passage than her *Prologue* addressed to the Virgin Mary. The one aspect of her description that might indicate worldliness is her desire to imitate the manners of court in the provinces where she dwells; but this is certainly naïveté rather than worldliness. That she wished "to been estatlich of manere, / And to ben holden digne of reverence" (I, 140-41) is entirely proper. It would be hard to imagine a person to whom it is more fitting to be dignified and respected than the head of a convent.

The Prioress tells of a little seven-year-old Christian scholar in a city in Asia who is a devout worshiper of the Virgin Mary. When he hears the older scholars singing a song in praise of the Virgin, he insists upon learning it himself. He always sings it on the way to and from school, and finally arouses the ire of the Jews by singing it as he goes through their district. They avenge the insult upon themselves by cutting his throat and throwing his body into a privy.

When he does not return home from school, his mother goes in search of him, and finally when she goes through the Jewry crying out to him, he begins to sing his beloved song, *Alma redemptoris*. His body is recovered and taken to a monastery, and the Jews are tortured and executed. Lying on his bier in the abbey, the boy continues to sing his song and also to explain that he will sing it until the grain which the Virgin had placed on his tongue is removed. The abbot removes the grain, and the little scholar lapses into silence and is interred in a tomb of clear marble. His case, the Prioress concludes, is similar to that of Hugh of Lincoln, who was also slain by the Jews.

No single source of either the *Prioress's Prologue* or *Tale* has been discovered. The *Prologue* draws freely from various Church offices and anthems, and there are many analogues of the tale, but the action of no other one is placed in Asia. The tragic ending of Chaucer's version is less frequently found than a happy ending, for in a genuine miracle of the Virgin it is not asking too much to have the little scholar restored to life.

The picture of the Prioress in the *General Prologue* is that of a

sentimental woman who wept over dead mice, coddled her lap-
dogs, and wept if one of them were dead, "Or if men smoot it
with a yerde smerte" (I, 149). She, in accordance with her sentimental nature, usually uses some endearing term when referring
to the "litel clergeon, seven yeer of age" (VII, 503): a "litel child"
(516), "for he so yong and tendre was of age" (524), "this innocent" (538), or "his litel body sweete" (682). His littleness, his
youth, and his innocence are constantly reiterated in terms tend-
ing to maintain a high pitch of pathos.

Moderns see a sharp contrast between the Prioress's devotion to
the child and her ferocity toward the Jews. From a present-day
point of view, it seems as if Chaucer is saying that the Prioress,
considerate as she is of mice, dogs, and children, hardens her
heart in a most unchristian fashion towards the Jews. In other
words, the belief is that Chaucer satirizes her. There are satiric
touches in her portrait in the General Prologue, and if there, why
not in her tale? It is, however, safe to say that he had no intention
of being satiric. To the Christian of the Middle Ages, the Jew
was a creature outside the pale; he had blackened his character
by the crucifixion of Christ, and nothing he had done since that
event had had any redeeming merit. The Jew was a usurious
murderer of pious Christian children and had not a single benev-
olent impulse—a monster, in short. In Chaucer's times, the Christian was unbelievably cruel to his fellow Christian, and for the
Jew, who was hardly thought to be human, there was no compas-
sion at all. Because we admire Chaucer, we incline toward the
belief that he had a more humane view of the matter than did the
ordinary person of his age.

The Prioress's Tale stems from a situation that the ordinary
person thoroughly believed: the ritual murder of Christian children by Jews. It was originally thought that Jews kidnapped
Christian babies and crucified them at the Easter season, and
from this belief grew the idea that the Jews had the habit of mur-
dering Christian children whenever the opportunity to do so presented itself. The Prioress refers to the slaying of Hugh of Lincoln,
whose story is told in a number of ballads. There is a general sim-
ilarity between the Hugh ballads and the Prioress's Tale, although
there is a difference in details. In the Prioress's Tale the Jews kill
the little clergeon because he offends them with his interminable
singing of the song in praise of the Virgin, but in the Hugh bal-

lads the Jew's daughter murders Hugh simply because she shares the wretched nature of her race.

The *Prioress's Tale* had a sobering effect on the Pilgrims, but the Host speedily livens things up with japes. He also lays the groundwork for one of the most delightful parts of the *Canterbury Tales*. His eye lighting on Chaucer, he rebukes him for having an abstracted manner—a manner, by the way, at variance with that depicted in the *General Prologue*, in which Chaucer in short order conversed with each of the twenty-nine Pilgrims who entered the Tabard Inn. Actually this shift on Chaucer's part from the good mixer to the withdrawn brooder involves no great contradiction. As a courtier, diplomat, customs official, and Clerk of the King's Works, he must have been able to associate easily with people when he wanted to. In his other identity as a poet he must often have fallen into abstractions, as one does not produce such works as *Troilus and Criseyde* and the *Canterbury Tales* without engaging in prolonged periods of contemplation.

The Host, with rude jocularity as to an equal, indicates that Chaucer is endowed with more than sufficient waist and that he would be a doll for a small and fair-faced woman to dandle on her knee. Some scholars have held that Chaucer was saying he himself was small and fair of face, but this interpretation is erroneous; he later indicates that he is six feet tall. His "elvyssh" face does not mean that he is a little fairy of a fellow but that he, as he rode along the Pilgrims' Way, looked upon a world invisible to ordinary eyes, such as those of Harry Bailly, for instance.

Upon the command to tell a "tale of myrthe," Chaucer says that he will tell the only story that he knows. This bit of modesty is in marked contrast to the passage in the prefatory matter to the *Man of Law's Tale* (II, 45-89), where Chaucer indicates that he is a prolific storyteller. In "The murye wordes of the Hoost to Chaucer," Chaucer shows superb comic technique; he makes a butt of himself, as he does elsewhere in his works. Small and mediocre writers seek to make butts of others, and only the great ones have the courage to aim the arrows of ridicule at themselves. This sort of thing almost invariably pleases readers, who have a comfortable feeling of superiority when they contemplate someone else's inferiority.

And so Chaucer begins the tale of *Sir Thopas*, and it is a delightful parody of the Middle English metrical romances that were popular in the fourteenth century. With remarkable skill he exactly imitates their jog-trot meter, and every line of his poem is a takeoff on a line in a romance.

Chaucer tells about a bold and beautiful knight, Sir Thopas, a resident of Flanders, who one day rides out into a fair forest of spices inhabited by gaily singing birds and gentle beasts. Finally, wearied with spurring his steed, he dismounts and lies upon the grass in love-longing. He had dreamed that he would love an elf-queen, as no mere human woman was worthy to be his mate. With this in mind he remounts his horse and rides to the country of Fairy, where he is met by a quarrelsome three-headed giant, Sir Elephant, with whom he decides to fight some other day. Sir Elephant makes him retreat by casting stones at him with a sling.

The next day Sir Thopas drinks sweet spiced wine and eats gingerbread. Then he arms for the combat with the giant, and, after he has stuck a lily into his helmet, he mounts his horse and rides forth. When Sir Thopas is likened to a number of heroes of romance he is, of course, made into a caricature. But Chaucer's doggerel nonsense becomes too much for the Host, who rudely breaks off the tale and bids Chaucer tell something else with more meaning to it.

It is a great pity that this remarkable piece of comic writing should be so little appreciated. It is true that every writer who mentions it extolls it to the skies. Enthusiastic professors assure their students that here is superb fun, but the general reader and the student in the classroom remain unmoved by mirth, and for the best of reasons: they are totally innocent of knowledge of the literary types that Chaucer is parodying. And there are few things flatter and less amusing than a parody of an unfamiliar original.

Apparently the Host must be numbered among those who do not recognize what Chaucer is up to in *Sir Thopas*. His interruption of the tale is, with the exception of his blast at the Pardoner, the least civil passage in the *Canterbury Tales*. His condemnation of the tale is absolute, and his concluding injunction is for Chaucer to turn to prose and tell something of mirth or of doctrine. Chaucer meekly agrees to obey and says that his "litel tretys" will be both a moral and a merry tale. His statement is one-third true; it is moral, but it is decidedly neither little nor merry. A close translation of *Livre de Melibée et de Dame Prudence*,

Chaucer's *Tale of Melibee* is quite generally sneered at in modern times as being overwhelmingly dull.

Melibee relates the story of Melibeus (which name means the drinker of honey), his wife Prudence, and their daughter. When Melibeus is absent in the fields, three of his foes invade his home, beat his wife, and inflict five serious wounds on his daughter. It is brought out that the foes are the world, the flesh, and the devil, and the five wounds are through the five senses. Melibeus is very angry, but Prudence, with apt quotations from a wide variety of authors, calms him and causes him to dry his tears. She advises that he hold a congress of advisers to help him decide what to do about the injuries his daughter has sustained. Melibeus summons surgeons, physicians, the old, the young, friends, reconciled enemies, flatterers, and wise advocates learned in the law.

Some of these folk advise vengeance; some, the mounting of a guard over his house to see that the outrage is not repeated. Others urge deliberation in doing anything at all; some counsel as speedy action as is possible; some suggest war and others peace. When Prudence finally requests an audience, Melibeus gives five reasons for not following any advice that she might give. She, however, with a heavy bombardment of quotations, refutes his reasons and again asks to be heard.

First she tells him who should be listened to and who disregarded, how they should be examined, and under what circumstances a change of counsel is warranted. She points out that when Melibeus summoned the members of his congress he erred in choosing people who would make unreliable advisers. She then, at exhaustive length, and enforcing everything she says with at least one learned quotation, councils Melibeus to be reconciled with his foes. He endeavors to argue with her, but he is no match for her; she beats him down on all points with the weight of her authorities. The idea is that Melibeus should make peace with God and be reconciled with his earthly enemies, and finally he falls into her train of thought. She sends for the adversaries, who praise her great wisdom and wish to be at peace with Melibeus. He desires to make known the decision to his friends. Prudence sends for the wise and good people who had been at the congress, and they all applaud the decision. Melibeus thus finally comes to a realization of what a wise woman his wife is.

Actually, this tale is not nearly so bad as it has been made out to be. Of course, it has not the salty tang of the *Miller's Tale*. To answer the question why Chaucer included it in the *Tales*, we can simply say that both he and the people of his age undoubtedly liked it. He thought well enough of it to translate it, and the suggestion, which has been seriously advanced, that he put it into the *Tales* as an extended practical joke is nonsense. *Sir Thopas* was a practical joke, and there is sufficient indication that it was not to the taste of the Pilgrims. Chaucer had the good judgment, moreover, to cut short the joke when he made his point; so, if *Melibee* had been intended as a jest, it would have been so labeled and then broken off somewhere far short of its present end. It is true that Chaucer's age had a high regard for moral instruction, and a great amount of extant Middle English literature is pure didacticism. It was just such pieces as *Melibee* that earned Chaucer his early reputation of being "wise" and "learned," a reputation that persisted for generations before anyone perceived anything especially humorous about his works. But whether moderns like it, *Melibee* exerted influence on at least four tales and one prologue of the poet's work. It certainly cannot be considered, therefore, as a mere extended trifle.

While comment by the Pilgrims on *Melibee* is not highly laudatory, it certainly is not condemnatory. The Host likes it and wishes that his wife Goodelief had heard it, and his wish introduces an amusing bit of confession: the Host, doughty fellow that he is and ruler of the pilgrimage, is henpecked.

After telling of the trials and tribulations of his married life, the Host addresses the Monk with sincere but completely misdirected admiration, complimenting him on his evidently good physical condition, his presumed official status in the monastery, and his sexual potentialities. Such speeches as the Host's are well-meaning but frequently embarrassing to the object of them and bystanders alike. But the Monk bears up patiently and indicates that he will tell either the life of St. Edward or some, or all, of the hundred tragedies that he owns. It is clear at this point that the conception of the Monk had changed in Chaucer's mind since he had written his description in the *General Prologue*. The Monk of the *General Prologue* was no student: "What sholde he studie and make hymselven wood, / Upon a book in cloystre alwey to poure?" (I, 184-85). The scorner of book-learning in the *General Prologue* has become in the *Monk's Prologue* not only a person with a cell stocked with stories, but one who can give a definition of tragedy. The outdoorsman has become the scholar.

There was an excellent reason why Chaucer should have someone in the band tell a series of tragedies. He had already written them and it would be a great pity to have them go to waste. While we can sympathize with his desire to utilize work already done, we can wonder at his choice of the Monk as the teller, because he, as described in the *General Prologue*, was an inappropriate narrator of tragedy.

It is generally agreed that many of the tragedies were early work on Chaucer's part, and that he inserted some fairly recent tragic heroes into the middle of the series. The two Petros, the Barnabo Visconti, and the Hugelino are thought to be late work. Of all of the stories, the one about Hugelino, which was derived from Dante, is far the best. There is a depth of feeling and a pathos in it that rivals anything else in Chaucer's works.

The hearing of one doleful tragedy after another is too much for the Knight, who with a "Hoo!"—the shout used by heralds to stop armed conflicts—halts the Monk in the telling of the sixteenth story and jeopardizes his own hitherto unblemished reputation for courtesy (I, 70-72). He explains his taste in narratives: he likes stories in which the principal characters rise in the world and dislikes those in which they fall from happiness and prosperity. This little confessional indicates a certain lack of sophistication on his part, but his taste is identical with that of the Host, who invariably calls for a merry tale from the Pilgrims. Indeed, when the Knight has brought the Monk to a halt, the Host plucks up courage to add to the Knight's condemnation of the stories. Had it not been for the clinking of the bells on the Monk's bridle, good Harry Bailly would have been overwhelmed with sleep. He, therefore, calls upon the Monk for a tale of hunting, which is what might reasonably have been expected from him in the first place.

But when the Monk makes a chilly refusal to comply with the Host's demand, Harry Bailly calls upon the Nun's Priest to tell something to gladden their hearts. It is worthy of note that "Thanne spak oure Hoost with rude speche and boold, / And seyde unto the Nonnes Preest anon" (VII, 2808-09). The Host has a keen sense of decorum, as might be expected of a successful inn-keeper. A little later his request to the wellborn and highly situated Prioress to tell her story (VII, 444-50) is an example of mealymouthed courtesy rarely equaled in the rest of English literature. He does not dare to initiate the stopping of the *Monk's Tale*, even though it bores him to distraction; the Monk is too much the Host's social superior for him to start anything that might indicate a lack of respect. But once it is started by the Knight he feels at liberty to continue it. With the characters from his own social level or below he uses "rude speche and boold."

It is significant that the Host addresses "*the* Nonnes Preest" (VII, 2809). The mention of "preestes thre" (I, 164) in the *General Prologue* has generally been felt to be some kind of error. There are several explanations of the passage, but the Host's words in the *Nun's Priest's Prologue* indicate that Chaucer envisaged only one Nun's Priest. One, the father confessor of the Prioress's nunnery, would be reasonable and right; he would shepherd the Prioress and the other Nun who was her chaplain and protect them from the dangers and inconveniences of the road. But three priests traveling with two nuns has an air of holiday gaity that is somewhat short of seemly.

A fairly logical explanation of the matter is that Chaucer intended to return to the place in the *General Prologue* where the Second Nun and the three priests are mentioned and do more work upon it. Of all the Pilgrims, the Second Nun and the Nun's Priest (or Priests) are the only ones not described in any way. It is entirely within the bounds of possibility that Chaucer meant to draw their portraits but never got around to doing it. A possible reason for the lack of a description of the Second Nun is that it would be the only duplication among the Pilgrims; Chaucer had just described the first nun, the Prioress, and perhaps shrank from the task of immediately describing the second one. A natural assumption we make in reading the *Canterbury Tales* is that Chaucer finished the *General Prologue* before pacing further into his project. There are critics, however, who believe that the *Prologue* is actually in an unfinished state and that Chaucer made additions to it as he developed the *Tales* as a whole and would have made many more had he gone on with his task.

Chaucer chose for the *Nun's Priest's Tale* an incident from the stories centering around the beast-epic of Reynard the Fox, but just what his immediate source was we do not know. It is, however, certain that he greatly expanded his original. Some of his elaboration consists of the amusing picture of the widow and her establishment, the discussion of predestination versus free will, and the extensive questioning of the validity of dreams as prophecies of the future. It is in this last matter that he really allows himself through one of his characters to investigate a subject of special interest to him. The *Book of the Duchess*, the *House of Fame*, the *Parliament of Fowls*, and the *Prologue* of the *Legend of Good Women* are all supposed to be records of dreams, and their nature is discussed in the *House of Fame* (1-65) and in *Troilus and Criseyde* (V, 358 ff.). It might be assumed that Chaucer, an intelligent man, would not believe that dreams foretell the future; but, in the *Nun's Priest's Tale*, Chauntecleer, the confirmed believer, has much the better of the argument, although he almost loses his life to make his point. It should be remembered that dreams play an important part in many Biblical stories. Chaucer's age accepted all of the Bible as literal truth, and there is no reason to suspect that Chaucer himself did not do likewise. Yet, in spite of Biblical authority, there persisted a gnawing doubt in his mind. The *Nun's Priest's Tale* is a gay story, light in tone. But because of the investigation of such intellectual matters as mentioned above, it is one of the more learned of the *Canterbury Tales*. So amusingly do theology and science issue from the mouths of a poor widow's barnyard fowls that we tend to overlook the fact that Chaucer is really treating serious subjects.

The Nun's Priest tells of a poor widow who lives in a narrow cottage in a dale; she has an assortment of farm animals, including a rooster and seven hens. The rooster, Chauntecleer, a peerless fowl, loves most one of his wives named Pertelote, a hen abundantly endowed with homely wisdom. One night Chaunticleer has a frightening dream of a doglike beast that attacks him. He is of the opinion that the dream means he will meet with some sort of calamity.

Pertelote scoffs at the idea that dreams foretell the future. She cites authorities to prove their worthlessness as prognostications, and she asserts that Chauntecleer's system is out of order and that what he needs is a dose of laxative. Chauntecleer, considerably affronted, attempts to refute her contention that dreams are lacking in signification. He cites more and better authorities than

Pertelote has been able to quote, and he also tells a number of stories to reinforce his point. As the day progresses, however, his fears are quieted and he goes about his barnyard business.

Later in the day he espies a creature hiding among the plants of the garden. He is instinctively fearful, but the creature, a fox, assures him that he merely wishes to hear Chauntecleer sing. Chauntecleer's father had been a notable singer, and he and the fox had had a certain association. Chauntecleer, says the fox, is an even better singer than his father. Chauntecleer, ravished by flattery, stands upon tiptoe and closes his eyes in preparation for crowing. Instantly the fox seizes him by the neck and makes off for the woods with him. A terrible clamor is raised in the widow's yard, and each living creature contributes to the uproar. Dogs and men set out in pursuit of the fox.

Chauntecleer finally gets enough possession of his wits to tell Don Russell, the fox, that he should turn and defy his pursuers. As soon as the fox acts on the suggestion and opens his mouth to speak, Chauntecleer breaks loose from his grip and flies up into a tree. The fox tries to cajole him down with the statement that he meant absolutely no harm at all, but Chauntecleer is not fooled again and so is delivered from his danger.

Rarely has a tale of such charm been composed as the *Nun's Priest's Tale;* everything is pleasant—setting, characters, plot, and conclusion. The characters are magnificent. What a wonderful combination of learning, sophistication, and gullibility is Chauntecleer, and what a practical, down-to-earth, small-town housewife is Pertelote! The manner in which Chaucer has Chauntecleer and Pertelote barnyard fowls at one moment, people at the next, and a combination of the two when it suits his purpose is brilliant. At one moment Chauntecleer is quoting Latin, and mistranslating it to deceive his unlearned wife, and immediately after is uttering "Cok! cok!" like any other rooster.

But not for a moment do we assume that the *Nun's Priest's Tale* was written merely to amuse. It seems to be filled with symbolism. What it symbolizes poses a problem, and there have been a number of interpretations. J. Leslie Hotson[10] contends that the tale is a retelling of the murder in September, 1397, of the Duke of Gloucester by Thomas Mowbray, Duke of Norfolk, who was assisted by Nicholas Colfox, and of the duel of Mowbray and Bolingbroke. This theory, which is undoubtedly ingenious, has met with little acceptance. One thing against it is that the tale would have had to be composed very late in Chaucer's lifetime, perhaps after he had given up writing. There are other interpretations, but they are even less convincing than Hotson's.

Everyone agrees that the *Nun's Priest's Tale* is a fable, and usually a fable has a generalized rather than a specific moral. It might be that Chaucer was merely telling the world at large to avoid flattery and keep its eyes open and its mouth shut. These might be sufficient morals for the ordinary fable, but Chaucer, or the Nun's Priest, so emphasizes the necessity that the reader grasp the lessons in the work that we are driven to conclude there is a specific application:

> But ye that holden this tale a folye,
> As of a fox, or of a cok and hen,
> Taketh the moralite, goode men.
> For seint Paul seith that all that writen is,
> To oure doctrine it is ywrite, ywis;
> Taketh the fruyt, and lat the chaf be stille.   (VII, 3438-43)

When an author insists that his work contains a moral that he wants specifically applied, he should provide some clue. It is possible that Chaucer has done just this, as there is a passage of direct address that cannot refer to anyone on the pilgrimage. It occurs just when Chauntecleer, ravished by flattery, cannot espy treason:

> Allas! ye lordes, many a fals flatour
> Is in youre courtes, and many a losengeour,
> That plesen yow wel moore, by my feith,
> Than he that soothfastnesse unto yow seith.
> Redeth Ecclesiaste of flaterye;
> Beth war, ye lordes, of hir trecherye.   (VII, 3325-30)

Since there were no lords with courts on the pilgrimage, this passage must have been inserted into the tale for some purpose. There was one lord in England who had a court—King Richard II; and if ever anyone needed warning against flatterers, it was he. Chaucer, who was in the employ of Richard and was his pensioner and who was, so long as Richard was on the throne, dependent upon him for his financial well-being, might have been trying to warn the King that his sycophantic associates were leading him into ruin.

If this interpretation is correct, we can add that it is not the only piece of advice Chaucer offered him. *Lak of Stedfastnesse,* which is universally accepted as also having been addressed to Richard II, indicates that society and, by inference, the court are in a bad way and that only virtue in the monarch can set things right. So, if Chaucer could offer the King one piece of advice, why not two? It would take courage for a pensioner-civil servant openly to tell the King that his best friends were a gang of flattering traitors. If the King did not resent the advice, the flattering traitors well might. This could account for Chaucer's having slipped his moral into the lightest and gayest of his tales; anyone who openly objected to it would in effect be confessing that he was guilty of the offense charged.

VIII   *Fragment VIII*

The *Second Nun's Prologue,* which begins a new group of tales (Fragment VIII), is a strange mixture. Written in rime royal, it begins with a short invective against idleness. To free us from this sin, Chaucer says that he has translated the life of St. Cecile. Throughout the following tale the industry of Cecile in waging her fight against heathenism is accentuated. No very definite source for this passage on idleness has ever been discovered.

Next, Chaucer presents in high style an invocation to Mary. It is derived from bits of Dante's *Paradiso,* the *Anticlaudianus* of Alanus de Insulus, and various parts of Latin hymns from the Hours of the Virgin. Two points of this section of the *Prologue* warrant comment. The first is VIII, 62, where the teller, who is presumably the Second Nun, refers to herself as an "unworthy sone of Eve." It is thus indicated that the original teller of this story was a male. Attempts have been made to set all straight by saying that nuns sometimes refer to themselves as sons of Eve, but the explanation is unconvincing.

The other noteworthy comment occurs in VIII, 78, "yet preye I yow that reden that I write." It would appear that at an earlier period than that of the composition of the *Canterbury Tales* Chaucer wrote this piece as an independent composition, with no thought of embedding it in a framework and with no intention of attributing it to anyone but himself. In the *Legend of Good Women* he mentions having written it:

> *And, for to speke of other holynesse,*
> *He hath in prose translated Boece,*
> *And maad the lyf of Seynt Cecile.*   (F, 424-26)

It thus appears that the "unworthy sone of Eve" was Chaucer himself, as was the "I" of "yet preye I yow that reden that I write."

An interesting variant that forecasts the passage in the *Second Nun's Prologue* against idleness occurs in the G text of the *Legend of Good Women;* instead of "holynesse," given in the F text above, he says, "And, for to speke of other besynesse" (412). Perhaps the G text of the *Legend* was written after Chaucer had assigned the Cecile story to the Second Nun, and the reference to busyness was included to accord with the reprehending of idleness in her *Prologue.* When he put the story into the *Canterbury Tales* he did not bother to do the slight bit of rewriting that would have adapted the story to a feminine teller. Perhaps, of course, Chaucer fully intended to go over the *Canterbury Tales* and straighten out all the little inconsistencies; we must never forget that the *Tales* are in an unfinished state. It is noteworthy, however, that nowhere does Chaucer say that the teller of the tale is the Second Nun. The attribution is wholly in the rubrics, which are not necessarily by Chaucer. Still, no one seriously doubts that he intended the story for her, who, of all the Pilgrims, would be the most logical teller of this pious tale about a saintly woman.

The interpretation of the name of Cecile in the last five stanzas of the *Prologue* is fine popular etymology, but we can excuse Chaucer of ignorance on the ground that he did not think it up himself. The name Cecilia is actually the feminine of Cecil, which means "dim-sighted." The *Second Nun's Tale* and the interpretation of the name Cecilia are derived from the *Legenda Aurea,* or *Golden Legend.* There are, however, features in Chaucer's version that are lacking in the *Legenda Aurea* but that can be found in the Greek *Life* by Simeon Metaphrastes, itself derived from the old Latin *Acta.* It seems probable that Chaucer used a now-lost account of the *Life* that combined the facts of the two sources.

The tale deals with Cecile, a maiden of Rome who was fostered from her birth in the Christian faith. When she is married to a youth named Valerian, she wears a hair shirt under her bridal robes. After the wedding she explains to Valerian that they will be married in name only, as she has an attendant angel who would slay her husband if he touched her with the intention of indulging in physical love. Valerian, naturally suspicious of such a story, wants to see the angel; but Cecile explains that, before he can do so, he must be baptized by Pope Urban. When he is purged of sin, he will be able to see what he requests.

Upon his return from being baptized, he sees the angel, who crowns Cecile with roses and him with lilies and then advises him to lead a clean life. Valerian, much impressed, has his brother Tiburce baptized also. At last, however, Roman officials arrest the brothers and take them before the prefect Almachius, who commands them to worship the image of Jupiter on pain of being beheaded. When they refuse, they are turned over to one Maximus for the execution of the sentence. Maximus is so impressed by the flight of their souls to heaven, accompanied as they are by angels, that he himself converts many people with the account of his experiences. Almachius has him beaten to death.

Cecile buries Maximus with Valerian and Tiburce and is in her turn arrested by Almachius, who condemns her to death when she proves steadfast in her adherence to Christianity. She is kept in a boiling bath for a day and a night, but she is totally unharmed by it, remaining cool and unheated throughout the ordeal. Finally an executioner strikes her three times on the neck with a sword (the law does not allow him a fourth stroke), but he does not succeed in killing her. With her neck almost completely severed, she lingers on for three days, spending the time in teaching the faith to the people. The people collect her blood in sheets as religious tokens. When she eventually dies, she is buried by Pope Urban and her house becomes the Church of St. Cecile.

This tale is an excellent example of a saint's life, containing as it does persons of great bodily and spiritual purity; the conversion of heathens; one fairly spectacular martydrom, besides several routine ones; and a miracle. It was to matters of this sort that

Chaucer, in the *Miller's Prologue*, advised the reader to turn if his taste did not run to harlotry and to churls' tales:

> *And therfore, whoso list it nat yheere,*
> *Turne over the leef and chese another tale;*
> *For he shal fynde ynowe, grete and smale,*
> *Of storial thyng that toucheth gentillesse,*
> *And eek moralitee and hoolynesse.* (*I, 3176-80*)

The *Second Nun's Tale* lacks interest for the modern reader; apparently it did not make a great impact on the Pilgrims either, for the *Canon's Yeoman's Prologue* merely says, "Whan ended was the lyf of Seinte Cecile" (VIII, 554). This comment does not even rise to the height of faint praise. Only the *Manciple's Tale*, of all the stories on which there is any comment at all, excites as little praise as this one.

This line is followed by a passage that is important in understanding how Chaucer envisaged the pilgrimage:

> *Er we hadde riden fully fyve mile,*
> *At Boghtoun under Blee us gan atake*
> *A man that clothed was in clothes blake,* (*VIII, 554-57*)

In other words, there were no tales told after St. Cecile until the Pilgrims had ridden five miles. As we read the *Canterbury Tales,* fragmentary as they are, we get the idea that the telling of one story followed hard upon that of another; at least, this is what we find in all of the fragments except this eighth one. Occasional pauses between stories would certainly be more realistic than uninterrupted storytelling from the beginning of the day until the end, and here Chaucer indicates a fairly long interval between tales. How long it would take a cavalcade to ride five miles would depend upon the terrain traversed and the gait of the horses, but, even if they trotted, the time would be considerable.

Whether or not Chaucer had the *Canon's Yeoman's Tale* in mind when he first envisioned the *Canterbury Tales* or whether it was something that occurred to him as he developed his project, we do not know. The addition of the Yeoman to the party is a realistic incident. If a fairly large group of pilgrims had been riding from London to Canterbury, it is the most natural thing in the world that they should be joined by at least a few people along the way. The Pilgrims who entered the Tabard Inn were "by aventure yfalle / In felaweshipe" (I, 25-26), and "aventure" could easily bring more travelers into the ranks. Most critics consider the *Canon's Yeoman's Tale* a late work; the fact that the *Canon's Yeoman's Prologue* and *Tale* are dramatic would tend to confirm this theory, because, as has been noted, as Chaucer worked, his sense of drama kept developing.

The *Prologue* is one of the most interesting head- or end-links in the entire *Canterbury Tales*. The unexpected appearance of the Canon and his Yeoman, the descriptions of the two characters, the realism of the conversation, the anger of the Canon and his flight, and the Yeoman's agreement to tell all that he knows about alchemy are all on a high artistic plane. Nowhere does Chaucer show a greater mastery of his calling than here.

The fact that there is no known source of the *Canon's Yeoman's Tale* has raised much speculation about why Chaucer wrote it. The theory originally propounded by Tyrwhitt,[11] that Chaucer himself had been swindled by an alchemist and in retaliation composed this tale, has gained little credence throughout the centuries. A sounder theory would be that Chaucer, well endowed with intellectual curiosity, made at least a superficial study of alchemy and as a result learned about the swindling practices of the alchemists. Being amused by them, he decided to recount them as one of the *Tales*. This theory receives some confirmation from the formlessness of the tale. It is nothing more than a string of anecdotes and lacks the unity that drives a story on a single plot-line from start to finish. It is in this way similar to two of Chaucer's other original stories, the *House of Fame* and the *Squire's Tale*. Both of them are so loosely constructed and episodic that Chaucer apparently left them unfinished because he had no idea where to go with them. They are both excellent works but are as devoid of unity as the *Canon's Yeoman's Tale*.

That Chaucer should have been interested in alchemy is in no wise remarkable. We can see in a number of places in his works that he was interested in what we call science, although much of what fascinated him is now contemptuously labeled pseudoscience. Alchemy in his day was perfectly reputable, and it remained so until it passed almost imperceptibly into chemistry. One of the objects of alchemy was to effect the transmutation of one metal into another, for which effort the alchemists have been ridiculed for centuries. What they were attempting to do, stated in different terms, was to rearrange atomic structure. Although alchemy developed into modern chemistry, the alchemist's problem was essentially that of the modern atomic or nuclear physicist.

The Canon's Yeoman begins his tale by saying that he has served his canon for seven years and still has not learned the alchemical science. He has lost greatly by his service, having nothing but an empty purse and a leaden complexion as a reward for all of his work. To impress the gathering of Pilgrims, he rattles off many names of materials and apparatus that belong to the craft; but he admits he does not understand it all. The alchemists, he says, search busily for the philosopher's stone. If they ever found it, all would be well, but the trouble is that they never do. When an experiment is in progress, the apparatus is sure to explode and scatter the materials all over the room. For such calamities various explanations are offered; but, whatever the reasons, the alchemists sweep up the metals and begin again.

The Canon's Yeoman then tells of a canon of his acquaintance who was much slyer than his own canon; in fact, he was an accomplished swindler. The canon borrows some money from a priest and pays it back in three days. This act stimulates the priest to finance some demonstrations to convert quicksilver into silver. By means of a hollowed piece of charcoal filled with silver powder, a palmed ingot, and a hollow stick used as a poker, the priest is deceived into thinking that ingots of silver have been produced from inexpensive raw materials. The exhibitions arouse the priest's cupidity; he pays the canon forty pounds for the formula for producing silver. As soon as the money is paid, the canon disappears, never to be seen by the priest again. The priest never could make the formula work, no matter how often he tried.

The character of the Canon's Yeoman is especially well presented. Essentially ignorant, he—in an effort to impress his audience—makes a wonderful display of the alchemical terms that he has picked up in the laboratory. That he tells his tale in pure exasperation and vindictiveness is quite in accord with his intelligence. He is "getting even" with his canon, whom he has come to dislike intensely. At the end of his story we sympathize with the Yeoman. He has wasted his life on alchemy and it is nothing but a swindle—yet there *might* be something to it after all!

IX   *Fragment IX*

The *Manciple's Prologue* begins Fragment IX. Chaucer places the opening at the little town of "Bobbe-up-and-doun," which is generally identified as Harbledown in the Bleen Forest or as Up-and-down Field in Thannington. An old theory that this tale was supposed to have been told on the journey homeward from Canterbury has recently been revived, but actually we have no knowledge about what Chaucer intended. The demand that the Cook tell a tale is somewhat unexpected, as he had begun a tale —which remains unfinished—immediately after the *Reeve's Tale.* We might assume that Chaucer intended to return to the Cook's fragment to complete it. Or he may have intended to cancel it but never got around to removing it from his manuscript. That the *Manciple's Prologue* is told in the morning is shown by the Host's rebuke of the Cook: "What eyleth thee to slepe by the morwe?" (IX, 16).

In this *Prologue* Chaucer brings in a relationship between the Cook and the Manciple that is supposed to exist in their everyday life in London outside the time-scheme of the *Canterbury Tales.* This is the only occurrence of this sort of thing, although other relationships have been suggested by critics. The Host, referring to the peculations of the Manciple mentioned in the *General Prologue,* says:

> But yet, Manciple, in feith thou art to nyce,
> Thus openly repreve hym of his vice.
> Another day he wole, peraventure,
> Reclayme thee and brynge thee to lure;
> I meene, he speke wole of smale thynges,
> As for to pynchen at thy rekenynges,
> That were nat honest, if it cam to preef.   (IX, 69-75)

The Manciple is not disposed to argue the matter of his own honesty; he says:

> . . . that were a greet mescheef!
> So myghte he lightly brynge me in the snare.

> *Yet hadde I levere payen for the mare*
> *Which he rit on, than he sholde with me stryve.*
> *I wol nat wratthen hym, also moot I thryve!*
> *That that I spak, I seyde it in my bourde.* (IX, 76-81)

That the Host apparently knows of the association, with all of its dishonesty, between the Manciple and the Cook, also indicates a relationship between the Host and the other two. It is just such a tantalizing glimpse as this of what might have been in Chaucer's mind that makes us greatly regret the highly fragmentary state of the *Canterbury Tales*.

The *Manciple's Tale* is one of Chaucer's lesser accomplishments. It is about Phebus Apollo's career while he lived on earth. He, who excelled in archery and minstrelsy, had in his house a snow-white crow that could talk. He also had a wife whom he dearly loved and tried to please in every way he could. The wife was, however, false to him with a man of little reputation. When Phebus returned home, the crow cried "Cuckoo!" It had witnessed the wife's cuckolding and was bent upon informing Phebus of it. When Phebus questioned the crow, it gave a detailed account of the whole affair.

Phebus in his ire killed his wife with an arrow and then in sorrow broke all of his musical instruments and his bow and arrows. He then accused the crow of having slandered his wife with wicked lies. To repay the crow for its supposed perfidy in maligning his wife, Phebus plucked out all of its white feathers, turned it black, and deprived it of its song and its gift of human speech. For this reason all crows are now black. When he had finished the anecdote the Manciple then gave a long moralizing passage taught him by his mother.

Derived from Ovid's *Metamorphoses*, the tale deals with a mythological personage and so does not have the great interest of most of the other tales which deal with people. Phebus Apollo never becomes human. This tale is generally held to be an early work, and there is nothing about it to indicate that it was specifically written for a Pilgrim. It fits the teller as poorly as any tale in the *Canterbury Tales*. Although the talking-bird story was fairly well known, the fact that it was given a setting from classical mythology argues a certain degree of education in the teller, and we are told in the *General Prologue* that the Manciple was not a learned man (I, 574). One feature of the tale, however, is its accentuation of one of the morals in the *Nun's Priest's Tale*. This emphasis upon the necessity of holding one's tongue and not being a babbler causes us to wonder whether Chaucer might have had some highly placed person in mind as the object of his warnings. It has been pointed out that the ideas of the moralizing passage were commonplaces to be found scattered through the works of a number of writers. This makes the passage all the more noteworthy. If Chaucer had translated or adapted it from a single work, we might not be curious about it. But when it is, in effect, an original composition by reason of its having been synthesized from many sources, we are privileged to speculate why Chaucer thought it worth his while to compose it.

X *Fragment X*

The *Parson's Prologue* is generally accepted as beginning a new fragment (X), although it begins with a reference to the *Manciple's Tale*. But it is entirely illogical to assume that the telling of that work lasted from morning (IX, 16) until four o'clock in the afternoon (X, 5). Why this long lapse of time occurs no one can explain. It is in the *Parson's Prologue* that Chaucer tells us he was six feet tall (X, 8-9); this was an unusual height for a man of the fourteenth century.

The Host says (X, 15-19) that all the tales have been told except this one and that his duties are almost completed. Did Chaucer intend this tale to be the last one on the homeward journey or was it the last before the Pilgrims entered Canterbury? No one knows. Nor can we say if Chaucer decided to abridge his plan to include only a one-way trip to Canterbury instead of having a round trip back to London.

The Parson is conjured to tell a tale. The Host's command to him ends with the oath "for cokkes bones" (X, 29). It will be remembered that the oath by the Host (II, 1169) in the *Epilogue of the Man of Law's Tale* brought down upon him the Parson's censure, which in turn produced the Shipman's accusation that the Parson was a Lollard. In the *Parson's Prologue* there is no rebuke for the swearing, although the Parson's character—stiff, pious, perhaps a bit narrow—does not seem to have changed since the earlier episode. There is, however, a clever echo of the Shipman's scornful words. The Shipman had said of the Parson: "He wolde sowen some difficulte, / Or springen cokkel in our clene corn"

(II, 1182-83). The Parson, now refusing to accede to the Host's request to "telle us a fable anon" (X, 29), says: "Why sholde I sowen draf out of my fest, / Whan I may sowen whete, if that me lest" (X, 35-36).

Morality is what he will tell, and it will be in "a myrie tale in prose" (X, 46). He admits his inability as a southern man to speak in the northern "rum, ram, ruf" (X, 43), or alliterative verse; he indicates that he does not have a high opinion of rhyme, either. Why Chaucer has him inveigh against alliterative verse is somewhat of a puzzle, as, of course, there is no alliterative verse in the *Canterbury Tales*. There has been speculation that Chaucer may have intended to have the Cook tell an alliterative tale between the *Manciple's Tale* and the *Parson's Tale*. All we can say about this theory is that we have no evidence that Chaucer could write alliterative verse; and, even if he had composed such a poem, the Cook, coming from Ware in Herefordshire, would have been an unlikely person to tell it. Someone from the north of England, where this type of verse continued in style long after it was abandoned in the London area, would have been more appropriate.

Before beginning his tale, the Parson apologizes for any mistakes that he may make in translating his original and says that he will stand to correction (X, 60). This disclaimer is usually taken as an apology on Chaucer's part for any slips that he might make in rendering his source into English. The apology was, however, needless so far as we are concerned, for we do not know what Chaucer's source was. Apparently there was a combination of two pious works, one about penitence and the other about the deadly sins. Whether Chaucer found the two already fused or effected the connection himself we do not know.

Certainly the Parson does not keep his promise to tell a "myrie" tale, but he keeps his word to tell it in prose. In his tale we again have, as in the *Tale of Melibee*, a piece not to the modern taste. But tastes vary in different ages, and Chaucer must have had a good opinion of the *Parson's Tale* to choose it for the conclusion of his great work. Moreover, he must have had confidence that his contemporary readers would find it as fascinating as he did.

The section of the *Parson's Tale* about the deadly sins is more interesting than the one about penitence. For one thing, it is significant in showing what was considered sin in Chaucer's day. There are many passages in this part of the work that occur in substantially unchanged form in some of the other *Canterbury Tales.* This fact has led to the supposition that the *Parson's Tale* is an early work and that Chaucer, either consciously or unconsciously, borrowed extensively from it as he composed the other *Canterbury Tales.*

The *Parson's Tale* shows how many of the Pilgrims were guilty of deadly sins. The suggestion has been made that the *Canterbury Tales* was intended to be an extended treatment of the seven deadly sins. Although this idea is somewhat hard to accept, it is fascinating to see how many of the Pilgrims can be branded as sinners.

If we look at what is said about pride, we find the Wife of Bath guilty of "superfluitee of clothynge" (X, 416). "Pride of the table" (X, 443) is one of the Franklin's sins. Certainly the Miller prided "hym in his strengthe of body" (X, 459). The Miller, the Reeve, the Friar, and the Summoner are surely guilty of envy: "Thanne cometh eek bitternesse of herte, thurgh which bitternesse every good dede of his neighebor semeth to hym bitter and unsavory. Thanne cometh discord, that unbyndeth alle manere of freendshipe. Thanne comth scornynge of his neighebor, al do he never so weel." (X, 509-10).

At least half of the Pilgrims are guilty of ire, either on the pilgrimage or as a way of life. The Friar's customary manner of dealing with rich men and sellers of victual is sinful. The Pardoner and the Merchant are guilty of avarice; the Franklin, the Miller, the Summoner, and the Cook of gluttony; the Friar and the Wife of Bath of lechery—and so it goes. The list above makes no pretense at being complete. Dull as some may find the *Parson's Tale,* it offers in a way far more commentary on the Pilgrims than all the rest of the *Canterbury Tales* combined.

After the *Parson's Tale* we have the Retractions in which Chaucer takes leave of his book. Whenever the Retractions are now mentioned, it is fashionable to say, "If they are genuine. . . ." There should be no doubt about their authenticity, as similar passages have been appended to the works of many writers. Nothing could be more proper for a son of the Church than to disavow all improper works that tend towards sin and to commend the proper ones to the attention of the godly. From a liberal modern point of view, many of the works that Chaucer repudiates are quite harmless; but, as they were not religious, they were worldly vanities and, as such, were to be cast away.

In the list of works in the Retractions, the *Legend of Good Women* turns up as *The book of the xxv. Ladies;* and, since this number occurs in many manuscripts, it appears as if it could be the number of biographies that Chaucer intended to write, although nineteen is a generally accepted number. *The book of the Leoun* is widely held to be derived from Machaut's *Dit dou Lyon,* with which Chaucer seems to have been familiar. We do not, of course, have Chaucer's *Book of the Lion;* but, if he actually translated it, it merited retracting, for it contained considerable satire against women. The "many a song and many a leccherous lay" (X, 1086) that Chaucer repudiates are also lost, for which fact we mourn.

CHAPTER 8

Chaucer Through the Years

I *Chaucer's Immediate Successors*

IT should be an easy matter to characterize Chaucer as a poet, but, as we look back over almost six centuries of allusion to him, doubts assail us. For Chaucer has been many things to many men. Each age since he lived has had its own literary opinion and thus its own opinion of Chaucer. Sometimes the opinion was good and sometimes there was little appreciation for him. And with this in mind, how can we now say that we have arrived at the ultimate truth about him? As Caroline F. E. Spurgeon says:

> To-day we prize Chaucer above all because he is a great artist, we delight in his simplicity, his freshness, his humanity, his humour, but it is possible that these may not be the only or even the principal reasons why he is liked three hundred years hence. If, as would seem to be the case, the common consciousness of a people becomes enriched with time and experience, enabling them to see ever more and more in the work of a great poet, the lovers of Chaucer three centuries hence will be capable of seeing more in him and will be able to come actually nearer to him than can those who love him to-day.[1]

In other words, we can have our opinion of him, but it is not necessarily true that our descendants will have the same opinion, just as we differ from many of our predecessors.

The first period of Chaucer criticism began while the poet was still alive. His contemporaries and immediate followers perceived that he was a great poet, and writer after writer hailed him as "master," a term which Lydgate, for instance, was never tired of employing. But Lydgate had no monopoly on the word, as Henry Scogan, Thomas Hoccleve, James I of Scotland, John Metham of Norwich, George Ashby, Stephen Hawes, and others so refer to him. With them he was "noble" Chaucer, and was usually commended as a master of rhetoric. Terms that these men frequently applied to him were "aureate" and "laureate" poet. "Aureate," of course, means "golden, splendid"; and it seems clear enough that "laureate" means about the same thing, a poet of excellent quality. This term "laureate" was taken up by some of the great tribe of undiscerning later writers who wrongly assumed that Chaucer held the official position of poet laureate.

Most of the early references are general in nature; their tenor is that Chaucer is a great poet skilled in the use of language. When the praise is at all specific, it is for him as a poet of love. Thus one of the earliest of all references to him, that by John Gower in the first version of *Confessio Amantis* (1390), has the goddess of love say:

> *And gret wel Chaucer whan ye mete,*
> *As mi disciple and mi poete:*
> *For in the floures of his youthe*
> *In sondri wise, as he wel couthe,*
> *Of Ditees and of Songes glade,*
> *The whiche he for mi sake made,*
> *The land fulfild is oueral.* (Bk. VIII, 2941-47)

There are other comments in a similar vein, and *Troilus and Criseyde* was the work most frequently alluded to by name in this early period. We, with our eyes focused upon the *Canterbury Tales*, perhaps wonder about this, but it has been well said as follows:

When the men of the fourteenth or fifteenth centuries thought of Chaucer, they did not think first of the *Canterbury Tales*. Their Chaucer was the Chaucer of dream and allegory, of love-romance and erotic debate, of high style and profitable doctrine. To Deschamps, as every one remembers, he was the 'great translator'—the gardener by whom a French poet might hope to be transplanted—and also the English god of Love. To Gower, he is the poet of Venus: to Thomas Usk, Love's 'owne trewe servaunt' and 'the noble philosophical poete.' [2]

This emphasis on Chaucer is not surprising. The French tradition, which Chaucer firmly established in England, was the vital influence in poetry for well over a century after his death. And, while it is true that the French poets did write about other things besides love, it was the aspect of love in their work that caught the attention of the successors of Chaucer, just as it had caught Chaucer's attention in the early part of his career. It is, therefore, not to be wondered that Chaucer's immediate successors considered him the first English poet. He was not, of course, the first; but, as he was the popularizer of the theme that captured universal attention, it was natural for his admirers to disregard all those who had come before him. Whether much of the poetry antedating Chaucer was generally available to his successors is unknown; thus it is possible that his contemporaries and immediate successors believed him to be the first English poets because they were ignorant of most of the poetry that had been written in English before his time.

We now recognize that the works of Petrarch and Boccaccio were a Renaissance influence on Chaucer. This particular influence was almost completely neglected by his immediate followers. We sometimes characterize the *Canterbury Tales* as coming in his "English period," meaning that all the influences that operated upon him were synthesized into something that had not existed before. The works of the English period were disregarded by his successors: they sang his greatness as a poet, but his greatness lay elsewhere for them than for us.

Since it was his rhetoric that first brought him renown, it is easy to see that his more formal early poems were read to the exclusion of some of the simpler *Canterbury Tales*. Caxton, for instance, in the Epilogue to *Boethius de Consolacione Philosophie* (c. 1479), refers to Chaucer as "the worshipful fader & first foundeur & embelissher of ornate eloquence in our englissh" (fol. 93b). Further on in the same work he says that Chaucer deserves prayers as the "enbelissher in making the sayd langage ornate & fayr." William Dunbar, in *The Golden Targe* (1503), mentions Chaucer's "fresch anamalit terms celicall" (line 256). In other words, Chaucer's easy colloquial style was at first consigned to limbo in favor of his "high style."

John Skelton seems to be alone in feeling that Chaucer wrote good plain English. In *Philip Sparrow* (1507?) he says:

> And now men wold haue amended
> his english, where at they barke,
> And marre all they warke:
> Chaucer, that famous Clarke,

> *His tearmes were not darcke,*
> *But pleasaunt, easy, and playne;*
> *No word he wrote in vayne.* (797-803)

It is interesting to have this commendation from Skelton, although in other works he reverts to the conventional idea that Chaucer was the grand master of polished eloquence.

II *Chaucer in the Sixteenth Century*

At the end of the fifteenth and at the beginning of the six-teenth centuries, Chaucer became the god of a group of poets—Robert Henryson, Gawain Douglas, William Dunbar, and Sir David Lindsay—known as the Scottish Chaucerians. They had extreme reverence for him and faithfully imitated his works in a multitude of poems. Henryson even wrote a continuation of *Troilus and Criseyde*, called *The Testament of Cresseid*, in which Criseyde, notorious for her infidelity, passes from man to man and finally becomes a woman of the streets.

In the sixteenth century the admiration for Chaucer shifted from his rhetoric to his learning and morality. Probably the shift occurred because the secret of reading his verse metrically by pronouncing the final "e's" of words was totally lost; and, instead of being a master of eloquence, he came to be considered a very rough poet. About his moral influence John Foxe, in *Actes and Monumentes* (1570), said: "As also I am partlye informed of certeine, whiche knewe the parties, which to them reported, that by readyng of Chausers workes, they were brought to the true knowledge of Religion. And not unlike to be true" (I, 965). And Raphael Holinshed, in *The Chronicles of England, Scotlande, and Irelande* (1577), said: "But now to rehearse what writers of oure English nation liued in the days of this Kyng [Henry IV], that renowmed Poete Geffreye Chaucer is worthily named as princi-pall, a man so exquisitely learned in all sciences, that hys matche was not lightly founde anye where in those dayes, and for reduc-ing our Englishe tong to perfect conformitie, hee hath excelled therein all other" (III, 58). This is a pretty tribute, even if Holin-shed has Chaucer gracing a reign that he saw very little of.

The idea that Chaucer was an exceedingly learned man was by no means restricted to the sixteenth century. Elias Ashmole, in 1652, in *Theatrum Chemicum Britannicum*, wrote: "Besides he that Reads the latter part of the *Chanon's Yeoman's Tale*, wil easily perceive him to be a *Iudicious Philosopher*, and one that fully knew the *Mistery*" (470). Ashmole, by "Mistery," meant the science, or the pseudo-science, of alchemy. And John Lewis, in 1720, in *The History of the Life and Sufferings of the Reverend and Learned John Wicliffe, D.D.*, wrote: "*Geoffrey Chaucer*. He is said to have been educated in *Canterbury* or *Merton* College with *John Wicliffe*, and thereupon to have commenced an accute Logician, a sweet Rhetorician, a pleasant Poet, a grave Philosopher, and an ingenious Mathematician, and an holy Divine" (210). Lewis is here repeating the old tradition that Chaucer was university educated; he is, however, showing great restraint, as many writers had Chaucer a student at both Oxford and Cambridge. Lewis' catalog of Chaucer's intellectual achievements was, however, a generally accepted one.

III *Chaucer and the Language*

In the passage by Holinshed above there is contained an idea that persists with some people to the present time, that Chaucer was the founder of the English language. Chaucer, of course, did not invent the English language. The London division of the East Midland dialect of the language was already in existence when Chaucer made his appearance on the scene; it had been developing for centuries. What Chaucer did was to use the language extremely well. That others also mastered it can be seen in the *Confessio Amantis* of John Gower. As literature the *Confessio* is far below Chaucer's works, purely because Gower did not have Chaucer's genius; but it is a mistake to think that Gower did not have a thorough mastery of English, for his use of it compares very well with Chaucer's. There is generally a smoothness and naturalness in Gower that is sometimes lacking in Chaucer.

Chaucer, it is true, introduced a large number of French words into English, but the introduction of these words did not change the essential character of the language. And certainly Chaucer was not alone in his use of French words; they had been coming into English for centuries before his time and were to continue to come in for centuries after his death. The case of Chaucer as the founder of the English language has been well summed up as follows:

Not only did the fourteenth century see English firmly and finally established as a literary language, but it saw the elevation of one dialect into a commanding position. Hitherto there had been rival claimants among the three groups of dialects, Northern, Midland, and Southern. Beginning with the fourteenth century, however, a single subdivision of one of these, the East Midland dialect of the capital, the court, and the universities, assumed a peculiarly favored position as the literary standard, and it was never seriously threatened thereafter. The causes of this elevation of East Midland are not far to seek. All things worked together to bring it about; if England was to be a really united realm, the speech of London could scarcely fail to be, in time, the standard for the whole country.

But one very important additional reason why London English became the standard dialect just when it did is quite certainly the influence of Chaucer. The happy accident that he was a Londoner born and bred, and wrote for a court that, though probably still bilingual, used the local dialect when speaking English, helped immeasurably to give the East Midland dialect a place apart from the others. It is easy to exaggerate here. In the past, phrases like "the father of the English language," "the first finder of our fair language," and "the well of English undefiled" have tended to magnify unduly the contribution of Chaucer to the English language. For even if he had never lived, London English would surely still have become the basis of standard English. On the other hand it is evident that a great part of English poetry, throughout the fifteenth century, is in direct imitation of Chaucer. The chorus of praise that arose from his contemporaries, and the eagerness of his successors to acknowledge him their master, are almost evidence enough of his powerful influence. But the point need hardly be labored, since the wonderful genius of Chaucer has never been more clearly perceived than in the twentieth century.[3]

Thus we see that we should give Chaucer his due as a great influence on the adoption of English as the literary language, but more than his due we need not give him. But it is frequently difficult for an enthusiast to preserve moderation in the praise of his hero.

Later ages, it may be said, viewed Chaucer's introduction of French words into the English language in two ways: some praised him for enriching the language, and others condemned him for polluting it.

From the sixteenth century until well toward the end of the eighteenth, Chaucer's verse was, with some rare exceptions, completely misread. Chaucer had been old-fashioned in the selective pronunciation of the final "e's" of words. The pronunciation of this letter in final position had been gradually passing out of use during a good part of the fourteenth century. Its loss as a syllable had worked no great hardship on the poets of the time, who quite generally wrote their verses with a number of accents or beats to a line, but without the regular alternation of accented and unaccented syllables that characterizes conventional verse. Nor were such poets under constraint to have a fixed number of syllables to a line. To achieve the regularity that marks most of his verse, Chaucer retained, or revived, the use of the final "e." With the passage of time, however, the secret of his verse became completely lost, and the men of the sixteenth century considered his versification rude. The narrative parts of Edmund Spenser's *Shepheardes Calender* are a good example of what the poets of the later sixteenth century thought Chaucer's verse to be. The imitations of Chaucer in pseudo-Middle English all are in meter that is very rough indeed. A term sometimes applied to his verse is "riding rhyme," by which is meant a loosely iambic pentameter line rhyming in couplets, apparently given its name because the Canterbury pilgrims spoke it as they rode.

But whether they understood his metrics or not, the greater Elizabethans thought very well of Chaucer. Spenser, as may be inferred from the above, took one of his meters from what he believed the elder poet wrote; and, in addition to the *Shepheardes Calender*, *Mother Hubberd's Tale* and *Daphnaïada* are also strongly reminiscent of Chaucer. Shakespeare thought well enough of him to borrow his plot for *Troilus and Cressida*, and, with Fletcher, that for *Two Noble Kinsmen*. *A Midsummer Night's Dream* shows strong influence from the *Knight's Tale*. Other Elizabethans such as Philip Sidney, Gabriel Harvey, Samuel Daniel, Michael Drayton, George Puttenham, and William Webbe were also his admirers.

IV Chaucer and the Seventeenth Century

It was in the seventeenth century that Chaucer's language began to cause genuine difficulties in the understanding of his works. As there were no Middle English scholars to prepare glossaries to accompany his poems, many of his words passed out of understanding. As a consequence he was considered a rude ancient from a misty age whose works were for the most part a closed book to the moderns of the time. The difficulty in understanding him caused him to be read but little, although he was mentioned often enough. For well over a century after his death, he had usually been mentioned in connection with Gower and Lydgate, but in the seventeenth century he was almost always coupled with Spenser, who was not much read at the time either, and for the same reason: a distaste for the language. He is frequently commended for his sense but often reprehended for the crudity of his expression. Henry Peacham, in 1622, in *The Compleat Gentleman,* said: "Of English Poets of our owne Nation, esteeme Sir *Geoffrey Chaucer* the father; although the stile for the antiquitie, may distast you, yet as vnder a bitter and rough rinde, there lyeth a delicate kernell of conceit and sweet inuention" (Ch. 10, 81-82).

Sir Thomas Pope Blount, in 1694, in *De Re Poetica,* said: "But though the place of his Birth is not certainly known, yet this is agreed upon by all hands, that he was counted the chief of the *English Poets,* not only of his time, but continued to be so esteem'd till this Age; and as much as we despise his old fashion'd Phrase, and Obsolete Words, *He* was one of the first Refiners of the *English* language" (42).

There were those, however, with the intelligence to perceive that if there was a fault, it lay not with Chaucer but with his readers. Sir Aston Cokayne, in 1658, in *Small Poems of Divers Sorts,* said:

> *Our good old Chaucer some despise, and why?*
> *Because say they he writeth barbarously.*
> *Blame him not (Ignorants) but your selves, that do*
> *Not at these years your native language know.*   (155)

It was in the seventeenth century that the bawdy side of Chaucer was emphasized. This is an amusing twist of fortune, for, as has been said, he was first esteemed as a noble poet of love, a purveyor of the most exalted sentiments. Apparently *Troilus and Criseyde* and the other early poems which were at first the most popular were supplanted by the tales of the Miller, the Reeve, the Merchant, and the Shipman. Samuel Sheppard, about the year 1650, in *The Faerie King,* referred to Chaucer as

"a Knight readen in vertues lore / who knew full wellen how to
Jape and Jeere" (fol. 65b). Edward Phillips, in 1675, in *Theatrum
Poetarum*, said of Chaucer that, "being by some few admir'd for
his real worth, to others not unpleasing for his facetious way,
which joyn'd with his old *English* intertains them with a kind of
Drollery" (sig. **2). The japing, jeering, and facetiousness all refer to Chaucer's obscenity, which the seventeenth century really
took to its heart. The "Drollery" in the quotation above refers to
the amusement that the people of the time got from words the
meanings of which they did not understand: surely a queer and
childish source of entertainment!

John Evelyn, in 1685, in *The Immortality of Poesie*, had more
to say in Phillips' vein:

> *Old* Chaucer *shall, for his facetious style,*
> *Be read, and prais'd by warlike* Britains, *while*
> *The Sea enriches, and defends their Isle.* (p. 91)

Joseph Addison, usually a fairly perceptive critic, assumed a
scornful attitude in *An Account of the Greatest English Poets*
(1694):

> *Long had our dull Fore-Fathers slept Supine,*
> *Nor felt the Raptures of the Tuneful Nine;*
> *Till* Chaucer *first, a merry* Bard, *arose;*
> *And many a Story told in Rhime and Prose.*
> *But Age has Rusted what the* Poet *writ,*
> *Worn out his Language, and obscur'd his Wit:*
> *In vain he jests in his unpolish'd strain*
> *And tries to make his Readers laugh in vain.* (I, 23)

Apparently even the improper stories of Chaucer left Addison
cold.

V *The Eighteenth Century*

That Addison was not expressing a universally held opinion is
evinced by John Oldmixon, who, in *Reflections on Dr. Swift's
Letter to the Earl of Oxford about the English Tongue* (1712),
indicated that Chaucer was highly thought of by some people at
least: "*Chaucer* will, no doubt, be admir'd as long as the *English* Tongue has a Being; and the changes that have happen'd

to our Language have not hinder'd his Works out living their
Contemporary Monuments of Brass or Marble" (24-25).

Oldmixon was, however, living in a new era of Chaucer appreciation which had been ushered in by John Dryden at the turn
of the century. Dryden, one of the many "modernizers," or trans-
lators, of Chaucer's works, had a keen appreciation of Chaucer's
many virtues, which he sets forth at length in the introduction to
*Fables Ancient and Modern, Translated into Verse from Homer,
Ovid, Boccace & Chaucer: With Original Poems* (1700), and
many writers who came after him echoed his sentiments.
Whether they actually appreciated Chaucer or were merely doing the fashionable thing in following the lead of the most important literary figure of the day is not clear. It was felt, however,
that if Chaucer was to be read at all generally, he must be
clothed in modern dress, and so for decades Chaucer was diligently translated. It must not be thought that Dryden was the
pioneer translator of Chaucer. Sir Francis Kynaston, in 1635, published *Amorum Troili et Creseidæ libri duo priores Anglico-
Latini*, a translation into Latin of the first two books of *Troilus
and Criseyde*. This fantastic achievement was greeted with ac-
claim; William Cartwright, in *To the worthy Author on his Approved Translation* (verses prefixed to Kynaston's work), said:
" 'Tis to your Happy cares wee owe, that we / Read *Chaucer*
now without a Dictionary" (250). Ed. Foulis, also in prefactory
verses to Kynaston, said:

> *Thus the Translation will become*
> *Th' Originall, while that growes dumbe;*
> *And this will crowne these labours: None*
> *See* Chaucer *but in* Kinaston.   (*sig. °4b*)

The vogue for translating Chaucer lasted until 1841, when the
last collection of modernizations to be published for nearly a
century was issued.

VI   *Modern Times*

Although the praise of Chaucer was by no means general
through the years, there having always been plenty of detractors,
there were those in every age to hail him as a truly great poet.
To us this seems but simple justice; but, when we consider that

in most of time past Chaucer could be read only in very corrupt texts in editions loaded with spurious, and all too often inferior works, we sometimes wonder how he maintained the reputation that he did. But in 1775 Thomas Tyrwhitt published *The Canterbury Tales of Chaucer. To which are added an Essay upon his Language and Versification; an Introductory Discourse; and Notes. In Four Volumes.* This splendid edition, containing as it did an accurate text, a good biography, and a highly perceptive interpretation and criticism of the works, may be said to usher in the modern age of Chaucer appreciation.

The fact that this was a fine edition did not by any means signify that Chaucer was universally well received for the rest of the eighteenth century or during the nineteenth. There was much opposition to him and his works by highly esteemed authors and critics, although at the same time there was a growing realization on the part of others of his true worth as a poet. As not everyone read Tyrwhitt's edition, the old prejudices died slowly, but die they did. With the founding of the Chaucer Society in 1868 by Dr. Frederick J. Furnivall, there began the fine scholarly and critical work that persists until the present time. Scores of careful and devoted scholars in England and the United States, and some on the Continent, have given their attention to all aspects of Chaucer study; the result is that there is now probably better apparatus for the study of Chaucer than for any other English poet.

VII *Chaucer's Qualities*

Although Chaucer is at present one of the best-loved English poets and is widely read with delight, he probably no longer exerts any appreciable literary influence. The fifteenth and sixteenth centuries were the time when his works really stimulated poetry—and plays—in others. And as we have said, the influence was largely from the poems exclusive of the *Canterbury Tales*, which have engendered remarkably little literature. C. S. Lewis says:

The *Canterbury Tales* are glorious reading, but they have always been sterile. If the later Middle Ages can offer us only the Prologue to *Thebes* and the Prologue to *Beryn*, we ourselves are not in much better plight. William Morris's discipleship to Chaucer was an illusion. Crabbe and Mr. Masefield are good writers; but they are hardly among the greatest English poets. If Chaucer's *Tales* have had any influence, it is to be sought in our prose rather than in our verse. Our great and characteristic poets—our Spenser, Milton, Wordsworth, and the like—have much more in common with Virgil, or even with *Beowulf*, than with the *Prologue* and the *Pardoner's Tale*. Perhaps none of our early poets has so little claim to be called the father of English poetry as the Chaucer of the *Canterbury Tales*.[4]

One of the qualities now most esteemed in Chaucer is his irony; scholars are constantly uncovering hitherto undiscovered examples of it, and we all relish it when it is finally uncovered. It is always possible, however, that we overdo our search for it. Lewis says:

We have heard a little too much of the 'mocking' Chaucer. Not many will agree with the critic who supposed that the laughter of Troilus in heaven was 'ironical'; but I am afraid that many of us now read into Chaucer all manner of ironies, slynesses, and archnesses, which are not there, and praise him for his humor where he is really writing with 'ful devout corage'. The lungs of our generation are so very 'tickle o' the sere.'[5]

This is a warning that it might be well to take. Once a person gets a reputation for irony, practically everything he says, even his most serious utterances, are considered deliciously funny to those who consider themselves the initiate.

Of Chaucer's humor there can be no doubt, and this is an aspect of his work that has long been appreciated, although, as said, there were periods when only his coarse humor was appreciated. Writers in the sixteenth and seventeenth centuries often applauded Chaucer's "wit." The modern reader must be on his guard when he comes to such a reference, since it did not, until the eighteenth century, have any reference to being funny. What the older authors meant was his "skill" or "wisdom," and sometimes "ingenuity" or "a quickness of the mind in seeing unexpected resemblances."[6]

We in this modern day make very little to-do about Chaucer's learning, the thing for which he was once chiefly celebrated. In fact, some modern critics minimize his learning—although he was amply learned. For us it is not so obtrusive as it apparently once was, for we are less interested in gaining information from him than we are in other aspects of his poetry. It is difficult to imagine a modern patiently reading *Melibee* for the good doctrine it contains, but that is exactly what our forefathers did.

We, like the admirers of Chaucer in the first century after his death, are unanimous in praising him as a master of style, although we look for different things than did the men of the fifteenth century. The passages of rhetorical grandeur that fascinated them we are likely to neglect for his simple, direct style—a style in which he has no equals in English. We now admire him as a master of metrics, as the men of several centuries did not. Of his marvelously subtle use of words we have now come to a great appreciation; only posterity can say whether it is a full appreciation. No longer do we consider him the founder of the English language, but we willingly admit that he used it superbly.

Chaucer was a magnificent storyteller, one of the greatest storytellers of English literature. Such a statement as this is easy to make, but difficult to particularize, for everything about the man is important in the telling of a story. A story is more than an elaborated plot; many poets have used the same plots, but the results have differed widely. An effort was made much earlier in this book to point out that a mere combining of sources accounts for almost nothing in the formation of a story. It is the passing of the elements through the brain of a great writer, who in telling his story transmits part of his own mind, that produces distinguished literature. When the raw material of sources passed through the mind of Chaucer, it emerged in tales that we would be much the poorer for not possessing.

One last quality in Chaucer should be mentioned: his tenderness. When we read his works, we constantly feel that we are in communion with a man of sensitive feelings, of tremendous sympathies. Chaucer never takes any of his characters, rascals though some of them may be, very seriously to task. We can only feel that Chaucer was unconsciously characterizing himself when he wrote his favorite line: "For pitee renneth soone in gentil herte."

Notes and References

Chapter Two

1. Edith Rickert, "Was Chaucer a Student at the Inner Temple?" in *Manly Anniversary Studies in Language and Literature* (Chicago, 1923).
2. James R. Hulbert, *Chaucer's Official Life* (Menasha, Wisc., 1912), pp. 6-36.
3. *Ibid.*, p. 65.
4. *Ibid.*, p. 57.

Chapter Three

1. *The Works of Geoffrey Chaucer,* Globe Edition, ed. by Alfred W. Pollard, *et al.* (London, 1928), p. xxxiv.
2. John L. Lowes, *Geoffrey Chaucer and the Development of his Genius* (Boston, 1934), p. 133.
3. *Ibid.*, p. 163.

Chapter Five

1. Bernard L. Jefferson, *Chaucer and the Consolation of Philosophy of Boethius* (Princeton, 1917), p. 149. This discussion derives much of its material from Jefferson's work.
2. Guillaume de Lorris and Jean de Meun, *The Romance of the Rose,* trans. by F. S. Ellis, 3 vols. (London, 1900).
3. Thomas R. Lounsbury, *Studies in Chaucer,* 3 vols. (New York, 1892, 1960), II, 3-166.
4. Sister M. Madeleva, *A Lost Language and Other Essays on Chaucer* (New York, 1951), p. 99.

Chapter Six

1. Although Boccaccio's *Filostrato* was Chaucer's main source for *Troilus and Criseyde,* the influence of at least thirty other works has been traced.
2. George L. Kittredge, "Chaucer's Lollius," in *Harvard Studies in Classical Philology* (Cambridge, Mass., 1917).

Chapter Seven

1. H. Snowden Ward, *The Canterbury Pilgrimages* (London, 1904), pp. 100-60.

2. Although Langland in *The Vision of Piers Plowman* is severe in his censure of wicked priests, he by no means indicates that there are no good ones.

3. Sister M. Madeleva, *op. cit.*, in Chapter 2, "Chaucer's Nuns," interprets the description of the Prioress as indicating that Chaucer was depicting a perfect nun rather than a sentimental worldling.

4. Nevill Coghill, *The Poet Chaucer* (London, 1947), p. 167.

5. F. N. Robinson, *The Works of Geoffrey Chaucer,* 2nd ed. (Boston, 1957), p. 697.

6. Marcette Chute, *Geoffrey Chaucer of England* (New York, 1958), p. 278.

7. Walter C. Curry, *Chaucer and the Medieval Sciences,* rev. ed. (New York, 1960), pp. 3-36.

8. Eileen Power, *Medieval English Nunneries* (Cambridge, 1922), p. 141, note 1. Nuns at some nunneries received four gallons of the superior beer and three gallons of the weaker kind each week.

9. George L. Kittredge, "Chaucer's Pardoner," in *The Atlantic Monthly,* LXXII (1893), p. 830; also in *Chaucer: Modern Essays in Criticism,* ed. by Edward Wagenknecht (New York, 1959), p. 118. Kittredge points out that it is said the Pardoner "exposes himself with unnaturally frank cynicism" and that his exposure "is dramatically impossible." Kittredge's defense of Chaucer is a much-referred-to landmark in Chaucer criticism.

10. J. Leslie Hotson, "Colfox *vs.* Chauntecleer," *PMLA,* XXXI (1924), pp. 726-81; also in Wagenknecht, as in note 11, pp. 98-116.

11. Thomas Tyrwhitt, *The Canterbury Tales of Chaucer. To which are added an Essay upon his Language and Versification; an Introductory Discourse; and Notes,* 4 vols. (London, 1775).

Chapter Eight

1. Caroline F. E. Spurgeon, *Five Hundred Years of Chaucer Criticism and Allusion, 1357-1900,* 3 vols., new ed. (Cambridge, 1960), I, cxxix. This chapter as a whole depends upon Miss Spurgeon's work for the general outline of the subject and for the illustrative quotations.

2. C. S. Lewis, *The Allegory of Love* (New York, 1958), p. 162.

3. Stuart Robertson, *The Development of Modern English,* revised by Frederic G. Cassidy, 2nd ed. (Englewood Cliffs, N. J., 1954), pp. 49-50. The references in this selection are to Lydgate's *Book of Thebes* and the anonymous *Tale of Beryn.*

4. Lewis, *op. cit.,* p. 163.

5. *Ibid.,* pp. 164-65.

6. Spurgeon, *op. cit.,* I, xcvii.

Selected Bibliography

Works

Baugh, Albert C. *Chaucer's Major Poetry*, New York, 1963. Excellent edition of most of Chaucer's poetry; words are glossed at the bottoms of the pages.

Robinson, F. N. *The Works of Geoffrey Chaucer*, 2nd ed., Boston, 1957. Chaucer's complete works, with up-to-date introductions and notes. The standard modern edition.

Skeat, Walter W. *The Complete Works of Geoffrey Chaucer*, 6 vols., Oxford, 1894-1900. Valuable for the copious notes and the most complete glossary of the works extant.

Secondary Sources

1. Chaucer's Background

Andreas Capellanus. *Art of Courtly Love*, translated by John Jay Parry. New York, 1959. Paperback, edited by Frederick W. Locke, New York, 1957. The best-known codification of the rules of courtly love.

Baldwin, Charles S. *Medieval Rhetoric and Poetic*. New York, 1959. Examination of rhetorical and poetic theories begins with classical treatises and works through the medieval period.

Coulton, George G. *Medieval Panorama*. London and Cambridge, 1938. Paperback, Meridian Books, New York, 1955. Fifty-two chapters on a wide range of medieval matters—religion, social life, literature, sport, education—presenting the English scene from the Conquest to the Reformation.

————. *The Medieval Village*. Cambridge, 1931. Paperback, Torchbooks, New York, 1960. Life of the peasant; the point of view is mainly English.

————. *Ten Medieval Studies*. 3rd ed. Cambridge, 1930. Paperback, Boston, 1959. Essays on friars, monks, and religion in general in the time of Chaucer. The author combats a number of generally held beliefs.

————. *Social Life in Britain from the Conquest to the Reformation*.

Cambridge, 1918. Selections from the writings of the medieval period describing fifteen phases of life, land and folk, town life, wayfaring and foreign travel, medicine and justice, and superstitions and marvels, etc.

Crombie, A. C. *Medieval and Early Modern Science.* 2 vols. First published as *Augustine to Galileo: the History of Science A.D. 400-1650.* London, 1952. Paperback, Anchor Book, New York, 1959. Growth of all branches of science from the classical period through the Renaissance.

Davis, Henry W. C., ed. *Medieval England.* Oxford, 1924. Derived from Barnard's *Companion to English History.* Reedited in 2 vols. by Austin Poole, Oxford, 1958. Nineteen essays on such matters as architecture, war, costume, heraldry, shipping, town and country life, art, trade, commerce, from the Old English period to the Renaissance; copiously illustrated.

Funck-Brentano, Franz. *The Middle Ages.* Tr. by E. O'Neill. New York, 1923. A good general history of Europe from the eleventh century to the end of the Middle Ages.

Haskins, Charles H. *The Rise of Universities.* New York, 1923. Paperback, New York, 1962. Three lectures on the founding of European universities; the subjects are the earliest universities, the professors, and the students.

Hepple, R. B. *Medieval Education in England.* London, 1932. Short pamphlet which gives an excellent account of the development of various types of medieval schools and whom and what they taught.

Huizinga, Johan. *The Waning of the Middle Ages.* New York, 1954. Paperback, Anchor Book, New York, 1956. Study of life, thought, and art in France and the Netherlands in the fourteenth and fifteenth centuries, showing how the medieval period gave rise to the modern age.

Jusserand, J. J. *English Wayfaring Life in the Middle Ages (XIV Century).* Tr. by Lucy T. Smith. 3rd ed. New York, 1939. Paperback, New York, 1962. Entertaining account of the multitudes that swarmed over the medieval highways; a large amount of the social history of the times as it bore on travel is included.

La Tour-Landry, Geoffroy de. *The Book of the Knight of La Tour-Landry.* Ed. by Thomas Wright. Rev. ed. London, 1906. Another edition was edited by G. S. Taylor. London, 1930. Fascinating book about morals and manners, written by a French father for his three motherless daughters.

Lewis, Clive A. *The Allegory of Love: A Study of Medieval Tradition.* Oxford, 1936. Paperback, Galaxy Book, New York, 1958. General treatment of the allegory of love and its application to Chaucer, Gower, Usk, Spenser, and others.

Lorris, W., and J. Clopinel. *The Romance of the Rose.* Tr. by F. S. Ellis. 3 vols. London, 1900. Poem of joint authorship that exerted a profound influence on Chaucer.

McKisack, May. *The Fourteenth Century, 1309-1399.* Oxford, 1959. An excellent interpretative history of Chaucer's century.

Pendrill, Charles. *London Life in the Fourteenth Century.* London, 1925. Examination of the topography, laws, sports, trades, customs, and so forth of Chaucer's time.

Pirenne, Henri. *Medieval Cities.* Princeton, 1925. Paperback, Anchor Book, New York, 1956. Origins of medieval cities and the revival of trade, expounding the theory that the growth of cities was a product of the growth of trade and commerce.

————. *Economic and Social History of Medieval Europe.* First appeared in Vol. VIII of *Histoire du Moyen Age,* by Henri Pirenne, Gustave Cohen, and Henri Focillon. Paris, 1933. Paperback, London, 1936; New York, 1937. Excellent discussion of the revival of commerce, the land and the rural classes, commerce to the end of the thirteenth century, international trade, urban economy and the regulation of industry, and economic changes of the fourteenth and fifteenth centuries.

Power, Eileen. *Medieval English Nunneries, c. 1275 to 1535.* Cambridge, 1922. Paperback, New York, 1954. Amusing examination of the life and conditions in nunneries of the late medieval period.

Rashdall, Hastings. *The Universities of Europe in the Middle Ages.* New ed. in 3 vols. Ed. by F. M. Powicke and A. B. Embden. Oxford, 1936. Vol. III is about English universities. Development of Oxford and Cambridge universities, with a long section on student life.

Rickert, Edith. *Chaucer's World.* Ed. by C. C. Olson and M. M. Crow. New York, 1948. Paperback, New York, 1962. Large collection of quotations from a wide variety of sources to illustrate the life and times of Chaucer; they are almost exclusively taken from documents written during Chaucer's lifetime. The English is modernized but still gives the flavor of the originals.

Robertson, D. W., Jr. *A Preface to Chaucer.* Princeton, 1962. Excellent treatise on the vital ideas of Chaucer's time, with the specific focus of attention on the poetry of Chaucer. One hundred and eighteen beautifully reproduced illustrations.

Salzman, Louis F. *English Industries in the Middle Ages.* New ed. Oxford, 1923. Treats of various kinds of mining, building, and manufacturing that were extensively pursued in Chaucer's time.

————. *English Life in the Middle Ages*. London, 1927. Chapters on country life, town life, home life, church and religion, education, literature, art and science, warfare, law and order, industry, trade, finance, women, and wayfaring.

————. *English Trade in the Middle Ages*. Oxford, 1931. Treatise on trade by land and water, both within England and outside; the money system, credit, etc.

Snell, Frederick J. *The Fourteenth Century*. Vol. II in the series "Periods of English Literature." Edinburgh and London, 1899. Treatment of English literature in the fourteenth century.

Taylor, Henry O. *The Medieval Mind*. 2 vols. New York, 1930. Extensive study of thought and emotion in the Middle Ages; the great intellects of the time are examined, as are such matters as feudalism, chivalry, scholasticism, symbolism, and allegory.

Thompson, James W. *The Medieval Library*. Chicago, 1939. Although the entire volume is interesting, Chapter XIII, "English Libraries in the Fourteenth and Fifteenth Centuries," is the one bearing on Chaucer's age. Also of importance is Part IV, "The Making and Care of Books in the Middle Ages."

Thorndike, Lynn. *A History of Magic and Experimental Science during the First Thirteen Centuries of Our Era*. 8 vols. New York, 1923-58. The first four volumes are those bearing on Chaucer's times.

Trevelyan, George M. *England in the Age of Wyclif*. New impression. London, 1935. Illuminating political and religious history of the England of Chaucer's time, Wycliffe and Lollardry being the point of focus. The book throws light on much of Chaucer's work.

Ward, H. Snowden. *The Canterbury Pilgrimages*. London, 1904. The life of St. Thomas à Becket, the growth of his cult, a detailed description of the Pilgrims' Way, and the decline of the Thomas cult are treated. The book makes clear why Chaucer's Pilgrims were on pilgrimage.

Watt, Francis. *Canterbury Pilgrims and Their Ways*. London, 1907. An account of the martyrdom of St. Thomas, the shrine, pilgrims and pilgrimages, a short biography of Chaucer, and the tracing of a number of routes from various cities to Canterbury.

Wells, John E. *A Manual of Writings in Middle English, 1050-1400*. New Haven, 1916. Supplements 1919, 1923, 1926, 1932, 1935, 1941; 1952 (containing the literature down to 1945, ed. by Beatrice D. Brown, Eleanor K. Heningham, and F. L. Utley); eighth supplement has index of matter treated in Supplements 1-7. A mine of information about all Middle English authors including Chaucer: MSS, editions, commentaries, criticism. A valuable book.

Selected Bibliography

2. Chaucer and His Works

Baum, Paull F. *Chaucer: A Critical Appreciation.* Durham, N. C., 1958. Observations on a large number of Chaucerian matters.

Bronson, Bertrand H. *In Search of Chaucer.* Toronto, 1960. Four perceptive lectures on various aesthetic and interpretative matters in Chaucer's works.

Bryan, W. F., and Germaine Dempster. *Sources and Analogues of Chaucer's Canterbury Tales.* Chicago, 1941. Scholarly treatise on the many sources and analogues of the various tales. The book makes its primary appeal to the advanced student.

Chaucer Society. *Life Records of Chaucer.* Pts. I & III, by W. W. Selby; Pt. II, by F. J. Furnival; Pt. IV, by R. E. G. Kirk. London, 1875-1900. Index, By E. P. Kuhl, in *Modern Philology,* 1913. A fascinating collection of practically all of the contemporary documents dealing with Chaucer. All sorts of matters that bear on Chaucer but do not necessarily mention him are quoted.

Chute, Marcette. *Geoffrey Chaucer of England.* New York, 1946. Paperback, New York, 1958. Readable biography of Chaucer and a critical examination of all of his works; it has an extensive bibliography.

Coghill, Nevill. *The Poet Chaucer.* London, 1947. A biography and a critical examination of most of Chaucer's works.

Coulton, George G. *Chaucer and His England.* 7th ed. London, 1946. Paperback, New York, 1963. About the England and the London of Chaucer's day and much about Chaucer himself and his poetry.

Curry, Walter C. *Chaucer and the Medieval Sciences.* Rev. and enlarged ed. New York, 1960. Examination of the medieval science used by Chaucer—medicine, physiognomy, astrology, alchemy, physiology, metoscopy, dream lore, etc. Curry also treats the matter of fate at considerable length. The book includes a general bibliography, with emphasis on recent periodical articles on scientific subjects. The thesis that Chaucer composed his characters from bits of scientific and pseudo-scientific lore should be accepted with caution.

Dodd, William G. *Courtly Love in Chaucer and Gower.* New York, 1959. Conventions of courtly love according to various authorities and an application of the conventions to the works of Chaucer and Gower.

Emerson, Oliver F. *Chaucer Essays and Studies.* Cleveland, 1929. Fifteen essays on various Chaucerian matters originally published in scholarly journals, by a notable Chaucer scholar.

Fansler, Dean S. *Chaucer and the Roman de la Rose.* New York, 1914.

Thorough comparison of Chaucer's works with the *Roman de la Rose* by topics. The author shows that although Chaucer found much in the *Rose*, he adapted it to his own uses so that it became much more than mere imitation. He shows that Chaucer drew upon both Guillaume de Lorris and Jean de Meun roughly in proportion to the contribution of each to the *Roman*.

French, Robert D. *A Chaucer Handbook.* 2nd ed. New York, 1947. Chaucer's times and life, and interpretations of the lesser works, of *Troilus and Criseyde*, and of the *Canterbury Tales.* A chapter on Chaucer's language and versification and an extensive bibliography are included.

Gerould, Gordon H. *Chaucerian Essays.* Princeton, 1952. Six brief interpretative essays on such matters as "Chaucer's Calendar of Saints," "The Social Status of the Franklin," "The Vicious Pardoner."

Griffith, D. D. *A Bibliography of Chaucer, 1908-1953.* Seattle, 1955. Continuation of Hammond's *Bibliographical Manual;* an essential book, giving a great deal of otherwise hard-to-find material such as theses and reviews.

Hammond, Eleanor P. *Chaucer, A Bibliographical Manual.* New York, 1908. A volume for the serious student: a mass of information on the MSS of the different works, the editions, modernizations and translations, sources and analogue, commentaries, and much else.

Hulbert, James R. *Chaucer's Official Life.* Menasha, Wisc., 1912. This valuable little book explains the nature of Chaucer's various public offices and shows how his career corresponded to that of others in similar posts.

Kern, Alfred A. *The Ancestry of Chaucer.* Baltimore, 1906. Study of the name Chaucer in medieval England and a long section on the poet's ancestors. Fourteenth-century England abounded with Chaucers, and the author sorts them out. A map and an elaborate pedigree of the Chaucer-Malyn family.

Kittredge, George L. *Chaucer and His Poetry.* Cambridge, Mass., 1915. Biography of Chaucer and critical appraisals of the chief works.

———. "Chaucer's Lollius." *Harvard Studies in Classical Philology.* Cambridge, Mass., 1917. The author indicates that when Chaucer wrote *The House of Fame*, he believed a Lollius had written on the Trojan War but when Chaucer wrote *Troilus and Criseyde*, he stated Lollius was his source as a fiction to lend truth, vividness, and authenticity to his work.

Kökeritz, Helge. *A Guide to Chaucer's Pronunciation.* New York, 1962. Pamphlet treating the principles of Chaucer's pronunciation, with thirteen pages of the poetry in phonetic transcription.

Selected Bibliography

Lawrence, William W. *Chaucer and the Canterbury Tales*. New York, 1950. A study of the structure and design of the *Canterbury Tales;* groups of tales and themes are considered, rather than individual tales.

Legouis, Émile. *Geoffrey Chaucer*. Tr. by L. Lailavoix. London and New York, 1913. Biography, a chapter on "The Making of Chaucer as a Poet," and a critical examination of Chaucer's works. Gives the French view of Chaucer and his works.

Lounsbury, Thomas R. *Studies in Chaucer*. 3 vols. New York, 1892. Reissued, New York, 1960. Highly readable book on many phases of Chaucer scholarship. One of the most valuable critical works on Chaucer, it has been quoted or referred to by almost all the writers who have come after Lounsbury.

Lowes, John L. *Geoffrey Chaucer and the Development of His Genius*. Boston, 1934. Background, life, and a critical examination of some of the works.

Madeleva, Sister M. *A Lost Language and Other Essays on Chaucer*. New York, 1951. Seven chapters on various Chaucerian matters. "Chaucer's Nuns," reprinted from a former volume, is interesting in that it is written by a Catholic nun; the interpretation of the Prioress is widely at variance with the usual one.

Malone, Kemp. *Chapters on Chaucer*. Baltimore, 1951. Critical examination of the major works.

Manly, John M. "Chaucer and the Rhetoricians," in *Proceedings of the British Academy*, XII. London, 1926. Study of Chaucer's familiarity with formal rhetorical theory; Chaucer's early works closely follow the strictures of the rhetoricians, but as he develops as an artist he gradually frees himself from definite rules.

———. *Some New Light on Chaucer*. New York, 1926. An entertaining examination of the historical background of many of Chaucer's Pilgrims, with tentative identifications of some of them with historical personages.

———. With Edith Rickert. *The Text of the Canterbury Tales, Studied on the Basis of All Known Manuscripts*. 6 vols. Chicago, 1940. Authoritative text of the *Canterbury Tales*, with all of the variant readings.

Patch, Howard. *On Rereading Chaucer*. Cambridge, Mass., 1939. Observations on humor, the court of love, medieval romances, satire, etc.

Rickert, Edith. "Was Chaucer a Student at the Inner Temple?" *Manly Anniversary Studies in Language and Literature*. Chicago, 1923. Information and arguments in favor of Chaucer's having been a student of the law.

Root, Robert K. *The Poetry of Chaucer*. Rev. ed. Gloucester, Mass., 1934. Brief chapters on Chaucer's England and his life and an extended analysis of the works; a much-quoted book.

Ruud, Martin. *Thomas Chaucer*. Minneapolis, 1926. Life and career of Geoffrey Chaucer's son, showing how wealthy and important he was.

Schoeck, Richard J., and Jerome Taylor, eds. *Chaucer Criticism: The Canterbury Tales*. Notre Dame, Ind., 1960. Also: *Chaucer Criticism: Troilus and Criseyde and the Minor Poems*. Notre Dame, Ind., 1960. Collections of critical essays that have in the main appeared in scholarly journals; most of the essays are recent. Paperbacks.

Spurgeon, Caroline F. E. *Five Hundred Years of Chaucer Criticism and Allusion, 1357-1900*. New ed. 3 vols. Cambridge, 1960. Collection of all of the mentions of Chaucer and allusions to his works from the time of his contemporaries down to 1900. The work also reproduces all of the known Chaucer portraits.

Tatlock, John S. P. *The Mind and Art of Chaucer*. Syracuse, 1950. Biography of Chaucer and critical examinations of *Troilus and Criseyde* and the first four of the *Canterbury Tales*.

————. And Arthur G. Kennedy, *A Concordance to the Complete Works of Geoffrey Chaucer and the Romaunt of the Rose*. Washington, 1927. Complete index to every word and everything in Chaucer's works; a necessity for textual study and very useful for a large number of other purposes.

Wagenknecht, Edward, ed. *Chaucer: Modern Essays in Criticism*. New York, 1959. Paperback. Twenty-six critical essays and a few chapters from books by various authors on the *Canterbury Tales, Troilus and Criseyde,* and the minor poems.

Index

(Page references to the author's works will be found under Chaucer's writings. The italicized numerals refer to the detailed discussions of the works.)

Index

Index

Spurgeon, Caroline F. E., 190
Stace, Geoffrey, 39-40
Stace, Thomas, 39
Staplegate, Edward, 45
Strode, Ralph, 47, 107
Sudbury, Archbishop and Chancellor, his poll-tax and murder, 25-26
Sweating sickness, 21
Swynford, Katherine, 16, 44, 52

Taverner, le, 39
Teseide (Giovanni Boccaccio), 66, 128
Testament of Cresseid (Robert Henryson), 193
Theatrum Chemicum Britannicum (Elias Ashmole), 193-94
Theatrum Poetarum (Edward Phillips), 198
Thebes, Book of (John Lydgate), 200
Theodoric, Emperor, 88
Thomas, Duke of Gloucester, *see* Gloucester
Translations of Chaucer's work, vogue for, 199
Trivet, Nicholas, 91, 138
Troilus and Cressida (William Shakespeare), 196

Tyler, Wat, 27
Tyrwhitt, Thomas, 182, 200

Urban V, Pope, 38
Urban VI, Pope, 38
Usk, Thomas, 191

Vache, Sir Philip de la, 84
Vert, le Song, 57
Villeins, taxes and tallages on, 21
Virgil (Publius Vergilius Maro), 86
Visconti, Bernabo, 46, 73

Weaving, became rural, 31
Webbe, William, 196
Westhale, Agnes de, 38-39
Westhale, Joan, 38
Wife of Bath on family sovereignty, 143; morality of, 140-41; femininity of, 139-40
Wife of Bath's Prologue, interruptions of, 142
William of Bavaria, 69
William of Hainault, 68
William of Ockham, 35
Wordsworth, William, 91
Wycliffe, 36-37, 123

York, Duke of, *see* Edmund of Langley